Standing Together

American Indian Education as Culturally Responsive Pedagogy

Beverly J. Klug

Published in Partnership with the
Association of Teacher Educators

ROWMAN & LITTLEFIELD EDUCATION
A division of
ROWMAN & LITTLEFIELD PUBLISHERS, INC.
Lanham • New York • Toronto • Plymouth, UK

Published in Partnership with the Association of Teacher Educators

Published by Rowman & Littlefield Education
A division of Rowman & Littlefield Publishers, Inc.
A wholly owned subsidary of The Rowman & Littlefield Publishing Group, Inc.
4501 Forbes Boulevard, Suite 200, Lanham, Maryland 20706
www.rowman.com

10 Thornbury Road, Plymouth PL6 7PP, United Kingdom

British Library Cataloguing in Publication Information Available

Library of Congress Cataloging-in-Publication Data

Klug, Beverly J.
Standing together : American Indian education as culturally responsive pedagogy / edited by Beverly Klug.
p. cm.
ISBN 978-1-61048-785-6 (cloth : alk. paper) — ISBN 978-1-61048-786-3 (pbk.) — ISBN 978-1-61048-787-0 (electronic)
1. Indian children—Education—United States. 2. Indian students—United States. 3. Multicultural education—United States. 4. Teachers—United States—Attitudes. 5. Social values—Study and teaching—United States. 6. Ethnicity—Study and teaching—United States. 7. Critical pedagogy. I. Klug, Beverly. II. Title.
E97.K57 2012
371.829'97—dc23
2012028671

♾™ The paper used in this publication meets the minimum requirements of American National Standard for Information Sciences Permanence of Paper for Printed Library Materials, ANSI/NISO Z39.48-1992.

Printed in the United States of America

This book is dedicated to American Indian children, their families, and their communities.

Contents

Acknowledgments

We would like to acknowledge the support of our families and constituents who have been with us on our journeys as we pursue the agenda of social justice for **all** students in our schools throughout the United States.

Introduction

Jane McCarthy

My work with American Indian populations over the past ten years has provided me with a glimpse of the struggles for self-determination played out so forcefully in public schools both on and off the reservation. As an invited guest on the reservation, I had the unusual role of "sister" to my Native colleagues. In this role, I attended ceremonies and was included in the political and educational life of the tribe. I listened to stories of my friends' and their parents' experiences with the boarding school movement.

What I heard and saw inspired me to question even more deeply what was happening to the culture of the tribes today in terms of the hegemonic homogenization of Native cultures taking place in schools. The advent of No Child Left Behind (2001) seemed to exacerbate this phenomenon as all efforts were geared toward passing the assessments with little consideration of cultural ways of learning and knowing. Even charter schools on the reservation, dedicated to preserving Native culture and language, were not immune to the pressures of achievement testing.

As the 2006–2007 President of the Association of Teacher Educators, I established a commission to study the education of the American Indian. Commission members were selected to represent a broad spectrum of Native and non-Native educators working with Indigenous populations.

We have sought to research the past stories of American Indian education, to describe current features of American Indian education, and to discover the future paths of American Indian education as Indigenous peoples arbitrate their destinies as sovereign nations within regions composing the United States, holding dual citizenship in both their Tribal nations and the United States. We have endeavored to describe culturally relevant programs that work (McCarthy and Benally 2003; Young 2009) and to suggest new approaches.

This volume represents some of the research and thinking that has resulted from our first three years of work. We have presented our work several times a year to diverse audiences at our Association of Teacher Educators (ATE) conferences. Our work has been influenced by the input and feedback from our colleagues who have generously critiqued and responded to our papers and seminars.

It is our hope that the ideas and research recounted in this volume will stimulate educators to think about the characteristics of the Native American students in their classrooms—both K–12 and college or university. We must think of the strengths American Indian students bring with them that can be built upon to facilitate powerful learning situations. We must utilize the richness of their diverse cultures to provide a stimulating educational environment that respects the dignity of all (see the work of Klug and Whitfield 2003).

Above all, we must listen to the dreams of the American Indian peoples for the education of their youth (see Lomawaima and McCarty 2006). We must empower American Indian students as citizens of a democracy to make decisions about their own futures (rich descriptions of such empowerment can be found in Abu-Saad and Champagne 2006). This volume is designed to stimulate thinking and discussion and to spur action on the part of educators to work for social justice in all aspects of our educational system and, in particular, for a much neglected sector, the education of the American Indian.

REFERENCES

Abu-Saad, I., and D. Champagne, eds. (2006). *Indigenous Education and Empowerment: International Perspectives.* Lanham, MD: AltaMira.

Klug, B. J., and P. T. Whitfield. (2003). *Widening the Circle: Culturally Relevant Pedagogy for American Indian Children.* New York: RoutledgeFalmer.

Lomawaima, K. T., and T. L. McCarty. (2006). *To Remain an Indian: Lessons in Democracy from a Century of Native American Education.* New York: Teachers College Press.

McCarthy, J., and J. Benally. (2003). "Classroom management in a Navajo middle school." *Theory into Practice* 42 (4): 296–304.

No Child Left Behind Act of 2001: Reauthorization of the Elementary and Secondary Education Act of 1965 (NCLB). (2001). *US code.* Title 20, section 6301 et seq.

Young, W. M. (2010). *Exemplary Teachers for Native American Students.* PhD diss., University of Nevada, Las Vegas.

Part I

A History of American Indian Education in the United States

This section of our book provides a look at the early years of formal Western European-style education provided for American Indian students in the United States. This information is imperative to those who are exploring the world of culturally responsive education for Native students and want to know about what has been done in the past and why traditional Western education has not been effective for these students.

Chapter 1, by Nuby and Smith, begins with an exploration of past governmental injustices and educational efforts leading to unequal treatment of Native students in the past to today's hope for a better future in an era of self-determination.

In chapter 2, Young presents an examination of the history of what occurred in one of many states with large populations of Native peoples, South Dakota. He provides for readers an example of how applied policies shaped local and state decisions concerning American Indian education. He delineates for us a legacy that has had lasting effects on the Native peoples in what was a full-fledged effort to deculturalize them. Finally, Young brings us through the period of reform beginning with the 1928 Meriam Report forward into a time of attempts to correct the damages resulting from those efforts.

Our third chapter, by Reyhner, offers us a window into the past of beginning efforts to make education relevant and responsive for American Indian students who had little to no experience with the dominant culture. He describes post-Meriam Native and non-Native educators employed by the U.S. Indian Office who realized that changes in the curricula employed by the dominant culture were needed to accomplish educational goals. Teachers not only took corrective actions to change their teaching but also shared their experiences with effective techniques for their students with others through their writings.

Reyhner continues through to the present time and the need for changes to current legislation in order to ensure academic achievement of American Indian students, including reinstatement of languages and cultures in schools serving Native populations. Like in Young's chapter, focus is also given to preparation of teachers and administrators to meet those needs.

In chapter 4, Marble provides us with an "inside look" into the personal experiences of a new teacher trying to find his way in how to educate Alaska Native students following changes in Alaska legislation to allow schools to be set up near students' villages, rather than have students continue to attend boarding schools far away from home. We learn about the impact of this experience on his life as an educator, on his students, and on the village community as he explores his past and realizes that so much of what he believes as an educator is rooted in these experiences on the Tundra.

We invite you, the reader, to consider your own ideas concerning the education of Native students. What are the questions you may have prior to exploring these chapters? As you read through part I, we want you to feel that you are traveling along this journey with us. Note that the appellations "American Indian," "Native American," "Native," and "Indigenous" are all used interchangeably to denote students belonging to indigenous sovereign Tribal nations in the United States.

Chapter 1

From Federal Intervention to Self-Determination

Looking Forward

Jacqueline F. Nuby: University of Montevallo and
James Smith: Cherokee High School

ABSTRACT

Since the time of the formation of the United States, the federal government has been involved in how to acculturate American Indians into the dominant Western culture as the steady demand for land from European settlers continued to increase. In addition, the diseases brought by European settlers wreaked havoc with Native American populations, leaving devastation in their wake as thousands of Natives died as a result.

These events, along with the poor treatment of American Indians by the federal government, led to undermining traditional Native communities and their practices for educating their children. As Native Americans were pushed out of their territories, the government determined that the way to enculturate them into European thinking was to have the children sent to boarding schools that were created where children would be involved in learning farming and industrial arts along with English and Christianity.

After it became evident through the 1928 Meriam Report that American Indians were living in great poverty and that the boarding schools had failed to provide a way for Natives to become assimilated, there was a call for rectifying these conditions through establishing a different way to educate American Indian children. This led to many significant events and measures taken during the 20th century leading to self-determination in the education of American Indian students.

Keywords: American Indian education, federal policy in American Indian education, self-determination

FROM FEDERAL INTERVENTION TO SELF-DETERMINATION: LOOKING FORWARD

The history of the United States' federal educational policies concerning Native Americans constitutes a national tragedy. From the time the United States government was established, the intent of the federal government was to intervene in Native American affairs. The goal was to perpetuate "Anglo" practices, which had prevailed since the Europeans first stepped foot on Native soil.

This federal educational policy consisted of uprooting Native Americans from their homes and forcing them into a disciplined, non-Indian educational environment, one which would strip the Indian child of his or her culture and substitute the English language and European values in its place. The result was the social and cultural disintegration of the family and tribe through misconceived and misdirected federal policies (Spring 2001).

After centuries of domination and ill treatment, the federal government passed legislation to protect the educational rights of Native Americans through self-determination. However, Native American schooling practices have been notoriously slow to adapt and change, even with the opportunity to determine schooling practices. Schools in Native American country are still rooted in an aged legacy, based on the time in which the Department of War administered schools for Native Americans (Adams 1995).

The purpose of this chapter is to present a historical view of the federal government's policy to intervene in the educational affairs of Native American people. It is also an account of the successful story of the efforts of Native Americans to become self-sufficient through determination. Now that self-determination is a choice, education leaders must examine the condition of Native American education, provide solutions to problems, and implement reforms that reflect Native American needs—educationally, socially, politically, and economically.

Traditional Education

Before Europeans came to America, the family, clan, tribe, or responsible mentors worked with youth until the information they needed, or tasks to be performed, were clearly understood. The lessons were an integrated part of daily life and ceremonies, not separate isolated events. Education was geared toward teaching children how to survive in their environments. Social education taught children the way to interact with family members, the clan, the tribe, or band (Reyhner and Eder 2004; Snipp 1989; Szasz 1999; Zinn 1999).

Vocational education taught young girls how to rear children, farm, and manage households. Boys were taught hunting, gathering, and fishing. Each tribe had its own religious ceremonies that taught the children the importance of spirituality. Storytelling passed on information from generation to generation. Members of the extended family taught the children by example, and children copied adult activities as they played and learned (Reyhner and Eder 2004; Snipp 1989; Szasz 1999; Zinn 1999).

The European Invasion

After the Europeans arrived, traditional customs for educating children were drastically altered. The European invasion and subsequent founding of the United States federal government brought tremendous changes in all parts of the lives of Native American people. The policies toward Native Americans were based on the mistreatment and misplacement of Native American people (Adams 1995; Zinn 1999).

The European intruders also brought horrific diseases, such as small pox and measles, for which Native Americans had no immunity. Thousands died as a result of contact with the white man's world, a world in which, they quickly discovered, they had little or no say about what happened to their future (Snipp 1989).

The "Indian Problem." When the federal government was established, it was faced with what came to be known as the "Indian Problem." To remedy this problem, the government established the Indian Bureau in the War Department in 1824 to deal with Native Americans. Through this bureau, which later became the Bureau of Indian Affairs (BIA), the federal government sought to "manage" the savages, as they were referred to, through Anglicized education, aggressive warfare, or by pushing Native Americans westward, far out of the way of the settlers (Belko 2004).

The Trail of Tears. Native Americans were seen as an impediment to the westward expansion of white settlers. Therefore, the Bureau of Indian Affairs stepped in to assist Europeans in their desires to move westward. In 1830, Congress passed the Indian Removal Act (Cave 2003; Prucha 2000). The government selected several tribes to remove from their territories in implementing this act: the Choctaw, Cherokee, Chickasaw, Seminole, and Muskogee Creek.

Although many white people, as well as Native Americans, were against the removal of Native Americans from their homelands, President Andrew Jackson ignored the dissention and approved the removal. The Cherokees attempted to fight removal legally by challenging the removal law in the Supreme Court. Initially, Chief Justice John Marshall sided with the Cherokee but later reversed his ruling with pressures from the white settlement proponents and President Jackson. After much battling and a visit to Jackson by Principal Chief John Ross, the Cherokee were unsuccessful in stopping their removal (Fitzpatrick 2006).

Through what was and is now called "ethnic cleansing," the military forces representing the United States government herded Native Americans into makeshift forts, deprived them of nutritious foods, and forced them to walk 1,000 miles on what came to be known as the "Trail of Tears." They were told that they would have their new homeland, Oklahoma, forever (Adams 1995). Under the generally indifferent army commanders, there were thousands of Native American deaths. Some estimate that approximately 4,000 Cherokee alone died as a result of the removal (Adams 1995; Zinn 1999).

This scenario was repeated over and over as other tribes were forced throughout the 1800s to move from their tribal lands as Anglo encroachment continued. In addition, Indian wars with tribes unwilling to "voluntarily" give up their lands provided additional excuses to take the lands by force as spoils of the victorious federal government (Madsen 1996; Walker 1985).

The boarding school era. To further Americanize Native Americans, the Indian Peace Commission of 1886 advised the Bureau of Indian Affairs to civilize Native Americans by blotting out "barbarous" dialects and enforcing their speaking of English only. To expedite this, Native American boarding schools and reservation schools were set up with the aim of eliminating Native languages and cultures.

Richard Pratt, an army officer, was the architect of the Bureau of Indian Affairs boarding schools. Pratt opened the first one in Carlisle, Pennsylvania, in 1879 (Spring 2001). He based it on an education program he had developed in an Indian prison. That year, children from the Cheyenne, Kiowa, and Pawnee tribes arrived at the school. The thought was that a new generation of young Natives, with new thought patterns, would return to their reservations and convert others to the "American way" (Spring 2001).

Children as young as four years old were taken to schools miles from all that was familiar to them. Their hair was cut off, and they were scrubbed with lye soap and doused in kerosene to delouse them. They were forced to wear military-style uniforms. They ate unfamiliar, unsavory food, which was, furthermore, in short supply; they were made to sleep in beds and sit in chairs, which were unfamiliar to them (Child 1993).

The boarding schools had strict rules against speaking Native languages and engaging in spiritual practices. Those who broke the rules were subjected to harsh punishments. They often had their mouths washed out with lye soap or were placed in confinement for disobeying rules. Some of the children had the whole outsides of their mouths raw and bloody as a result of using lye as a rinsing agent (Adams 1995; Holt 2001; Lomawaima 1987).

The boarding school was also used as a means to train Native American laborers. For the most part, the jobs they were trained for were menial jobs. Children of twelve and younger were forced to engage in industrial work, often for four hours a day or more. As a result, there was no way that a Native American generation of professionals, such as doctors, lawyers, or bankers, could be produced. The outcome was a feeling of inferiority or academic indifference in latter generations. The children had no role models to emulate because of their lack of ability to obtain a dignified, humane system of education (Archuleta, Child, and Lomawaima 2004; Cahape and Howley 1992).

Many children died while at boarding schools, either from diseases from which they had no natural immunity or from extreme homesickness. There are hundreds of graves at Carlisle Boarding School alone of children who suffered and died far from everything familiar to them. The children who survived were not much better off and, in some cases, in worse condition. When many Native Americans returned home, they found themselves unwelcome in their tribes. They were certainly not generally accepted in white society (Archuleta, Child, and Lomawaima 2004; Barrett and Britton 1997; Reyhner and Eder 2004).

Native Americans, at both the individual and community levels, experienced "intergenerational trauma" or "historical grief," passed down from generation to generation. The result has been distrust, anger, and confusion toward Anglos. This trauma, associated with disgrace, demoralization, and belittlement, became prevalent in Native American communities (Beiser 1974).

The General Allotment Act. Another means of robbing Native Americans of their cultures, heritages, and languages was by enacting legislation regarding Native American lands. The General Allotment Act, passed in 1887 and generally referred to as the Dawes Act, led to the distribution of the lands Native Americans had been promised in Oklahoma and other tribally reserved areas.

The land, which was tribally held, was divided into individually owned parcels, and then "surplus" lands were opened to settlement by whites. The Dawes Act (1887), with its emphasis on land ownership, immediately had a negative impact on the unity, self-government, and cultures of Native American tribes (Carlson 1981; Fitzpatrick 2006).

The Dawes Act (1887) was directly intended to force the deterioration of the communal lifestyle of Native American societies. In its place, there would be Anglo-oriented values, such as strengthening the individual family unit as compared to living communally as Native Americans had done for centuries.

The land granted to the allottees was not sufficient for growing crops and had little to no economic viability. The division of the land between heirs upon the allottees' deaths further led to land fractionalization. Additionally, land deemed to be "surplus" beyond what was needed for allotment was opened to white settlers (Carlson 1981; Deloria and Lytle 1983; Otis 1973). Because of the Dawes Act (1887), Native Americans lost approximately 90 million acres of treaty land, about two-thirds of the 1887 land base (Otis 1973).

The allotment policy depleted the land base, ending hunting as a means of existence. The men were forced into the fields to take on what had been the women's roles. The women were relegated to the domestic sphere. This act imposed a patrilineal nuclear household onto many matrilineal Native societies. Therefore, Native Americans' gender roles were altered. Women were no longer caretakers of the land and were no longer valued in the political sphere (Carlson 1981).

The Dawes Act (1887) was supposedly passed to encourage Native Americans to become farmers, but the land was unsuitable for farming and too small to support livestock. There was a twenty-five-year trust period to keep Native Americans from selling their land allotments. However, a 1907 law allowed them sell portions of their lands.

In addition, a policy of "forced patents" took additional land from Native Americans. Under this policy, government agents were to determine which Indians were "competent" enough to assume full responsibility for their allotments. Many Native Americans quickly sold their land to white purchasers. This resulted in a major loss of Native American lands (Carlson 1981).

Failure of federal policies. By the later nineteenth century, there was a widespread sense that the removal and reservation policies had failed. One person who brought national attention to the plight of Native Americans was Helen Hunt Jackson, a novelist and poet. Her classic book *A Century of Dishonor*, written in 1881, told the sad story of the way the federal government had broken treaty obligations (cited in Falk 1999). Humanitarian reformers repeatedly called for the government to support schools and end corruption on Indian reservations. Even though these reformers demanded good schools for Native Americans, it was still a widespread belief that they should be "Americanized" into society.

Shift in Policy

During the 1920s, federal policy began to shift away from Native American assimilation. Part of this had to do with John Collier, who conducted an investigation of Native American living conditions for the General Federation of Women's Clubs in 1922. Collier became a staunch advocate for preserving tribal cultures and land. His persistence resulted in a study that became well-known in history: the Meriam Report (Parman 1994; Rusco 1991).

The Meriam Report. In 1926, the U.S. Secretary of Interior chose Lewis Meriam to head a survey team to investigate Indian affairs. Meriam spent three years working on the project. The Meriam Report, or *The Problem of Indian Administration* (1928) [also known as the Indian Reorganization Act, 1928], was financed by the Rockefeller Foundation, much due to Collier's efforts (Philp 1999). The report dealt with the educational, industrial, social, and medical activities of the BIA, as well as with Indian property rights and economic conditions.

The report was a narrative and statistical criticism of the Dawes Act (1887), as well as of conditions on reservations and boarding schools. The conclusion of the report stated that any policy based on the idea that Indians should be permanently isolated was bound to fail. Instead, education should stress integration of Native Americans into civilization, rather than separating them from white culture (Meriam 1928; Philp 1977).

The Indian Reorganization Act of 1934. John Collier was named Commissioner of the Bureau of Indian Affairs under President Franklin Roosevelt. Under Collier's leadership, the Indian Reorganization Act of 1934 was passed by Congress.

The act ended the allotment process and provided for the election of tribal councils to represent the state and federal governments. Funds were also allocated to provide scholarships for Indian students and help Indians establish their own businesses (Philp 1968, 1977, 1999). The Johnson O'Malley Act (1934) was passed to promote cooperation between federal and state governments in improving Indian agriculture, education, and health care (Prucha 2000).

World War II. As Bernstein (1991) pointed out, World War II brought profound changes to Native American lives. The most significant of these changes was the opportunity to find well-paying jobs as a result of wartime shortages. Tens of thousands left the reservations to serve in the military. They took jobs in shipyards, lumbering, and other wartime industries. Unlike African Americans, they were not separated into different units. This served to increase the integration of many Native Americans into white society (Bernstein 1991).

The major postwar innovation in Indian policy was the establishment of the Indians Claims Commission, which compensated many Indians for fraud or unfair treatment by the federal government (Shoemaker 2002). However, many Native Americans were resentful because the Claims Commission based awards on land values in effect at the time of cession and refused to pay interest or adjust awards for inflation.

Termination, Relocation, and Native American Activism

During the 1940s and 1950s, there was an increase in Native American activism. In 1944, Indian leaders from fifty tribes formed the National Congress of American Indians (NCAI), the first major intertribal organization. Among their concerns were the protection of Indian lands and mineral and timber resources and improved economic opportunities, education, and health care for Native Americans (Cowger 1999).

Termination. During the 1950s, NCAI led opposition to a congressional policy known as "termination." In 1953, Congress passed a resolution that called for the government to transfer federal responsibilities for Native Americans to the states (Philp 1999). It also allowed states to assert legal jurisdiction over Indian reservations without tribal consent (Cowger 1999). The NCAI rebelled against this policy and called for self-determination rather than termination of tribal status (Fixico 1986).

Relocation. Many Native Americans were also against the relocation policy, another post-war government program. Under this policy, the Bureau of Indian affairs provided transportation, job placement, vocational training, and counseling to Native Americans who wanted to leave their reservations. Many Native Americans felt that relocation was termination in disguise (Fixico 1986).

The American Indian Movement. From the 1950s to the 1970s, a wide array of Native American groups began to organize and call for Native American rights. One of these was the American Indian Movement (AIM). Two of the most well-known leaders of the movement were Dennis Banks and George Mitchell. In the fall of 1972, AIM gained visibility when it led urban Indians and traditionalists along the "Trail of Broken Treaties" to Washington, DC. They seized the offices of the Bureau of Indian Affairs and occupied them for a week to dramatize Indian grievances (Esslinger 2003).

The seizure of Alcatraz, an abandoned federal penitentiary, gained public attention in 1969. The two hundred activists were there for nineteen months protesting the plight of Native Americans (Esslinger 2003). There was also the occupation of Wounded Knee, South Dakota, in 1973, the site of an 1890 massacre of three hundred Sioux by the army cavalry. The activists occupied the town for seven days to dramatize the injustices Native Americans suffered. In addition, they demanded the return of lands taken from Indians in violation of treaty agreements (Philp 1999).

While resistance in the 1960s and 1970s was at first scattered, Native American activists added unification to the movement by banding together across the United States. They came from all parts of the country and had many areas of interest. Some promoted educational independence while others focused on reclaiming Native American land as well as other issues (Philp 1999).

Indian Education Post–World War II

War on Poverty. In 1968, President Lyndon Johnson became the first federal official to use the term *self-determination* in respect to Indian policy. President Johnson's agenda was to highlight the need for economic and social programs for Native Americans. This was a part of Johnson's "War on Poverty" (Prucha 2000; Wilkins 2006).

A National Tragedy—A National Challenge. Out of the efforts of the activists and the support of President Richard Nixon, a subcommittee report, *Indian Education: A National Tragedy—A National Challenge*, was issued in 1969 (cited in Prucha 2000). The report stated that since the BIA was not able to solve the "Indian Problem" after more than a century, the government should back away and offer assistance to the tribes, who would then work to solve their own problems.

President Nixon presented a special message to Congress in 1970 in which he affirmed that Native Americans had been victims of white aggression. He stated that as a matter of human justice, the federal government should offer assistance but must act on the basis of what Native Americans themselves had been wanting: to be allowed to administer their own affairs (Senese 1986; Wilkins 2006).

Some hold that Richard Nixon was probably the one president in the twentieth century who exhibited a great concern for Native Americans' affairs (Cook 1994). In a message to Congress, Nixon recognized Native Americans' call for self-determination (Cook 1994).

The passage of the Indian Education Act in 1972 and the Indian Self-Determination and Education Assistance Act of 1975 brought attention to the need to provide federal money for special programs for Indian children, both on and off reservations, and allowed the tribes and Indian organizations to take over and run BIA programs, including BIA schools (Wilkins 2006). These two acts paved the way for Native American self-determination (Reyhner 1994).

Because of public and congressional concern about the state of Native American communities, two more reports were issued in 1990 (Prucha 2000). The focus of their agendas was on self-determination, the perpetuation of Native languages and cultures, and identifying more effective ways of educating Native children and youth (Charleston 1994). These reports were *Indian Nations at Risk* (Cahape and Howley 1992) and the White House Conference on Indian Education (1998) report.

With the final report of the White House Conference on Indian Education (1998), Executive Order no. 13096 (1998) was signed by President Clinton. In each report, recommendations were made to involve Native American leaders and educators in developing a research agenda on American Indian education.

Several Native American organizations, such as the National Indian Education Association (NIEA), provided a great amount of support that set the stage for self-determination. Some of the organizations were on the local, regional, or national levels. Out of these efforts came some important "firsts" for Native Americans. Ada Deer was the first American Indian appointed as secretary of the interior by President Clinton (Deloria and Lytle 1983).

Another first was the establishment of the Office of Economic Opportunity, which sought to directly involve the recipients of its aid and provide further impetus for self-determination in education. The Office of Economic Opportunity had great success with the Head Start preschool program, primarily because Indians were allowed to operate their own programs (Wilkinson 2005).

President Barack Obama reemphasized the importance of acknowledging the atrocities committed against Native Americans by the federal government (Guedel 2009). He signed a resolution passed by Congress recognizing the sad and painful experiences of Native Americans. In 2009, President Obama signed Native American Heritage Month into effect.

President Obama made an oath to Native Americans that as long as he was in the White House they would not be forgotten (White House 2009). Change, however, depends on everyone becoming part of the solution. Identification of problems and working to develop solutions will take effort from both the federal government and Tribal nations.

Looking into the Future

Now that self-determination is operational, it is time for unified Native American leadership to bring this concept into full fruition. True, programs to revitalize Native cultures have been initiated in schools; however, the quality of these programs is sometimes questioned. It is obvious that Native Americans need time to overcome a tragic past. There is a need, however, to promote a truly Native American curriculum, one that promotes traditional Native American values in every course.

As Obama stated, for anything to have lasting value, there must be Native American ownership (White House 2010). Ownership can only occur when there is committed Native American leadership (Tippeconnic 2000). Native Americans who can serve as positive role models and catalysts for improvement are vital. These leaders must have the ability to pull the tribal community together in a unified effort to assess the reforms needed and to put those reforms into effect.

REFERENCES

Adams, D. W. (1995). *Education for Extinction: American Indians and the Boarding School Experience, 1875–1928*. Lawrence: University Press of Kansas.

Archuleta, M. L., B. J. Child, and K. T. Lomawaima, eds. (2004). *Away from Home: American Indian Boarding School Experiences, 1879–2000*. Santa Fe: Museum of New Mexico Press.

Barrett, C., and M. Britton. (1997). "You didn't dare try to be Indian: Oral histories of former Indian boarding school students." *North Dakota History* 64 (2): 4–25.

Beiser, M. (1974). "A hazard to mental health: Indian boarding schools." *American Journal of Psychiatry* 131 (3): 305–6.

Belko, W. S. (2004). "John C. Calhoun and the creation of the Bureau of Indian Affairs: An essay on political rivalry, ideology, and policymaking in the early republic." *South Carolina Historical Magazine* 105 (3): 170–97.

Bernstein, A. R. (1991). *American Indians and World War II: Toward a New Era in Indian Affairs*. Norman: University of Oklahoma Press.

Cahape, P., and C. B. Howley, eds. (1992). *Indian Nations at Risk: Listening to the People: Summaries of Papers Commissioned by the Indian Nations at Risk Task Force of the U.S. Department of Education*. Charleston, WV: ERIC Clearinghouse on Rural Education and Small Schools.

Carlson, L. A. (1981). *Indians, Bureaucrats, and Land: The Dawes Act and the Decline of Indian Farming*. Westport, CT: Greenwood.

Cave, A. A. (2003). "Abuse of power: Andrew Jackson and the Indian Removal Act of 1830." *Historian* 65 (6): 1130–53.

Charleston, G. M. (1994). "Toward true native education: A treaty of 1992." *Journal of American Indian Education* 33 (2): 7–56. Final report of the Indian Nations at Risk Task Force, draft 3.

Child, B. J. (1993). *Boarding School Seasons: American Indian Families, 1900–1940*. Lincoln: University of Nebraska Press.

Cook, S. R. (1994). "What is Indian self-determination?" *Red Ink* 3 (1): 23–26.

Cowger, T. W. (1999). *The National Congress of American Indians: The Founding Years*. Lincoln: University of Nebraska Press.

Deloria, V., Jr., and C. M. Lytle. (1983). *American Indians, American Justice*. Austin: University of Texas Press.

Esslinger, M. (2003). *Alcatraz: A Definitive History of the Penitentiary Years*. Longboat Key, FL: Ocean View.

Executive Order no. 13096. (1998). "American Indian and Alaska Native education." *Federal Register* 63 (154): 42681–4.

Falk, J. S. (1999). *Women, Language and Linguistics: Three American Stories from the First Half of the Twentieth Century*. New York: Routledge.

Fitzpatrick, E. (2006). *History's Memory: Writing America's Past, 1880–1980*. Cambridge, MA: Harvard University Press.

Fixico, D. L. (1986). *Termination and Relocation: Federal Indian Policy, 1945–1960*. Albuquerque: University of New Mexico Press.

General Allotment Act of 1887 or *Dawes Act*. 24 Stat. 388.

Guedel, G. (2009). "Obama put to early test by tribes." *Native American Legal Update*, January 21. Retrieved from http://www.nativelegalupdate.com.

Holt, M. I. (2001). *Indian Orphanages*. Lawrence: University of Kansas Press.

Indian Education Act of 1972. (2000). *U.S. code*. Title 20, sec. 3385 et seq.

Indian Removal Act of 1830. (1988). *U.S. code*. Title 25, sec. 174.

Indian Reorganization Act of 1934. (2000). *U.S. code*. Title 25, sec. 461.

Indian Self-Determination and Education Assistance Act of 1975. (2000). *U.S. code*. Title 25, sec. 450f.

Johnson O'Malley Act of 1934. (2000). *U.S. code*. Title 25, sec. 452 et seq.

Lomawaima, K. T. (1987). "Oral histories from Chilocco Indian agricultural school, 1920–1940." *American Indian Quarterly* 11 (3): 241–54.

Madsen, B. D. (1996). *The Bannock of Idaho*. Moscow: University of Idaho Press.

Meriam, L., comp. (1928). *The Problem of Indian Administration*. Baltimore: John Hopkins Press. Education Resources Information Center. Retrieved from http://www.eric.ed.gov (accession number ED087573).

Meriam Report or *The Problem of Indian Administration*. (1928). 48 Stat. 984. [Also known as the Indian Reorganization Act.]

Otis, D. S. (1973). *The Dawes Act and the Allotment of Indian Lands*. Civilization of the American Indian 123, ed. F. P. Prucha. Norman: University of Oklahoma Press. Orig. pub. 1934. History of the allotment policy. In vol. 9 of *Readjustment of Indian Affairs: Hearings on H.R. 7902 before the House of Representatives Committee on Indian Affairs*, 428–89.

Parman, D. L. (1994). *Indians and the American West in the Twentieth Century*. Bloomington: University of Indiana Press.

Philp, K. R. (1968). *John Collier and the American Indian, 1920–1945*. Lansing: Michigan State University Press.

———. (1977). *John Collier's Crusade for Indian Reform, 1920–1954*. Tucson: University of Arizona Press.

———. (1999). *Termination Revisited: American Indians on the Trail to Self-determination, 1933–1953*. Lincoln: University of Nebraska Press.

Prucha, F. P., ed. (2000). *Documents of United States Indian Policy*. 3rd ed. Lincoln: University of Nebraska Press.

Reyhner, J. (1994). *American Indian/Alaska Native Education*. Bloomington, IN: Phi Delta Kappa Educational Foundation.

Reyhner, J., and J. Eder. (2004). *American Indian Education: A History*. Norman: University of Oklahoma Press.

Rusco, E. R. (1991). "John Collier: Architect of sovereignty or assimilation?" *American Indian Quarterly* 15 (1): 49–55.

Senese, G. (1986). "Self-determination and American Indian education: An illusion of control." *Educational Theory* 36:153–64.

Shoemaker, N. (2002). *Clearing a Path: Theorizing the Past in Native American Studies*. New York: Routledge.

Snipp, C. M. (1989). *American Indians: The First of this Land*. New York: Russell Sage Foundation.

Spring, J. (2001). *Deculturalization and the Struggle for Equality: A Brief History of the Education of Dominated Cultures in the United States*. New York: McGraw-Hill.

Szasz, M. C. (1999). *Education and the American Indian: The Road to Self-determination Since 1928*. Albuquerque: University of New Mexico Press.

Tippeconnic, J. W., III. (2000). "Reflecting on the past: Some important aspects of Indian education to consider as we look toward the future." In "Determination since 1928," special issue 3, *Journal of American Indian Education* 39 (2): 39–48.

Walker, D. E., Jr. (1985). *Conflict and Schism in Nez Perce Acculturation: A Study of Religion and Politics*. Moscow: University of Idaho Press.

White House. (2009). *Remarks by the President during the Opening of the Tribal Nations Conference and Interactive Discussion with Tribal Leaders*. Washington, DC: Department of the Interior. Retrieved from http://www.whitehouse.gov/the-press-office/remarks-president-during-opening-tribal-nations-conference-interactive-discussion-w.

———. (2010). *White House Tribal Nations Conference Progress Report: Forging a New and Better Future Together*. Retrieved from http://www.atalm.org/sites/default/files/white_house_tribal_nations_report.pdf.

White House Conference on Indian Education. (1998). *The Final Report of the White House Conference on Indian Education: Executive Summary*. Education Resources Information Center. Retrieved from http://www.eric.ed.gov (accession number ED353124).

Wilkins, D. E. (2006). *American Politics and the American Political System*. Lanham, MD: Rowman & Littlefield.

Wilkinson, C. (2005). *Blood Struggle: The Rise of Modern Indian Nations*. New York: Norton.

Zinn, H. (1999). *A People's History of the United States*. New York: HarperCollins.

Chapter 2

Historical Roots of Native American Education in South Dakota

William Young: Oglala Lakota College

ABSTRACT

Beginning with the Fort Laramie Treaty of 1868, the effects of subjugation of the Sioux nation and efforts to deculturalize them as American Indians played devastating roles on the health and welfare of the people. The educational system was used to provide the means for doing so by eliminating the protection of traditional cultures and substituting dominant cultural values through taking the children from their communities. The children were forced to attend boarding schools far from home or within the ones that were established in South Dakota.

For some Native children at the time, this provided a way to become "warriors" and prove themselves in the new order. However, for many students today, the removal of the protective barrier of traditional culture has led to very high numbers of American Indian student dropouts. This chapter provides a unique glimpse into the devastating effects of the educational policies on one Tribal nation, from the earliest efforts to assimilate American Indians through the policies of the No Child Left Behind Act (2001).

In order to address the hegemony present in our educational system, there must be respect and inclusion of Native cultures in the curriculum and pedagogy utilized in schools. A new model for education, one that includes changes in teacher education and encourages cultural understandings, holds the key to making needed changes within our schools for the sake of our American Indian students and the Sioux nation in particular.

Keywords: Sioux nation, American Indian Education, South Dakota

HISTORICAL ROOTS OF NATIVE AMERICAN EDUCATION IN SOUTH DAKOTA

The historical roots of modern Indian education in western South Dakota began with the Fort Laramie Treaty of 1868. The toll of war, disease, and starvation led to the negotiation of manifold treaties, most significantly the 1868 treaty. This treaty, in the attempt to pacify and placate, granted all of the land stretching from the Missouri River to the Big Horn Mountains to the Sioux[1] people.

A portion of the treaty reads: "No white person or persons shall be permitted to settle upon or occupy any portion of the territory or without consent of the Indians to pass through the same" (Brown 1971, 373). The 1868 agreement at Fort Laramie explicitly gave the Sioux western South Dakota; however, when gold was discovered in the Black Hills in 1874, the floodgate of prospectors opened, and the treaty was blatantly violated (Cook-Lynn 2005).

The Sioux, upset by this breach of treaty rights, fought back. After a series of skirmishes on the High Plains, the Indians were subdued and forced onto reservations. Spring (2010, 32) writes that "the reservation system combined with education was considered the best method for dealing with what then Commissioner of Indian Affairs Luke Lea called the 'wilder tribes.'" Just a few years later, in 1871, the U.S. Congress declared that Native Americans were "wards of the government" (Adams 1995, 7).

The reservation system was an attempt to deculturalize Native Americans. *Deculturalization*, according to Spring (1997), refers to the stripping away of a people's culture by replacing it with a new one. The goal of this forced movement onto the reservations was the transformation of a nomadic people into an agrarian society. Clearly, tending crops under difficult conditions left little time for war. This transformation has also been referred to as *acculturation* (Bruner 1996). Acculturation has been described as the cultural change that occurs when two or more cultures are in persistent contact.

Acculturation through Education

A particular kind of acculturation is *assimilation*, in which one culture changes significantly more than the other culture and, as a result, comes to resemble it (Spring 2010). Garcia and Alher (1992) state that this process is often deliberately established through force to maintain control over conquered people, but it can occur voluntarily as well. The method employed by the U.S. government for maintenance of control after the conquest of the Native Americans throughout the country was that of assimilation.

In South Dakota, the most important step in replacing the Native Sioux culture with the dominant culture was the forced assimilation of the Sioux peoples. The government thought that the best path toward assimilation was through education. "Education was the means whereby we emancipated the Indian child from his home, his parents, his extended family, and his cultural heritage" (U.S. Congress 1969, 9).

It was, in effect, "an attempt to wash the 'savage habits' and 'tribal ethic' out of a child's mind and substitute a white middle-class value system in its place" (U.S. Congress 1969, 9). To accomplish this goal, the policymakers established three models for education: the reservation day school, the reservation boarding school, and the off-reservation boarding school (Adams 1995). According to Adams (1995, 29), the primary reason for failure of both the day school and the reservation boarding school to assimilate Native students happened to be the schools' "proximity to the tribal [communities]."

Policymakers determined that a solution might be found in the formation of off- reservation boarding schools. While the most famous off-reservation boarding school was the Carlisle Indian School in Pennsylvania, South Dakota had its own share of boarding schools. Off-reservation boarding schools were established in Pierre in 1891, Flandreau in 1893, Chamberlain in 1898, and Rapid City in 1898 (Adams 1995).

The first national off-reservation boarding school was established in 1879 in Carlisle, Pennsylvania, by Richard Pratt (Spring 2010). Pratt, a former Civil War prison warden turned Indian educator, has been attributed with the quote that the goal of Indian education was to "kill the Indian to save the man" in every student (Churchill 2004). Furthermore, Spring

(2010, 33) credits Pratt with the slogan of the Carlisle Indian School that reflected the emphasis on changing cultural patterns of Indians: "To civilize the Indian, get him to civilization. To keep him civilized, let him stay."

The above quote, with the emphasis on "let him stay," was clearly evident in that the children usually spent a minimum of eight continuous years away from their families and communities in South Dakota, as in other areas of the country (Garrett 1996). In Pratt's argument, the time spent in off-reservation boarding schools was necessary to immerse "Indians in our civilization and when we get them under [hold] them until they are thoroughly soaked" (Spring 1997, 33).

The off-reservation boarding schools, according to Riney (1999, 7) in his book *The Rapid City Indian School*, "were the government's most powerful weapon against tribes and tribal cultures." Sending students to the off-reservation boarding schools was a major factor in the acculturation effort.

Boarding school education. Through the first half of the nineteenth century, the idea of assimilation guided all boarding-school curriculum development for Native American education. According to Yazzie (1999), Native American students endured a series of forced introductions to a new "civilized" culture. The replacement of Native languages with English, demand for allegiance to the U.S. government, and destruction of Indian customs emerged as the major educational polices for Native students during this time (Spring 2010).

For decades, Native American students tried to make sense of what they learned in history, math, and reading lessons while living in a separate society. Clearly, the position of American Indian students from Tribal nations in South Dakota was being made obvious to these students while they were supposedly studying the history of "their" country as well as engaging in other educational pursuits.

Lomawaima (1999, 17) writes, "Children found themselves in difficult, often hostile circumstances where their own language, religion, culture, behavior, and individualism were under constant, systematic attack." Often the attempt to civilize Indian students was brutal and even sadistic. Being cognizant of these oppressive conditions, why would some Sioux families willingly send their children to the boarding schools?

By the beginning of the *boarding school experience* (Adams 1995), the open warfare of the High Plains was largely over. In a very real sense, going to school for Native people was a substitute for going to war. In a different sense, and for the government, too, the school was a way to continue a conflict by other means. Riney (1999, 4) writes about how some Sioux saw the boarding school as an opportunity:

> Ota Kte (Luther Standing Bear) remembered his father, Mato Najin (Standing Bear), who had many times told his son the value of bravery on the battlefield. It was better to die young on the battlefield, even away from home, than to suffer old age. Yet Mato Najin had made peace with his enemies and no longer fought. Perhaps taking the chance to go east [to the Carlisle Indian School] would prove Ota Kte's bravery.

This is not to say that the Native Americans and Sioux generally did not place great value on education. The Sioux of the Pine Ridge Indian Reservation sent so many of their young people to the Rapid City Indian School that the superintendent had to discourage more pupils from making the journey to the school (Riney 1999).

While writing about the Chilocco Indian School of the Desert Southwest in her book *They Called It Prairie Light*, Lomawaima (1994, 19) notes: "In the Indian Territory, education was by and large a desired commodity." The Native Americans recognized that acquiring an education, even under a system that was foreign to them, was an opportunity to show their bravery and a chance to succeed academically.

Changes in educational policies. The educational polices of the United States government described above continued into the 1900s as some people started to critically examine the role that the U.S. government should play in Indian education. For the first time, the U.S. government considered the cultural aspects and educational needs of Native Americans. However, efforts to provide an education more respectful of Native American cultures have been sporadic throughout American Indian educational history.

The first discussion that legitimized cultural considerations in the Bureau of Indian Affairs (BIA) school curricula began with the release of *The Problem of Indian Administration*, better known as the Meriam Report of 1928 (Yazzie 1999). The Meriam Report signaled a significant change for the U.S. government's policies for Indian Education (Yazzie 1999). The report stated that "the most fundamental need in Indian education was a change in government attitude" (Meriam 1928, 346).

Another salient change was the desire of the U.S. government to move away from the boarding school polices and toward a local approach to providing education. Federal policy after the Meriam Report (Meriam 1928) began to stress community day schools as well as the support of Native cultures (Spring 2010). Even so, including information about Sioux culture and history in the curricula for American Indian students in South Dakota proceeded very slowly, probably due to fears concerning addressing the truth about the "Indian Wars" and the massacre at Wounded Knee (EyeWitness to History 1998).

Elimination through termination and relocation. Despite the criticism of Native American education after the release of the Meriam Report (Meriam 1928) and the subsequent move away from the boarding school policies, education did not markedly improve for Native American students. In fact, in some ways it became worse. During the 1940s and 1950s, federal Indian policy was directed at termination of both tribes and reservations (Spring 2010).

During this period of termination, vast tracts of Native American lands were sold. This plunged Native Americans into deeper poverty (Garrett 1996). In South Dakota, the Sioux were divested of 9,000,000 acres of their land through the selling of "surplus" land to non-Native farmers, ranchers, and homesteaders. As a result, many consider the Yankton Sioux to now be landless (Johnston 1948). During this time, the U.S. government reduced tribally held land bases from 140 million acres to just under 50 million acres (U.S. Congress 1969). The most productive land, the most valuable land, was taken from Native people and often sold for a fraction of actual value to neighboring white farmers and ranchers (U.S. Congress 1969).

Again, the federal policy was moving toward assimilation through relocation (Spring 2010). The policy was an attempt to break up tribes and relocate Native Americans to urban settings. A negative aspect of the relocation effort was its intention to achieve sociocultural integration of Native Americans within the dominant culture. The relocation effort was met with great resistance, and Native Americans found an ally in the Kennedy administration in the 1960s. Although the relocation effort failed, there remain comparatively large pockets of Native Americans in urban settings in South Dakota, as in other states.

A New Era for American Indian Education

In 1969, the U.S. Senate Special Subcommittee on Indian Education, part of the Senate Committee on Labor and Public Welfare, issued the report *Indian Education: A National Tragedy—A National Challenge* (U.S. Congress 1969), also known as the Kennedy Report. Apparently recognizing the errors of the past, the special committee reported that the historical literature revealed that the dominant policy of the U.S. government toward the Native Americans had been one of forced assimilation and the desire to divest the Native Americans of land.

The Kennedy Report (U.S. Congress 1969) documented the significant failure of American public education to address Native learners' needs. The report identified the federal government's policy of coercive assimilation of American Indians and Alaska Native peoples as the fundamental cause of this failure.

The most significant attribute of the Kennedy Report (U.S. Congress 1969) was the recommendation of "maximum participation and control by Indians in establishing Indian education programs" (Spring 1997, 120). With the Kennedy Report (U.S. Congress 1969) as a springboard, schools and programs began to move toward meeting the needs of Native Americans for the first time since colonization.

Strides were being taken to ensure the efficacy and solvency of education for Native American students. One of the first steps forward was the passage of the Indian Education Act of 1972 (Reyhner 1994). The act was aimed toward providing financial assistance to meet the needs of Native American students (Spring 2010).

The next and most important step was the Indian Self-Determination and Education Assistance Act of 1975, which gave tribes the power to contract with the U.S. government to run their own education and health programs (Spring 2010). This was meaningful not only for the reservation schools, but also because it allowed the Sioux to influence their education at off-reservation schools.

Educational Success of Native American Students in South Dakota Today

The education afforded to Native Americans has improved, but students "continue to be disproportionately affected by poverty, low educational attainment, and access to fewer educational opportunities than other students" (Beaulieu 2000, 35). Sheets (2003, 112) criticizes, "In reality, as U.S. citizens our children are methodically violated in our public schools and their entitlement to equal educational opportunities is criminally denied."

Many factors have been illustrative of this fact thus far. Beaulieu (2000) finds that Indian students often start school unprepared to learn, their achievement rate is often lower, the dropout rates for Indian students are high, and few Indian students enter and finish college.

Moran and others (2008) report that Native Americans and Alaska Native students have an average dropout rate (among all of the different tribal nations) of 33 percent, about twice the national average and the highest dropout rate of any ethnic or racial group cited in the United States. The current dropout rate for members of the Sioux nation in South Dakota is 50 percent (South Dakota Department of Education 2011), much higher than dropout rates of the averaged American Indian populations as a whole.

While some Native Americans drop out of school because their needs are not being met, Reyhner and Eder (1992, 36) wrote that others are "pushed out because they protest, in a variety of ways, how they are being treated." According to Villegas (1988), the act of dropping out may be a form of resistance to the dominant culture and its oppressive conditions in society, although the behavior itself is probably counterproductive in that it can function to disempower minorities further.

Spring (1999, 93) considers the position of culture in schools serving American Indian students. He suggests that students' "loyalty to their native culture versus accommodation to the dominant culture premised on the belief that neither abandoning one's own culture nor gaining respect and acceptance will do anything to change the basic political and economic relations in society" has been a contributing factor to the high dropout rate of Native students.

Examining successful teaching practices for Native American students. With the aforementioned rates of nonpersistency for Native American students, researchers should be motivated not to continue to document the manifold negative aspects of the inferior education that Native Americans receive but rather to investigate what exemplary teachers are doing to help keep Native American students in the classroom. In South Dakota, as in other regions, the goal should be on increasing the graduation rate for American Indian students.

What educators must do is examine the place of culture and teaching practices in classrooms in order to best influence the education of Native American students. Whitbeck and others (2001) argue that traditional culture functions as a protective mechanism when used to guide curriculum. Deyhle and Swisher (1997, 182) report that "research based on cultural strengths and culture integrity has yielded significant sustainable results for some schools and communities."

A solution to the academic failure of Native students seems to be found in the ability of teachers to mitigate social and economic factors influencing poor academic performance by immersing themselves in the communities in which they teach (Demmert 2001). Tippeconnic (2000, 39) has argued that the key to success is two-fold: "first, to hire competent teachers who know how to teach Indian students; and second, . . . increase parental and tribal involvement" in schools.

The emergent question seems to be what do such teachers do differently in their classrooms to foster success for Native American students? It appears that literature provides a road map for the best practice in the education of Native Americans with the role of culture as its roots. Whitbeck and others (2001), like Coburn and Nelson (1987), found that maternal warmth, extracurricular activities, a sense of enculturation, and self-esteem relate positively to school success. These findings support a growing body of research on Native American cultural traditions supporting Native youths' school success.

Whitbeck and others (2001) believe that living a traditional cultural lifestyle may result in cultural discontinuity, which occurs when Native American students find themselves in an environment that contradicts their traditional values. Both teachers and students come to the classroom with expectations about how people should behave (and speak and think and feel) derived largely from their experiences outside the classroom (Jordan 1985). If teachers and students come from different cultural backgrounds, they may differ in those expectations on a great many fronts.

However, traditional culture imbues children with pride in cultural heritage and gives them the direction they need to negotiate their way through the cultural contradictions in school (Whitbeck et al. 2001). With the role of traditional culture so plainly important to school success for Native American children, teachers have yet another insight about how best to teach their students through integrating cultures within the schools.

Reyhner's (1992) research indicates that particularly critical factors for Indian students' success include smaller schools, caring and trained teachers, active teaching methods, appropriate curriculum, appropriate testing/student retention, and parental involvement. This seems to be consistent with what promotes school success in general, and South Dakotan schools need to heed this research.

Much work remains to be done. Researchers should continue to investigate the manifold challenges inherent in educating Native American students. "Much of the current diversity scholarship, in spite of its quantity and quality, appears to advance a mindset satisfied with magic, hope, and advocacy—rather than pedagogy" (Sheets 2003, 113). As Tippeconnic (2000, 39) suggests, "We have not learned how to put this research into practice, or have determined the best ways to prepare teachers or to teach students." It is what is done with this knowledge that affects change.

Preparation of new teachers of American Indian students. Researchers need to continue to ask deep questions to probe for findings that will help put this research into practice in order to prepare teacher candidates and teachers for the struggle to narrow the achievement gap for Native American students. We must be cognizant and respectful of the education research produced by American Indians themselves, who have an "insiders' view" of educational issues (Swisher 1996), while at the same time working together as Native and non-Native researchers effecting change (Lomawaima and McCarty 2002).

Rather than being satisfied with the mindset of magic, hope, and advocacy that Sheets (2003) leveled against educators and researchers alike, we need to embark on deep investigations of best teaching practices for Native American students that will ultimately yield tangible results in the classroom. Educators need to know what works and how to implement best practices for Native learners.

Future research should, according to Bowman (2003, 99–100), build a new "Native American learning theory that builds on culturally relevant pedagogy, research, and evaluation strategies, which would ultimately inform kindergarten through graduate level educational policies, departments, and organizations." Teacher educators need to know how to best prepare teacher candidates, as well as in-service teachers, to meet the needs of diverse learners.

Implementing research results in classrooms. The investigation alone is not enough. Teachers must use this research to impact Native students' learning and achievement. While, admittedly, many factors exist that are not within the scope of influence of the classroom teacher, our teacher candidates must become educated in culturally responsive methods to focus on those factors that can be addressed in the classroom.

The current method of preparing teachers to work in a multiethnic teaching situation is less than exemplary because the needs of all learners are not being met. "To support democracy, educators must seek to eliminate disparities in educational opportunities among all students, especially those students who have been poorly served by our current system" (Banks et al. 2005, 233).

In addition to the staggering rate of nonpersistency at the high school level, apparent discrepancies exist due to high-stakes testing. In general, according to Fox (1999), American Indian students have traditionally scored exceedingly low on standardized achievement tests. Nichols and Berliner (2007) write that the curriculum imposed by high-stakes testing for Native Americans seems to be especially damaging; the curriculum is narrowed, and it is also culturally irrelevant for the children it is supposed to educate.

With an intense focus on high-stakes testing, teachers feel forced to design curricula that are boring and alien to their students (Nichols and Berliner 2007). In their book *Collateral Damage*, Nichols and Berliner (2007, 57) state, "It is widely known that if the disaffected or weakest students can be pushed out of schools or allowed to dropout [sic], then the test scores at the school or district that loses these students will go up."

If this is the case, then schools have a vested interest in the failure of some students (Nichols and Berliner 2007). Nichols and Berliner (2007) believe that schools are driving out students through a test-oriented curriculum and abandoning the kind of culturally relevant curriculum that might keep them in school. "This will have the effect of increasing the already high dropout rates while at the same time potentially raising the scores at the schools, thus making it difficult for school personnel to address this issue" (Nichols and Berliner 2007, 72).

Educators of conscience cannot afford to allow the pressure of high-stakes testing, with the attendant threat of fiscal punishment for their schools, drive students out. This is just as important in South Dakota as in every other state in the nation as the current state of education nationally is being dictated by these conditions.

Changing the Climate in South Dakota Classrooms for Native Students' Success

A discussion of the importance of culture in schools is salient if the overarching goal is to keep Native American students in the classroom and guide them toward graduation. According to Bruner (1996), culture provides the tools for organizing and understanding our world in communicable ways. Implicit in the discussion of understanding Native American students is the understanding of poverty and the students' home environments and their influences on education.

Educators must critically examine culture and teaching practice to best influence the education of Indian students. "Traditional culture may function as a protective mechanism when it is used to guide curriculum" (Whitbeck et al. 2001, 2).

Demmert (2001, 18) argues that "social and economic factors influencing poor academic performance could be mitigated by teachers who become involved in community activities and spend time with community members." Teachers must be able and willing to mitigate these factors.

The school is not neutral ground for proving talent. Villegas (1988, 260) illustrates the reality of hegemony in education: "As the educational system is currently organized, it functions to maintain the advantage of the socially powerful." To maintain power, a dominant culture emphasizes the history of conquest at the expense of other histories.

The advantages of the socially powerful have been preserved with resulting disastrous effects for nonwhite students. This is evident in the expectation that the subservient culture must conform to a dominant cultural norm (Starnes 2006, 185).

Ogbu (1992, 9) argues that one significant reason that the dominant culture has preserved this power is due to the belief that involuntary minorities "have greater difficulty crossing cultural/language boundaries in school than voluntary minorities with primary cultural differences." This belief occurs because of the nature of the relationship between involuntary minority cultures and the dominant white American culture. Involuntary minorities' cultural differences have initially arisen to serve as boundary-maintaining and coping functions under subordination and have evolved into oppositional qualities of struggle.

Villegas (1988, 262) purports that "the problem of academic failure is much more complex than differences between the language or culture of home and school. The differences that create difficulties for both teacher and pupils stem from the struggle for power in society" and would require political action to resolve. Ogbu (1992) describes the parasitic relationship between the dominant and dominated groups: dominant groups maintain their power by using it to define what is valued in school and society while dominated groups exert their power by resisting oppressive authority.

This argument would seem to allow educators to throw up their collective hands and absolve themselves of responsibility for the lack of student success. Rather, Pewewardy and Hammer (2003) shift responsibility for change back to the individuals who are closest to education, in other words, to those who make the decisions and hold the attitudes and beliefs in schools concerning the achievement of ethnically diverse students.

This is reflected in Ogbu's (1992) assertion that minority students do not succeed or fail only because of what the schools do or do not do but also because of the action of the community. The social structure and relationship within minority communities seems to have a significant impact on students' attitudes toward school. There may be a mismatch between students' home environments and school environments (Cajete 1999) or differing expectations for schools on many fronts (Jordan 1985). Thus educators, schools, and communities must help foster cultural pride (Whitbeck et al. 2001).

Yazzie (1999) has pointed to the growing body of research suggesting that better learning occurs when teachers transform their educational practices and the curriculum to reflect the children's home cultures. If the infusion of culture, as the research literature suggests, has apparent benefits, then educators must transform their teaching practices and the ways in which they educate Native American students. The crux is in how that cultural transformation occurs.

Today, many Native American youth experience cultural conflicts and difficulties in identity development due to differences between the values and expectations of their tribal traditions and those of mainstream American social and educational systems (Garrett 1996). This situation is reflected in the education for Native American students in South Dakota as well.

These factors have important ramifications for finding new ways of teaching Native American students in South Dakota, including understanding that language and/or the degree of traditionalism can isolate students, thereby impacting learning either positively or negatively. Through identifying with tribal traditions, teachers may be able to build relationships with students and families, thus strengthening their teaching.

In conclusion, although the obstacles for narrowing the achievement gap for Native American students in South Dakota are numerous and those challenges are clearly daunting, the solution may be found in the preparation of teachers. Reflective, well-trained, culturally responsive/reflective, community-building educators can make a significant difference in the lives of Native American youth (Klug and Whitfield 2003; Ladson-Billings 1995; Yazzie 1999).

The powerful impact of this model of gifted, culturally sensitive educators is not to be underestimated. It requires teachers who have taken it upon themselves to learn about the Sioux culture, attend community events, get to know community members who can act as mentors, and are unafraid of being criticized for doing so by members of the dominant culture. In the words of Yazzie (1999, 84), "If Indigenous agriculture, jazz music, Broadway theater productions, tribal courts, and medical research are all embodiments of culture, so is schooling."

REFERENCES

Adams, D. W. (1995). *Education for Extinction: American Indians and the Boarding School Experience, 1875–1928*. Lawrence: University of Kansas Press.

Banks, J., M. Cochran-Smith, L. Moll, A. Richert, K. Zeichner, P. LePage, L. Darling-Hammond, and H. Duffy. (2005). Teaching diverse learners. In *Preparing Teachers for a Changing World: What Teachers Should Learn and Be Able to Do*, ed. L. Darling-Hammond and J. Bransford, 232–76. San Francisco: Jossey-Bass.

Beaulieu, D. (2000). "Comprehensive reform and American Indian education." *Journal of American Indian Education* 39 (2): 29–38. Retrieved from http://jaie.asu.edu/v39/index.html.

Bowman, N. (2003). "Cultural differences of teaching and learning: A Native American perspective of participating in educational systems and organizations." *American Indian Quarterly* 27 (1): 91–102.

Brown, D. (1971). *Bury My Heart at Wounded Knee: An Indian History of the American West*. New York: Holt, Rinehart and Winston.

Bruner, J. (1996). *The Culture of Education*. Cambridge, MA: Harvard University Press.

Cajete, G. (1999). "The Native American learner and bicultural science education." In *Next Steps: Research and Practice to Advance Indian Education*, ed. K. G. Swisher and J. W. Tippeconnic III, 162–78. Charleston, WV: Appalachia Educational Laboratory.

Churchill, W. (2004). *Kill the Indian, Save the Man: The Genocidal Impact of American Indian Resident Schools*. San Francisco: City Lights.

Coburn, J., and S. Nelson. (1987). *Characteristics of Successful Indian Students: Research and Development Program for Indian Education*. Portland, OR: Northwest Regional Educational Laboratory.

Cook-Lynn, E. (2005). Review of *The Plains Sioux and U.S. Colonialism from Lewis and Clark to Wounded Knee*, by Jeffrey Ostler. *Wicazo Sa Review* 20 (1): 199–201.

Demmert, W. (2001). *Improving Academic Performance Among Native American Students: A Review of the Research Literature*. Charleston, WV: Appalachia Educational Laboratory.

Deyhle, D., and K. Swisher. (1997). "Research in American Indian and Alaska Native education: From assimilation to self-determination." *Review of Research in Education* 22:113–94. Retrieved from http://www.jstor.org/stable/1167375.

EyeWitness to History. (1998). "Massacre at Wounded Knee, 1890." http://www.eyewitnesstohistory.com/knee.htm.

Fox, S. (1999). "Student assessment in Indian education, or what is a roach?" In *Next Steps: Research and Practice to Advance Indian Education*, ed. K. G. Swisher and J. W. Tippeconnic III, 162–78. Charleston, WV: Appalachia Educational Laboratory.

Garcia, R. L., and J. G. Alher. (1992). "Indian education: Assumptions, ideologies, strategies." In *Teaching American Indian Students*, ed. J. Reyhner, 13–32. Norman: University of Oklahoma Press.

Garrett, M. T. (1996). "Two people: An American Indian narrative of bicultural identity." *Journal of American Indian Education* 36 (1): 1–21.

Indian Education Act of 1972. (2000). *U.S. code*. Title 20, sec. 3385 et seq.

Johnston, M. A. (1948). *Federal Relations with the Great Sioux Indians of South Dakota: With Particular Reference to Land Policy Under the Dawes Act*. PhD diss., Catholic University of America, Washington, DC.

Jordan, C. (1985). "The role of culture in minority school achievement." *Kamehameha Journal of Education* 3 (2): 135–49.

Klug, B. J., and P. T. Whitfield. (2003). *Widening the Circle: Culturally Relevant Pedagogy for American Indian Children*. New York: RoutledgeFalmer.

Ladson-Billings, G. (1995). "Toward a theory of culturally relevant pedagogy." *American Education Research Journal* 35: 465–91.

Lomawaima, K. T. (1994). *They Called it Prairie Light: The Story of Chilocco Indian School*. Lincoln: University of Nebraska Press.

———. (1999). "The unnatural history of American Indian education." In *Next steps: Research and Practice to Advance Indian Education*, ed. K. G. Swisher and J. W. Tippeconnic III, 3–31. Charleston, WV: Appalachia Educational Laboratory.

Lomawaima, T. and T. McCarty. (2002). *Reliability, Validity, and Authenticity in American Indian and Alaska Research*. Charleston, WV: ERIC Clearinghouse on Rural Education and Small Schools. Education Resources Information Center. Retrieved from http://www.eric.ed.gov.

Meriam, L., comp. (1928). *The Problem of Indian Administration*. Baltimore: Johns Hopkins Press.

Moran, R., B. D. Rampey, G. S. Dion, and P. L. Donahue. (2008). *National Indian Education Study 2007 Part I: Performance of American Indian and Alaska Native Students at Grades 4 and 8 on NAEP 2007 Reading and Mathematics Assessments*. Washington, DC: National Center for Education Statistics, Institute of Education Sciences, U.S. Department of Education.

Nichols, S., and D. Berliner. (2007). *Collateral Damage: How High-stakes Testing Corrupts America's Schools*. Cambridge, MA: Harvard Education Press.

Ogbu, J. (1992). "Understanding cultural diversity and learning." *Educational Researcher* 21 (8): 5–14, 24.

Pewewardy, C., and P. C. Hammer. (2003). *Culturally Responsive Teaching for American Indian Students*. Charleston, WV: ERIC Clearinghouse on Rural Education and Small Schools. Education Resources Information Center. Retrieved from http://www.eric.ed.gov (accession number ED482325).

Reyhner, J. (1992). "American Indians out of school: A review of school-based causes and solutions." *Journal of American Indian Education* 31 (3): 37–56. Retrieved from http://jaie.asu.edu/v39/index.html.

———. (1994). *Teaching American Indian Students*. Norman: University of Oklahoma Press.

Riney, S. (1999). *The Rapid City Indian School, 1898–1933*. Norman: University of Oklahoma Press.

Sheets, R. (2003). "Competency vs. good intentions: Diversity ideologies and teacher potential." *International Journal of Qualitative Studies in Education* 16 (1): 111–20.

South Dakota Department of Education. (2011). *No Child Left Behind 2011 Report Card*. Retrieved from http://doe.sd.gov/NCLB/reports/2011/reportcard/2011state.pdf.

Spring, J. (1997). *Deculturalization and the Struggle for Equality: A Brief History of the Education of Dominated Cultures in the United States*. 2nd ed. New York: McGraw-Hill.

———. (1999). *Wheels in the Head: Educational Philosophies of Authority, Freedom, and Culture from Socrates to Human Rights*. New York: McGraw-Hill.

———. (2010). *Deculturalization and the Struggle for Equality: A Brief History of the Education of Dominated Cultures in the United States*. 6th ed. New York: McGraw-Hill.

Starnes, B. (2006). "What we don't know *can* hurt them: White teachers, Indian children." *Phi Delta Kappan* 87 (5): 384–92.

Swisher, K. G. (1996). "Why Indian people should be the ones to write about Indian education." *American Indian Quarterly* 20 (1): 83–90.

Tippeconnic, J. W., III. (2000). "Reflecting on the past: Some important aspects of Indian education to consider as we look toward the future." *Journal of American Indian Education* 39 (2): 39–48. Retrieved from http://jaie.asu.edu/v39/V39I2A4.pdf.

U.S. Congress. Senate. Committee on Labor and Public Welfare. Special Subcommittee on Indian Education. (1969). *Indian Education: A National Tragedy—A National Challenge*. 91st Cong., 1st sess. S. Rep. 91–501.

Villegas, A. (1988). "School failure and cultural mismatch: Another view." *Urban Review* 20 (4): 253–65.

Whitbeck, L. B., D. R. Hoyt, J. D. Stubben, and T. LaFramboise. 2001. "Traditional culture and academic success among American Indian children in the upper Midwest." *Journal of American Indian Education* 40 (2): 49–60. Retrieved from http://jaie.asu.edu/v40/V40I2A3.pdf.

Yazzie, T. (1999). "Culturally appropriate curriculum." In *Next Steps: Research and Practice to Advance Indian Education*, ed. K. G. Swisher and J. W. Tippeconnic III, 84–106. Charleston, WV: Appalachia Educational Laboratory.

NOTE

1. The term *Sioux* is used to designate the Lakota, Dakota, and Nakota collectively.

Chapter 3

A History of American Indian Culturally Sensitive Education

Jon Reyhner: Northern Arizona University

ABSTRACT

This chapter details the history of Indian education beginning with the abysmal results of the boarding-school era and the failed attempts to educate American Indian children through the use of assimilation with the dominant culture in schools. Most importantly, it focuses on the recommendations for education included in the 1928 Meriam Report released by the Institute for Government Research, the Brookings Institute, located at Johns Hopkins University (Meriam 1928).

Among the report's authors, W. Carson Ryan, Jr. and Henry Roe Cloud—Winnebago and first American Indian Yale graduate and holder of a master's degree in anthropology—recommend acknowledging the importance of the role of culture in the education of children and youth. They call for culturally sensitive education for American Indian students that follows the philosophy of Dewey's progressive education movement (College of Education and Social Services), involving democratic decision making and active learning in classrooms.

Following these recommendations, the administrators of the U.S. Indian Office actively supported educational efforts capitalizing on American Indian cultures, languages, and knowledge produced by each tribal nation. They provided in-service activities during the summers for teachers to learn culturally responsive methodologies for teaching, as well as biweekly news magazines covering these topics.

The chapter chronicles other efforts to provide culturally sensitive education for Indigenous students. It ends with the failure of the No Child Left Behind Act (2001) to advance education for American Indian students in today's America.

Keywords: American Indian education, history of culturally sensitive education

A HISTORY OF AMERICAN INDIAN CULTURALLY SENSITIVE EDUCATION

Throughout the history of American Indian Education in the United States—whether provided by Christian missionaries, the U.S. government, or public schools—the main thrust was to assimilate American Indians into the dominant culture with English-only schooling that gave little or no recognition to, or appreciation for, the cultures of the various Indian nations. Based on the National Study of American Indian Education carried out from 1967 to 1971, Estelle Fuchs and Robert J. Havighurst conclude,

> With minor exceptions the history of Indian education had been primarily the transmission of white American education, little altered, to the Indian child as a one-way process. The institution of the school is one that was imposed by and controlled by the non-Indian society, its pedagogy and curriculum little changed for the Indian children, its goals primarily aimed at removing the child from his aboriginal culture and assimilating him into the dominant white culture. Whether coercive or persuasive, this assimilationist goal of schooling has been minimally effective with Indian children, as indicated by their record of absenteeism, retardation, and high dropout rates. (1972, 18)

As a long-time Indian Bureau teacher and agent notes, the U.S. government's Indian Bureau "went on the assumption that any Indian custom was, per se, objectionable, whereas the customs of whites were the ways of civilization" (Kneale 1950, 4). However, there were the "minor exceptions" that Fuchs and Havighurst (1972) note—attempts at culturally appropriate education—at some times and in some places.

These efforts were made to provide culturally sensitive education designed to meet the needs of American Indian students, including listening to what American Indian families and communities wanted for their children. This chapter focuses particularly on efforts made in the 1930s and 1940s in schools run by the U.S. Indian Office to promote culturally responsive Indian education.

The Meriam Report and Progressive Education

In the 1920s, a comprehensive independent study of U.S. government policy toward American Indians was undertaken by the Institute for Government Research, the Brookings Institute, at Johns Hopkins University. Commonly known as the Meriam Report (Meriam 1928), this study emphasizes the need for specialized curriculum and instructional practices for Indian students, as stated in the following:

> It is true in all education, but especially in the education of people situated as are the American Indians, that methods must be adapted to individual abilities, interests, and needs. A standard course of study, routine classroom methods, traditional types of schools, even if they were adequately supplied—and they are not—would not solve the problem. The methods of the average public school in the United States cannot safely be taken over bodily and applied to Indian education. Indian tribes and individual Indians within the tribes vary so much that a standard content and method of education, no matter how carefully they might be prepared, would be worse than futile. (Meriam 1928, 347)

It was deemed necessary that "everything in the Indian life and surroundings will have to tie in the educational program in a manner now seldom observed" (Meriam 1928, 351). In regard to teaching reading, the Meriam Report notes, "There is such a chance to build up for the Indian schools reading material that shall have some relation to Indian interests, not merely Indian legends . . . but actual stories of modern Indian experiences" (Meriam 1928, 372–73). Furthermore, "it is the task of education to help the Indian, not by assuming that he is fundamentally different, but that he is a human being very much like the rest of us, with a cultural background quite worthwhile for its own sake and as a basis for changes needed in adjusting to modern life" (Meriam 1928, 354).

The authors of the education section of the Meriam Report (Meriam 1928) included W. Carson Ryan Jr. and Henry Roe Cloud (Winnebago), the first American Indian Yale graduate who also received a Yale master's degree in anthropology in 1914. Like Sioux doctor and author Charles Eastman, Roe Cloud was a student at the bilingual Santee Normal Training School. Ryan went on to serve as the U.S. Indian Service's Director of Education from 1930 to 1935, and he wrote an introductory article with Rose Brandt, the Indian Service's Supervisor of Elementary Education, in the February 1932 issue of the journal *Progressive Education* that was devoted to Indian education. In their introduction, they call for summer institutes for Indian Service teachers to include:

1. Environmental experiences of children as a basis for school procedure and curriculum content.
2. Philosophy of progressive education, basing school work on activities and at the same time recognizing and providing opportunities for various learning outcomes rather than beginning and ending teaching procedures mainly with subject matter. (Ryan and Brandt 1932, 83)

In the same issue, a teacher at Eastern Navajo School in Crownpoint, New Mexico, saw the school lunch as the place to start teaching English, with students learning names for utensils and different kinds of food. She notes how "sand tables" (raised sand boxes used to sculpture a miniature scene) were used in Indian schools:

> The sand table provides another center of never-failing interest and opportunity for vocabulary building. Here are constructed houses such as we live in, barns, schoolhouse, sidewalks, windmill, stores, chicken houses, pens, fences, troughs, trees, tanks, church, garages, trucks, cars—all illustrative of the school and agency or the home community. Usually, the first sand-table scene consists of the school village. (Heger 1932, 143)

Literacy learning in English. A first-grade boarding-school teacher at Fort Apache, Arizona, in "Teaching Navajo Children to Read," notes that students should not be expected to read English without first developing some oral English vocabulary. Too often, students would read aloud well (or pronounce the words right) but not comprehend what they read. She maintains, "The child's own experiences should form the basis of his reading materials" (Lawhead 1932, 133). Beginning students needed "simple sentences" and "plenty of action." Her students would make original drawings for their favorite stories and dramatize scenes from them. She also used a sand table to "make the story."

In a section titled "Language Experiments of Indian Children," the 1932 special issue describes a process similar to the "language experience approach" (Ashton-Warner 1986; Stauffer 1970) to teaching reading:

> The children talk over their experiences in group discussion, the teacher keeping a written record on the blackboard of their comments. These are later presented to the children to be read on large charts or in the form of booklets which have been hektographed or written on typewriters having Primer type faces. ("Language Experiments" 1932, 154)

A sample description of "Navajo Father" used with first graders was:

> Navajo father wears a shirt and pants. Navajo father wears a green headband. He wears red kil'chi on his feet. He wears a blanket to keep him warm. Navajo father wears blue earrings. He wears beads on his neck.

Navajo father works. He plows the ground. He plants corn and watermelons. He makes the hogan. He chops the tree. He chops wood. He takes care of goats and sheep. He rides the horse. ("Language Experiments" 1932, 154)

In an article titled "We Make Our Own Books" in the Indian Service publication *Indians at Work*, Brandt (1935) describes how older students wrote books for younger ones using familiar vocabulary. For example, a book written by fourth graders had chapters on home life, history, customs, ceremonials, and legends.

In her autobiography describing her experiences as an Indian Service teacher starting in the 1920s and retiring in 1954, Polingaysi Qöyawayma (Hopi) notes the importance "on teaching from the known to the unknown" and that "there should be no parrot learning" where students memorized how to sound out words without comprehending their meaning (1964, 150). Criticizing the use of non-Indian curriculum, she declares,

What do these white-men stories mean to a Hopi child? What is a 'choo-choo' to these little ones who have never seen a train? No! I will not begin with the outside world of which they have no knowledge. I shall begin with the familiar. The everyday things. The things of home and family. (Qöyawayma 1964, 125)

She replaced European folk tales with familiar Hopi legends and songs, and she was reprimanded for her temerity by her immediate supervisors for not teaching only in English. However, higher ups in the Indian Service—including Roe Cloud and John Collier, commissioner of Indian affairs from 1933 to 1945—applauded her work and commissioned her to do workshops on her teaching methods for Indian Service teachers. Collier had been extremely critical of the U.S. Indian Service in the 1920s, and, under him, Willard Beatty, the president of the Progressive Education Association (PEA), became the Indian Service's director of Indian education, serving from 1936 to 1952. Ryan then took over Beatty's position of president of the PEA.

On September 1, 1936, the same day Henry Roe Cloud became supervisor of Indian education, Beatty launched a fortnightly newsletter to reach his widely dispersed staff (from Alaska to Florida). The first issue described two six-week college-credit institutes held the past summer with 190 attendees at Pine Ridge, South Dakota, and 200 attending the institute at Fort Wingate, New Mexico. At the Wingate institute, "anthropology was seen in its relationship to the teaching problem" ("Summer Institutes" 1936, 3), and classes were offered in spoken Navajo.

The Sioux language was taught at the Pine Ridge institute ("Summer Institutes" 1936). The index for the first year of *Indian Education* listed eight articles under the heading "anthropology." A discussion about ethnocentrism in the first issue became extended into a whole article on "In-group and Out-group" in the fourth issue.

The third issue of the newsletter describes a series of Indian readers printed and distributed to all Indian schools, edited by Rose Brandt, based on the "belief that Indian children, like white children, learn to read more easily and with greater enthusiasm when the subject matter that they are reading deals with experience close to child life" ("Indian Readers" 1936, 5). The issue also includes an article on why Indian boarding schools failed.

A 1940 summary of the inter-American [Patzcuaro] conference on Indian affairs written by Beatty notes,

Possibly the most fundamental change which has taken place in the objectives of Indian educators grows out of a recognition of the fundamental values in Indian cultures, and a desire to preserve these values while making available to the Indian the advantageous element of the dominant culture. Most important of these older culture elements which is receiving recognition is the native language. (1940, 7)

In *Journey to the People*, Indian Service teacher and children's author Ann Nolan Clark (1969) recalls how Beatty encouraged experimenting with teaching approaches and methods. She states that all the Indian-school teachers in the late 1930s were using "experience reading charts" where the teacher wrote down student descriptions of class activities on chart paper.

However, Clark's students, rather than learning to read, would memorize what she wrote and singsong it back. "But these were charts, and to the children charts were charts and had no connection with books" (Clark 1969, 56). She even folded paper and bound it with yarn to make booklets, but still her Tesuque Pueblo students did not see these as books and were still against books because they saw books as some sort of white-man's magic closed to them.

Buying a mimeograph machine with her own money, Clark's "book-hating third graders with ceremony and pomp were henceforth the Tesuque Printers" (Clark 1969, 58) and printed *A Third Grade Home Geography*, written by Clark about everyday life in the pueblo. Beatty helped Clark get this book published in 1941 by the Viking Press under the title *In My Mother's House*, which was named a Caldecott Honor Book.

Clark's initially reluctant readers went on to Haskell and Sherman Indian schools, and one went on to college, and another became an artist. Clark went on to help write a whole series of books for Indian students in the 1940s, including *The Hen of Wahpeton* (1954), *Little Herder in Autumn* (1940), *The Pine Ridge Porcupine* (1941), and *Young Hunter of Picuris* (1943), some of which were bilingual and printed at Haskell and Phoenix Indian schools.

Clark (1969, 88) writes of the need

> for children to have books written for them that will help them develop an understanding of themselves, their potentialities and resources, and the pressures and problems of their immediate world. It is the need for books to be written that will help give them an insight into, and an acceptance of, the larger world outside their own.

She declares that "books for children should help develop an appreciation of life and all that life means and holds and promises" (Clark 1969, 97).

Shoshone teacher Esther Burnett Horne (Horne and McBeth 1998) recalls that Indian Service teachers were encouraged to take progressive education courses during the 1930s, a welcome break for her from sanding student desks in the summer. These courses encouraged her to integrate different subjects into thematic units. She describes a farm unit where

> children might begin by making and decorating the farm buildings out of cardboard boxes. We then might study concepts associated with farm life, like keeping records of the sale of produce. . . . I found this method of teaching interesting and challenging but also difficult to use in teaching my students enough of the basics. I felt that sometimes the students were shortchanged by the use of this method alone, and I supplemented it with materials correlated to the state course of study. (Horne and McBeth 1998, 76–77)

During the summer of 1935, Horne took two anthropology classes at the University of New Mexico, plus Indian art classes at the Albuquerque Indian School. She spoke highly of Willard Beatty because he "had a deep respect for Native American culture" (Horne and McBeth 1998, 69). In the summer of 1936, Horne was asked to demonstrate how to incorporate Native American materials into the classroom to other Indian Service teachers at Pine Ridge.

There, Horne was also able to take an ethnology course from the anthropologist Dr. Ruth Underhill, a student of Columbia University professor Franz Boaz, who is considered the "father of American anthropology" and originator of the concept of cultural relativism (Horne and McBeth 1998). Underhill had taught a similar summer institute for Indian schoolteachers at Santa Fe in 1934 (Heyer 1990) and served as assistant supervisor of Indian education from 1934 to 1942 and then as supervisor from 1942 to 1948.

A 1943 *Indian Education* article emphasizes that for "pre-primer to high school seniors there is a need for reading materials based upon the life situations of the readers" (Beatty 1944). The article called for "first the experience or activity, then the written record, then the reading" (Beatty). Stories, including group-made reading material, were to be made into mimeographed books for the children.

The following year, an *Indian Education* article on "Writing for Pleasure" (1944) calls for starting with "one sentence diaries." Teachers were told that "the secret of creative writing with children is simple . . . first . . . let the child pick his own subject . . . second take the good, praise it, save it, and ignore the bad" ("Writing for Pleasure" 1944, 6).

Indian Service linguist Robert Young writes: "On the Navajo Reservation, for example, the vast majority of the people were either illiterate, or read the English language after the fashion of parrots—pronouncing the words without understanding the meaning" (1944, 2). Young finds that many Navajos feel that the "acquisition of the White Man's language is tantamount to taking on his civilization" (1944, 3).

To overcome this resistance to assimilation, Young (1944) promotes teaching reading and writing in the children's Native language. A month later, an article in the same publication reprinted an article from *Schools and Society* on "Learning a Foreign Language Faster," which calls for giving students "a real, lifelike opportunity to do so by withholding book reading and writing during the first year or two until the child becomes a fluent speaker ("Learning a Foreign Language Faster" 1944, 7).

In a 1950 article on choosing schoolbooks, Willard Beatty warns against "word calling," an exercise without comprehension, and notes, "Beginning reading only makes sense when the things that the child reads about are things with which he is familiar and which he understands. One of the important attitudes toward reading, which a child should gain in the early grades, is that it is fun to read" (1950, 2). He reminded teachers, "Modern trends in education are directed toward students working in small groups, as opposed to the older method of teaching en masse" (1950, 4).

Project learning. In *How We Think*, John Dewey (1933) calls on teachers to engage their students in "constructive occupations" or "projects" that engage students' interests, have intrinsic worth, awaken curiosity, and are carried out over an extended period. Projects should integrate as many of the basic subjects taught in schools as possible, and the "project method" was used successfully with American Indian students in the 1940s.

In an article, anthropologist Ruth Underhill (1944, 5) declares that Tohono O'odham children traditionally "learned through activity, in a system surprisingly like our modern project method." In an article on day school methods for Dakota Sioux students, the Indian Service's associate supervisor of education, Gordon MacGregor (1948, 6–7), writes:

> The project method is exceptionally well suited to educating the Dakota because it follows their own method of learning by doing and following the example of others. By bringing the children to participate and to share in the work and the responsibility for completion of a project, this method also reinforces the training for cooperative work already begun in the family.

MacGregor (1964) notes that this method had been used for seven or eight years very successfully in Pine Ridge schools. He found that the competition between students and individualism fostered by traditional American teaching methods was difficult for young Sioux children to understand, as they were taught at home to work cooperatively and not to outshine their peers (MacGregor 1964).

Indigenous education has been criticized for being too vocational and slighting academics in the past, with racism seen as a factor that lowered academic expectations for Indigenous students (see e.g., Barrington 2008). However, Beatty himself was a graduate of a model vocational high school in San Francisco and saw the value for everyone of a challenging curriculum that combined academics with vocational education (Stefon 2009).

Beatty, in a 1944 collection of articles from the Indian Service's *Indian Education* biweekly newsletter, includes 17 articles in a section on "Culture: Background for Learning." Those articles emphasize that teachers need to understand, appreciate, and build on the cultural backgrounds of American Indian and Alaska Native students (Beatty 1944).

Self-Determination

World War II sapped the U.S. Indian Service of both funding and personnel, and the war's aftermath led to a period where a Republican-controlled Congress sought to terminate Indian Reservations. The post–World War II termination era brought a return to assimilationist English-only education for American Indians.

However, at the same time, the establishment of the United Nations and various declarations concerning human rights called for letting peoples determine their own destinies. In the United States, this helped lead to a policy of self-determination for Indian peoples starting in the 1960s. In addition, new studies of Indian education pointed to the continued failure of assimilationist educational policies (Fuchs and Havighurst 1972: Navajo Division of Education 1986).

This shift in policy led to the establishment of Indian-controlled schools, starting with the establishment of Rough Rock Demonstration School in 1966 and a resurgence of interest in culturally responsive and bilingual education (McCarty 2002). Unfortunately, in the twenty-first century, the insights gained by Ann Nolan Clark, Polingaysi Qöyawayma, Esther Burnett Horne, and many other teachers who actually worked with Indian students are becoming lost in the efforts under the No Child Left Behind Act of 2001 (NCLB).

Conclusion

Recognizing the importance of linguistically and culturally appropriate education, United Nations Educational, Scientific and Cultural Organization (UNESCO 1953) released *The Use of Vernacular Languages in Education*. Its authors declare, "It is axiomatic that the best medium for teaching a child is his[1] mother tongue" (UNESCO 1953, 11), and they conclude,

> On educational grounds we recommend that the mother tongue be extended to as late a stage in education as possible. In particular pupils should begin their schooling through the medium of the mother tongue, because they understand it best and because to begin their school life in the mother tongue will make the break between home and school as small as possible.
>
> We consider that the shock which the young child undergoes in passing from his home to his school life is so great that everything possible should be done to soften it. . . . The use of the mother tongue will promote better understanding between the home and the school when the child is taught in the language of the home. (pp. 47–48)

In 1991, the U.S. Department of Education's Indian Nations at Risk Task Force (INAR) recommended, as one of four national priorities, "establishing the promotion of students' tribal language and culture as a responsibility of the school" (INAR 1991, 22). In the transmittal letter of the Task Force's final report, William Demmert, Jr. (Tlingit/Sioux) and former secretary of education Terrel H. Bell write:

> The Task Force believes that a well-educated American Indian and Alaska Native citizenry and a renewal of the language and culture base of the American Native community will strengthen self-determination and economic well-being and will allow the Native community to contribute to building a stronger nation—an America that can compete with other nations and contribute to the world's economies and cultures. (Demmert and Bell 1991, iv)

American Indians and other Indigenous groups have continued to lobby the United Nations to support their right to self-determination and culturally appropriate education, and in 2007, they were successful in getting it to adopt the United Nations Declaration on the Rights of Indigenous Peoples, which states:

> 1. Indigenous peoples have the right to establish and control their educational systems and institutions providing education in their own languages, in a manner appropriate to their cultural methods of teaching and learning. . . .
> 3. States shall, in conjunction with indigenous peoples, take effective measures, in order for indigenous individuals, particularly children, including those living outside their communities, to have access, when possible, to an education in their own culture and provided in their own language. (United Nations 2008, art. 14)

Culturally appropriate education is both a basic human right and good educational practice. The best way to contextualize education for student understanding is to relate their schooling to their cultures, communities, lives, and land. Students need to learn both the knowledge and skills included in tribal, state, and national standards, and they and their teachers also need to respond to local concerns and have some choice in what type of learning projects they can become engaged.

A recent Canadian study of ten schools identified as having exemplary success with Indigenous students finds:

> All schools worked to provide culturally relevant learning experiences and affirm students' pride in their identity. Aboriginal language immersion programs were present in about half the schools and in some this was the language of instruction until Grade 6. Most offered local cultural classes—some of which were accredited, and the remainder infused cultural content across the core curriculum. In all schools, the importance of the traditions and culture was affirmed by displays, ceremonies, excursions on the land, and the use of elders and local resource people. (Fulford 2007, 12)

A contemporary ground-breaking Hawaiian study of culture-based education by the Kamehameha Schools Research and Evaluation Division, using data from 600 teachers, 2,969 students, and 2,264 parents, finds:

> First, culture-based education (CBE) positively impacts student socio-emotional well-being (e.g., identity, self-efficacy, social relationships). Second, enhanced socio-emotional well-being, in turn, positively affects math and reading test scores. Third, CBE is positively related to math and reading test scores for all students, and particularly for those with low socio-emotional development, most notably when supported by overall CBE use within the school. (Kana'iaupuni, Ledward, and Jensen 2010, 1)

Culture is ever-present in schools. As Shawn Kana´iaupuni writes:

> Culture refers to shared ways of being, knowing, and doing. Culture-based education is the grounding of instruction and student learning in these ways, including the values, norms, knowledge, beliefs, practices, experiences, and language that are the foundation of [an indigenous] culture. Because U.S. society typically views schools through a Western lens—where Western culture is the norm—what many do not recognize is that all educational systems and institutions are culture-based. Hence, the term is conventionally used to refer to "other" cultures, and, in this case, indigenous cultures. (2007, 1)

In a Hawaiian study, Brandon Ledward and Brennan Takayama (2008, 4) categorize culture-based activities into seven broad themes:

PILINA ´OHANA: Involvement of the family in education;
PILINA KAIĀULU: Incorporation of community members into the classroom and the classroom into the community;
HAKU: Development of original compositions;
MĀLAMA ´ĀINA: Land stewardship and environmentally based projects;
KŌKUA KAIĀULU: Active service promoting community well-being;
HŌ´IKE: Authentic performances and demonstrations of competency;
OLA PONO: Practical application of life and cultural skills and the teaching of values.

Closely related to culture-based education has been place-based education (Boyer 2006), which has promoted teaching students about their specific locality and its people and their cultures and languages. Studies by Paul Platero (1986) and Donna Deyhle (1989) find that the most frequent reason given by American Indian students for dropping out of school was that they were bored. They got tired of being told to read textbooks with content that they could not relate to their lives and in which they could not see either themselves or their communities (Reyhner 1992).

Castagno and Brayboy (2008) not long ago reviewed the state of culturally responsive education for American Indian students. They argue that "the increased emphasis on standardization and high-stakes accountability under NCLB seems to have resulted in less, rather than more, culturally responsive educational efforts and more, rather than no, Indigenous children left behind in our school systems" (Castagno and Brayboy 2008, 942).

In a second review, Brayboy and Castagno (2009, 31) compare the two dominant models of Indigenous education discussed in the United States, "the assimilative model and the culturally responsive model." They conclude that "the research is quite clear: there is no evidence that the assimilative model improves academic success; there is growing evidence that the culturally responsive model does, in fact, improve academic success for American Indian/Alaska Native children" (Brayboy and Castagno 2009, 31).

However, Brayboy and Castagno (2009, 37) find that "none of the research suggests that Indigenous youth should learn tribal cultures and languages at the expense of learning mainstream culture, English, and the typical 'academic' subjects generally taught in schools." In other words, "a both/and approach" has been advocated that recognizes, appreciates, and builds on Indigenous students' cultural heritages while at the same time teaching them about other groups of people and their cultures.

Ignoring the research on proven methods for teaching Native students, some of which were described in this chapter, the NCLB Act of 2001 has proposed to close the achievement gap between American Indian and non-Indian students by using methods based on "scientific" educational studies—studies that did not focus on American Indian students and ignored the role of culture and motivation in student success (Reyhner and Hurtado 2008). We need to continue to present the evidence that the best way to teach Native students is to return to education that is culturally sensitive and appropriate for them. One of the most promising efforts in that direction is that of Indigenous language-immersion schools that have been very successful for the Māori in Aotearoa/New Zealand and for Hawaiians in Hawai'i and have been experimented with in other parts of the United States (see e.g., Hill and May 2011; Reyhner 2010).

REFERENCES

Ashton-Warner, S. (1986). *Teacher*. New York: Simon & Schuster.

Barrington, J. (2008). *Separate but Equal? Māori Schools and the Crown, 1867–1969*. Wellington, New Zealand: University of Victoria Press.

Beatty, W. (1940). "Indian education in the Americas." *Indian Education* 43: 5–8.

———. (1944). *Education for Action: Selected Articles from "Indian Education," 1936–43*. Chilocco, OK: Education Division, U.S. Indian Service.

———. (1950). "Choosing school books." *Indian Education* 194: 1–4.

Boyer, P. (2006). *Building Community: Reforming Math and Science Education in Rural Schools*. Fairbanks, AK: Alaska Native Knowledge Network. http://www.ankn.uaf.edu/publications/building_community.pdf.

Brandt, R. K. (1935). "We make our own books." *Indians at Work* 2 (2): 25–27.

Brayboy, B. M. J., and A. E. Castagno. (2009). "Self-determination through self-education: Culturally responsive schooling for Indigenous students in the USA." *Teaching Education* 20 (1): 31–53.

Castagno, A. E., and B. M. J. Brayboy. (2008). "Culturally responsive schooling for Indigenous youth: A review of the literature." *Review of Educational Research* 78: 941–93.

Clark, A. N. (1940). *Little Herder in Autumn*. n.p.: United States Office of Indian Affairs, Education Division, Government Printing Office.

———. (1941). *The Pine Ridge Porcupine*. Lawrence, KS: Haskell Institute Printing Dept.

———. (1943). *Young Hunter of Picuris*. n.p.: United States Office of Indian Affairs, Education Division, Government Printing Office.

———. (1954). *The Hen of Wahpeton*. n.p.: United States Office of Indian Affairs, Education Division, Government Printing Office.

———. (1969). *Journey to the People*. New York: Viking.

College of Education and Social Services. University of Vermont. *A Brief Overview of Progressive Education*. Burlington: University of Vermont. Retrieved from http://www.uvm.edu/~dewey/articles/proged.html.

Demmert, W., Jr., and T. H. Bell. (1991). *Indian Nations at Risk: An Educational Strategy for Action: Final Report of the Indian Nations at Risk Task Force*. Washington, DC: U.S. Department of Education.

Dewey, J. (1933). *How We Think*. 2nd ed. Boston, MA: Houghton Mifflin, 1998.

Deyhle, D. (1989). "Pushouts and pullouts: Navajo and Ute school leavers." *Journal of Navajo Education* 6 (2): 36–51.

Fuchs, E., and R. J. Havighurst. (1972). *To Live on this Earth: American Indian Education*. Garden City, NY: Doubleday.

Fulford, G. (2007). *Sharing Our Success: More Case Studies in Aboriginal Schooling*. Kelowna, BC, Canada: Society for the Advancement of Excellence in Education. Retrieved from http://saee.ca/upload/SOSMoreCaseStudies.pdf.

Heger, N. I. (1932). "Before books in an Indian school." *Progressive Education* 9:138–43.

Heyer, S. (1990). *One House, One Voice, One Heart: Native American Education at the Santa Fe Indian School*. Santa Fe: Museum of New Mexico Press.

Hill, R., and S. May. (2011). "Exploring biliteracy in Māori-medium education: An ethnographic perspective." In *Ethnography and Language Policy*, ed. T. L. McCarty, 161–83. New York: Routledge.

Horne, E. B., and S. McBeth. (1998). *Essie's Story: The life and Legacy of a Shoshone Teacher*. Lincoln: University of Nebraska Press.

INAR (Indian Nations at Risk Task Force). (1991). *Indian Nations at Risk: An Educational Strategy for Action: Final Report of the Indian Nations at Risk Task Force*. Washington, DC: U.S. Department of Education.

Indian readers. (1936). *Indian Education* 3 (October): 5–6.

Kana'iaupuni, S. (2007). *A Brief Overview of Culture-based Education and Annotated Bibliography*. Culture in Education Brief Series. Honolulu: Kamehameha Schools Research and Evaluation Division.

Kana'iaupuni, S., B. Ledward, and U. Jensen. (2010). *Culture-based Education and its Relationship to Student Outcomes*. Honolulu: Kamehameha Schools, Research and Evaluation Division. Retrieved from http://www.ksbe.edu/spi/PDFS/CBE_relationship_to_student_outcomes.pdf.

Kneale, A. H. (1950). *Indian Agent*. Caldwell, ID: Caxton.

"Language experiments of Indian children." (1932). *Progressive Education* 9: 144–79.

Lawhead, H. E. (1932). "Teaching Navajo children to read." *Progressive Education* 9: 131–35.

"Learning a foreign language faster." (1944). *Indian Education* 98: 7. (Reprinted from *Schools and Society*).

Ledward, B., and B. Takayama. (2008). *Ho'opilina kumu: Culture-Based Education Among Hawai'i Teachers*. Culture in Education Brief Series. Honolulu: Kamehameha Schools Research and Evaluation Division.

MacGregor, G. (1948). "Federal schools meet Sioux needs." *Indian Education* 167: 6–8.

———. (1964). *Warriors without Weapons: A Study of the Society and Personality Development of the Pine Ridge Sioux*. Chicago: University of Chicago Press.

McCarty, T. L. (2002). *A Place to be Navajo: Rough Rock and the Struggle for Self-determination in Indigenous Schooling*. Mahwah, NJ: Lawrence Erlbaum.

Meriam, L., comp. (1928). *The Problem of Indian Administration*. Baltimore: Johns Hopkins Press.

Navajo Division of Education. (1986). *Executive summary: Navajo area student dropout study*. Window Rock, AZ: Navajo Nation.

No Child Left Behind Act of 2001: Reauthorization of the Elementary and Secondary Education Act of 1965 (NCLB). (2001). *U.S. code*. Title 20, sec. 6301 et seq.

Platero, P. (1986). *Executive Summary: Navajo Area Student Dropout Study*. Window Rock, AZ: Navajo Nation, Navajo Division of Education / Platero Paperwork.

Qöyawayma, P. [Elizabeth Q. White]. (1964). *No Turning Back: A Hopi Indian Woman's Struggle to Live in Two Worlds*. As told to Vada F. Carlson. Albuquerque: University of New Mexico Press.

Reyhner, J. (1992). "American Indians out of school: A review of school-based causes and solutions." *Journal of American Indian Education* 31(3): 37–56.

———. (2010). "Indigenous language immersion schools for strong Indigenous identities." *Heritage Language Journal* 7 (2): 138–52.

Reyhner, J., and D. S. Hurtado. (2008). "Reading First, literacy, and American Indian/Alaska Native students." *Journal of American Indian Education* 47 (1): 82–95.

Ryan, W. C., Jr., and R. K. Brandt. (1932). "Indian education today." *Progressive Education* 9:81–86.

Stauffer, R. (1970). *The Language-experience Approach to the Teaching of Reading*. New York: Harper & Row.

Stefon, F. J. (2009). "Willard Beatty and progressive Indian education." *American Indian Culture and Research Journal* 33 (4): 91–112.

Summer institutes. (1936). *Indian Education* 1 (September 16): 2–4.

Underhill, R. M. (1944). "Papago child training." *Indian Education* 103: 5–8.

UNESCO (United Nations Educational, Scientific and Cultural Organization). (1953). *The Use of Vernacular Languages in Education*. Monographs on Fundamental Education 8. Lucerne, France: C. F. Bucher AG. Retrieved from http://unesdoc.unesco.org/images/0000/000028/ 002897eb.pdf.

United Nations. (2008). *United Nations declaration on the rights of Indigenous peoples*. Retrieved from http://www.un.org/esa/socdev/unpfii/documents/DRIPS_en.pdf.

"Writing for pleasure." (1944). *Indian Education* 95: 5–8.

Young, R. W. (1944). "To read and write native languages." *Indian Education* 98: 2–8.

NOTE

1. The use of "his" for both males and females was preferred during the time of this writing.

Chapter 4

Tundra Schools Then and Now

Thirty Years of Possibilities

Stephen T. Marble: Southwestern University

ABSTRACT

I was one of many teachers in Alaska hired to teach in village schools following the landmark *Tobeluk v. Lind* (1979) legislation that decreed that Native Alaskan[1] secondary students would have the option of attending local high schools rather than secondary boarding schools in far-away cities. At the time, this decision, and its unknown consequences, presented a radical change from former policies.

Returning to the small village school in rural Alaska where I taught thirty years ago, I explored how the subsequent years of village secondary schooling have influenced the village, the school, and my former students. As a village teacher, along with fellow educators, I sought to meld both the dominant and Native cultural interests into educational experiences that would be most beneficial for all. Now I was interested in seeing how the village had fared under the pressures of differing, conflicting dominant-culture values and educational practices.

As I shared stories with Native students I had taught, their families, and the community, I found myself once again face-to-face with many of the dilemmas I had faced as a teacher. Reconsidering these quandaries thirty years later, I rediscovered my core authentic values that formed the basis of my personal philosophy regarding teaching and learning developed in the course of living and teaching on the tundra.

Keywords: Native Alaskan education, culturally responsive teaching, cross-cultural teaching

TUNDRA SCHOOLS THEN AND NOW: THIRTY YEARS OF POSSIBILITIES

The educational, economic, and cultural consequences of the massive shift to village high schools have scarcely been chronicled, let alone studied in depth. The magnitude of some changes may obscure others that are more subtle but may in the long run prove to be more profound. (Cotton 1984, 32)

The Journey: I Land—Again

It was September 2008. The pilot banked into final approach, eased the throttle back, and the Cessna 207 crunched onto the gravel runway just as the stall warning began to be-e-e-e-p. He taxied up to the metal hanger where two young men sat smoking on their four wheelers and, with a final rev of the prop, spun the plane to a stop. The name on the tail of the plane was different, but otherwise this could have been the same 207 I flew in when going to the village in 1978. Certainly, the pilot wasn't the same. Before, the pilot had been a white guy about twice my age; this time the pilot was Native and hadn't yet been born when I first flew out to Kasigluk.

I held my excitement in check. It had taken a long time to return to the village where I taught high school from 1978 to 1984, and a few more minutes did not matter. The agent pulled up his four wheeler and trailer and began unloading the plane. When I asked for a ride into town, he looked me over carefully. Was I going to the school? I nodded and then asked if he remembered me.

At first there was no hint of recognition, but when I finally said my name, he grinned familiarly, nodded as if he had been expecting me, and pointed at the trailer. I climbed in, and we bumped away along the mud track as the mail plane tore off down the runway to the next stop. I smiled; I was back.

I was dropped off near the pump house in back of the school, and before I took ten steps, I heard someone shouting out my name. Turning, I saw Yeako, a former student, waving as he approached. In the heartbeat it took to turn, three decades evaporated as if no time had passed. And, just as quickly, I was in the strange position of explaining myself, answering questions raised by my sudden reappearance after many years.

Over the next five days, many conversations followed a similar pattern. Was I returning to teach again? It was the beginning of the school year, so the connection seemed obvious. Was I coming to take over from the principal? No, I promised; I was on vacation and had just come to find out what had happened after all these years. I would only be staying a short while but hoped to be able to return yet again if all went well.

"What?" "A vacation to the Tundra?" "Right."

In truth, a number of questions prompted my visit. A smoldering desire to return to the village had recently flamed into a purposeful quest as I realized how deeply the experience had influenced my teaching practice. A sabbatical leave provided time and support to return to see firsthand what had happened to my students, the school, and the village over the years. I had left seeking answers to questions I could never find while living in the village. Ironically, I now realized that some questions could be answered nowhere else.

First and foremost, I wanted to visit old friends, renew relationships, and find out what had happened to the students attending in 1978 when we opened the state-supported high school program. What impact had the experience of schooling at home had on their lives, I wondered. But other motives complicated the picture. For example, I wanted to reflect on my own professional growth as an educator, and receiving long overdue feedback from my former students would be helpful. I required future teachers to reflect on their experiences, and a taste of my own medicine seemed in order.

I also wanted to know how the relationship between the school and the village had evolved in the intervening years. How had the evolving context of educational reform manifested itself in the village? Had the No Child Left Behind Act (2001) impacted village schools compared to the days I taught there, long before standards and benchmarks and adequate yearly progress? Sometimes it is just easier to do something than to keep thinking about it, so here I was, back after 30 years to remember, renew, and see with a fresh—and more experienced—eye.

Historical Perspectives

Through the mid-1970s, secondary educational opportunities for Alaskan Natives were extremely limited. An assortment of formal and informal practices separated the responsibility for educating whites and Native Alaskans between the state and the Bureau of Indian Affairs (BIA). Although many Native villages had BIA elementary schools (through grade 8), BIA policy required those seeking secondary educations to attend boarding schools, usually located in the lower forty-eight states (Cotton 1984).

In 1966, the number of students interested in secondary schooling in rural Alaska exploded. Bowing under pressure to serve the growing interest in secondary schooling, the state initiated two strategies designed to support village student attendance at existing high schools through (1) home boarding programs and (2) regional high school dormitory programs.

Students, however, fared little better under these programs than under the BIA boarding-school policies they replaced (Kleinfeld and Bloom 1973). Village secondary students, separated from their families and exposed to the social problems and pressures of towns and cities, continued to perform very poorly (Kleinfeld and Bloom 1973). In 1973, a study at the University of Alaska, Fairbanks, found that 96 percent of the village students entering Bethel Regional High School in 1971–1972 failed in their first year. The investigators recommended closing down the regional boarding schools and opening village schools (Kleinfeld and Bloom 1973).

The state was heading in a different direction, however; one that linked education closely to economic opportunity. Cotton (1984) argues that the state planned to shift people out of subsistence lifestyles common in the village and into the labor and cash economy with the promise of educational and vocational programs in hub towns.

As late as 1975, the state was defining new regional attendance areas that meant rural students would continue to travel to towns like Bethel for secondary education (Cotton 1984). However, the state's course changed dramatically and decisively with a landmark legal challenge popularly called the "Molly Hootch case" but legally titled *Tobeluk v. Lind* (1979), the *consent decree*—a contractual agreement between litigants leading to final judgment in the courts—that revolutionized educational opportunities for rural Native Alaskans.

Anna Tobeluk was a student in Nunapitchuk, one of the tundra villages in Southwest Alaska. She joined a list of plaintiffs suing the state for failing to provide village high schools. In 1976, a consent decree resolved the case, resulting in the state's agreement to create a high school program in each of 126 villages if the village desired one.

> That very fall Anna and 25 classmates in grades 10 through 12 enrolled in Nunapitchuk High School, one of 42 village high schools newly opened in conformity with the consent decree. Classes were held in a drafty, one-room clinic building so cold that the students wore parkas in class through much of that first winter. Use of such a clearly inadequate facility was a sign of the village's impatience to have a local high school: the village could have opted to wait until new classrooms were constructed. In this, Nunapitchuk was typical. Almost every village with an unused building larger than a broom closet pushed ahead with a high school program. (Cotton 1984, 31)

These historic events led directly to my own experiences as a village teacher. I was living in Anchorage, Alaska, when I was hired to staff one of the newly created high school programs just a few miles from Nunapitchuk. I was offered the position over the telephone on a Friday night one week after school had officially started in late August 1978.

When I asked what I should bring, the assistant superintendent replied, deadpan: "A warm sleeping bag and a year's supply of food." Two days later, after a frantic shopping spree and late-night packing, I flew from Anchorage to Bethel on Sunday afternoon. Monday was spent completing paperwork and an "orientation" at the district office. Tuesday afternoon I flew out to the village with all my gear. Wednesday morning found me standing in front of the thirty-five or so students in the new one-room school.

This was my first teaching position. As inexperienced as I was, the school as a whole was even less prepared. The village had waited until the last possible minute to decide to open a high school, and all the materials we needed were either on order or in shipment. Like the school in nearby Nunapitchuk, we worked in a village building, though it was hardly drafty: we only needed to wear our parkas when the heater failed! We had tables and chairs provided by the community center that the school now occupied full time: no books, paper, pencils, or chalk.

We borrowed materials from the BIA elementary school in the village to hold us over and essentially created the high school program out of our imaginations. I use the first-person plural because, though I was the "teacher," there was already quite a staff hired locally, including a principal, an aide, a Yu'pik teacher, a cook, a janitor, and a secretary. Local schools meant local jobs.

Three years later, the new K–12 school was finished at the bluffs a mile away, and we moved into our new quarters, complete with every possible amenity: full-court gym, well and pump, showers, computers, library, and even a telephone. The State of Alaska had come through on every promise for a first-class school facility. Cotton (1984), the attorney for the plaintiff in *Tobeluk v. Lind* (1979), explained the impact of the case very clearly:

> Anna's lawsuit has revolutionized the delivery of secondary education in rural Alaska. No longer does the entire village turn out each fall on the gravel airstrip to see off teenagers bound for boarding school for the next nine months. That scene has yielded to a more joyous celebration each spring; graduation ceremonies in the village's high school gym. Villages, which a decade ago were almost devoid of teenagers throughout the school year, now have their high school youngsters living at home. Dropout rates are down and graduation rates up. A native village without a high school has become, virtually overnight, a rarity. (Cotton 1984, 32)

Challenges Facing Tundra Teachers

Thrilled as I was to get a job teaching high school in the 1970s, I was woefully unprepared. My preservice teacher-education courses had stressed behaviorism, classroom management, and Madeline Hunter–style lessons. The disciplines in high school were completely isolated from each other and concentrated on using textbooks and strategies designed for students who were fluent in English and deeply embedded in American urban culture. My "classroom"— with thirty-five Native Alaskan students and twenty-two independent courses daily—was unlike anything anyone had ever described for me as "school."

But even more importantly, I was completely unaware of the political and social contexts in which I now found myself. My father, an experienced Foreign Service officer, told me that the village was the most unique environment he had ever encountered. On first arrival, I brought along few strategies for coping with the dilemmas that would engulf my professional and personal life, and those were quickly exhausted. My approach was typical of most outside teachers heading for bush schools: uninformed but good-hearted and willing.

The challenges for outsiders were significant. I suddenly found myself in the midst of a community of three hundred or so individuals who had been developing intense personal relationships with one another and the outside world for generations. There were, for example, two distinct church communities—the Moravians and the Russian Orthodox—each with its own history, practices, and even holidays. The Russian Orthodox church had been introduced when Alaska was under Russian control. The Moravian missions came later, in the late 1800s.

The school accommodated the two different church calendars with a winter break that spanned both Christmas celebrations and time in the spring for both Easters. Everyone knew who went to which church—that is, everyone but me. Church membership was one of the more visible relationships that bound and separated the village. It didn't take long to realize just how difficult, if not impossible, becoming a full member of the community would be.

Learning about village language and culture. A limited understanding of the Yu'pik language and culture further hampered me. In fact, most information about both language and culture came from other teachers only slightly better informed than I was. Older folks in the village spoke Central Yu'pik Eskimo and strongly supported efforts to teach Yu'pik to the younger generation. District policies and practices reinforced this goal, actively promoting bilingual instruction and an innovative K–3 Yu'pik-immersion program.

However, district policies also advocated for fluent proficiency in English. In some eyes, outside teachers who spoke no Yu'pik represented a clear threat to the traditional language and culture. My ongoing attempts to learn the complicated language produced more hysterical laughter than meaningful dialogue.

Village teachers traversed a perilous path indeed. As agents of the school system, teachers represented the normative interests of the dominant outside culture, something they did most naturally. Long before state and national content standards, the No Child Left Behind Act (2001), and adequate yearly progress (AYP), "bush teachers"—those who taught in the Alaskan villages far from metropolitan areas—eagerly looked for ways to help their students to be *academically successful*. Of course, the district defined "success" in terms of standardized test scores, and typically, most village students received very low results on standardized tests.

As teachers struggled to push scores higher with "tough love" practices (e.g., sports participation depended on adequate academic performance; students were given repeated drills and test-taking practices), they were reinforced by state and district policies. At the same time, the interests of the village were poorly articulated and essentially unknown to teachers from the *Outside*, a term widely used to describe the world of cities or out of state.

Caught in the undefined spaces between internal and external competing interests, teachers from the Outside found themselves further split between the interests of students and parents. For example, when the whole basketball team took off in bad weather to fly several hundred miles to a weekend basketball tournament, there would be a moment when the students' desperate longing to play and the parents' concern for their children's safety collided.

Though we had a strict no pass–no play rule, when a high school basketball star was denied a chance to play in the big tournament one Christmas, the repercussions nearly cost the principal his job. Classroom decisions needed to address these conflicting objectives, frequently simultaneously.

The most teachers and local administrators could hope to do was to mediate some of the more extreme policies to accommodate local knowledge and history. But the tensions between the culture of the village, with the values of its guiding elders, and the culture of the school, with its values derived from its external command structure, were powerful and persistent.

I came to visualize the school's policies and goals as a giant grid of rules and procedures that overlay village life, a life linked more to the open space the village actually occupied. And in this open space of the traditional village, children learned by doing in the natural unfolding of their lives—by trying and adjusting their efforts until successful, not by being told by teachers.

In an insightful essay, Rasmussen (2002) describes this tension between the traditional and school visions of learning and knowledge in Nunavik communities. The traditional approach built on the abundance of knowledge to be learned from everyday interactions in the world while schools promoted knowledge as a limited resource controlled by teachers.

> So when Nunavik Inuit say "culture cannot be taught with a piece of chalk," or when the elder Malaya Nakasuk laughs and says "you cannot teach the Inuit way of life from a book"—they are trying to remind Qallunaat [whites] that life is an ocean of unfoldment and growth, Inuit should not have to hunt for an accredited tap every time they feel the thirst of curiosity. Traditional values, says Nakasuk, used to be "learned as part of daily camp life" in "interactions among people who lived . . . closely linked to the land." But in Nunavut, the reality of abundance of wisdom from elders and communities is being replaced by the enforced Qallunaat illusion that learning is scarce and only obtainable through state-sanctioned education outlets administered by accredited (ninety-five percent Qallunaat) teachers. (Rasmussen 2002, 92)

The traditional approach to learning was illustrated for me during my first year when Zack, one of the school aides, took me for a ride in his wooden boat. His boat looked odd coming across the river. The bow rode way too high out of the water, making it difficult for the driver in the stern to see where he was going.

Zack had piled several bags of sand to hold down the bow, but even so, he needed to stand on a chair to control the outboard and to see where he was going. Zack explained that this was his first boat, and in the course of laying out the ribs, he had made a serious miscalculation. The more experienced boat builders saw this but did not correct him, knowing that Zack's next boat would be even better.

Life in the classroom worked at cross-purposes to the way life worked outside the school, in the everyday world. Inside, teachers deployed teaching strategies designed to engage learners in classroom dialogue, question-response, and group work, none of which seemed to work particularly well. Students were often uncomfortable in the forced-verbal settings that classroom discussions required. Questions were often answered with raised eyebrows, a local nonverbal form for "Yes."

It was impossible to group students for collaborative work without taking into account their lifelong associations with each other both inside and outside the school; students who did not get along would not work together. Lacking full understanding of these issues and the appropriate strategies to deal with them, we teachers stumbled along, hoping we were at least not doing harm.

Meanwhile, the world outside the classroom—the constant song of the changing seasons and human celebrations—called loudly to the students. When migrating birds, a major food source of the tundra villages, first returned in the spring, the boys would disappear for days, hunting. Of course, attendance and grade policies in the district did not allow for such absences. As teachers, we were challenged to come up with inventive ways to keep the boys in school long enough to finish the year.

Accommodating student needs. Fortunately, I worked with a principal who had lived in the village a long time and a staff that was aware of these challenges. Together, we negotiated local policies that paved the way toward accommodating local needs. We went to school every other Saturday to finish early enough in the spring to allow hunting. We used salmon-fishing expeditions to the Kuskokwim River to study the biology of salmon and to provide local food for lunches during the winter.

I accompanied students on numerous trips, not only to sporting events, but also, for example, to Platinum to see the Bering Sea shore, to Anchorage to explore the city, and even to San Francisco and Hawaii for one memorable three-week senior-class expedition into the outside world and its ways of being. The school suspended the standard curriculum for weeks, offering instead Native-arts courses, hosting elders from across the Yukon-Kuskokwim Delta to lead students in learning traditional crafts and arts.

Roles of teachers in tundra societies. It was very rare that teachers transcended their Outside past to become a significant part of the village landscape. Most bush teachers inherited their roles in the social order from teachers who came before them. Most commonly, but not always, the pressure to develop an identity—local or outsider—drove an irreconcilable wedge into the cultural gap between teachers and village.

The differences between the teachers, representatives of the alien dominant culture who met as professionals to solve the problems of teaching and learning, and the people of the village, who met to discuss the direction and management of the community, created an us/them boundary that few managed to penetrate. Invariably, teachers began to speak of the villagers and even of the students as "they."

Because limited support networks existed for teachers, there were only very rare opportunities to step outside our lived experiences to consider the situation of teaching in tundra environments from more informed perspectives. Old-timers survived by moving from village to village, by going Outside for a while, or by moving into town to take on district jobs. These strategies provided them with a privileged but frequently misinformed perspective.

I was constantly awash in the complexities arising from these challenges during the seven years I spent teaching on the tundra. I had assumed that when the village voted to open a state-supported school, the vote represented widespread acceptance for all the things a school would offer, including access to new ideas. In retrospect, the decision to open a village school was more a reactionary resistance to the BIA and boarding-school options then available, and less a statement of support for schooling as a process. And not all the changes the school brought with it were welcome.

For example, when we first opened, the BIA elementary school multipurpose room use was redefined to include a high school night. Since we had no gym, the boy's basketball team began to use high school night to practice. But many of the older students were also members of the village men's league and continued to play on men's night as well.

Someone noticed the double standard, and the high school boys were given a choice: play on men's night or high school night, but not on both. Overnight, seven students, each many years out of eighth grade but with no high school education, dropped out of school. Without hesitation, they abandoned their relationship with the school in order to maintain their status as young men in the village.

Policy adjustments and definitions were common in the beginning as the new school endeavored to define itself in the village environment. During this process, I began to deeply question my own role and purpose as a teacher; after all, what was or should be my contribution to the future of my students and their life in the village? Though certainly up for the adventure, I was uncomfortable playing the role of cultural colonial serving the interests of the external dominant culture through the institution of the school. Whenever I tried to nail down why I was teaching in the village, I would get lost in the contradictions.

I eased some of my discomfort by telling myself that I was not teaching culture; I was teaching individuals. It was, I argued, not about teaching the stuff—the content—through coverage and recall. It was about teaching the learners, starting where the learners were and proceeding in ways that not only made sense but also had value. This early constructivist perspective helped some, but ultimately, I could no longer be confident that my efforts—informed only by my own practice and reflection—were making a positive difference for my students. It was time to go.

Back to the Future

Thirty years later, I expected the calculus of village teaching to change over the decades; in fact, I was prepared for the village to have become unrecognizable. Recent events—including the turn of the millennium, social networking, global warming, 9/11, economic meltdowns, and the 2008 presidential election—all promoted the perception that our world has been altered beyond recognition. Even the pace of change had accelerated with the spread of communications and information technology. Why should the village be exempt?

When I had first moved up in 1978, twenty-two villages shared four radiotelephone lines. To make a call out, you had to hold the receiver up to your ear, listen across the wires for someone signing off, and then rapidly click the cradle to compete for a dial tone. If your TV antennae stood high enough and pointed toward Bethel, you could receive the one channel, public educational television, when it broadcast for a few hours each evening.

Every household had a CB radio, and in the evening, it was like bedtime at the *The Waltons* (a popular television program shown on the Columbia Broadcasting Systems [CBS] from 1972 to 1981) as everyone signed off: "Goodnight, Irene." "Goodnight, Junior!" The most common means of communication between villages was the *Tundra Drums*, a radio show from Bethel that broadcast family news—travel plans, births, deaths, and weddings—on request.

Now, here I was, once again immersed in village life. It was as if time had collapsed, the intervening years erased. I felt I was living in one of those puzzles where you are asked to look at two closely similar pictures and circle the fifteen things that are different. My visit created a time warp, a folding of the present to touch the past. Everyone I met seemed fixated on how much had changed. In fact, nearly every conversation included the topic of change. I was asked repeatedly "Is it different?" "Has it changed?" "Do you remember . . . [whatever]?" "Do you remember me?"

There were, of course, many things that had been unaffected by the passing years, reinforcing the sense that the past and present were simultaneous. The metal shed at the airport, the colors splashed across the fall tundra, the school building inside and out, the sounds of mixed Yu'pik and English spoken with village accents—all these were familiar reminders of life in the village.

There were other—less physical—reminders. For example, children were still the center of the world. One friend immediately asked me how many grandchildren I now had, chastising me for having none; after all, she had fourteen! My former students, except for one who had remained unmarried, all spoke about their children and grandchildren with pride.

Children have always held a privileged place in village families. My most profound connections with the village had come through my own family; an early tragic pregnancy was later followed by the birth of a son, and—though he was very young when we left—many remembered him and asked about how he was.

I was proud to be able to talk about my (only) three children, now grown and moving on with lives of their own. Children might be considered living treasure; if this is true, the people in the village were indeed rich. The 300 or so residents living there in 1978 have now become roughly 450, with the largest demographic comprising children under eighteen years of age.

But over the thirty years, there *were* significant changes. Most importantly, the Yukon-Kuskokwim Delta was no longer isolated from global concerns—including energy and its production and consumption. Visible from the plane as we approached, three massive wind turbines, clearly seen even on satellite images, loomed over the houses and school, generating power for the village cooperative.

The power station promised a steady supply of power for everyone, complete with oil storage and overhead power lines running throughout the village, across the tundra to the old village a mile up river, and then across to Nunapitchuk, three miles away. An ensured supply of electricity encouraged a whole host of uses for it—including computers, e-mail, satellite TV, telephones in every house, UHF radios in homes and boats, and even a gas station with an electric pump!

As my visit progressed, I began to sense another—less visible—change underway. The day I flew out to the village, the Alaska Permanent Fund checks were mailed, amounting to over $3,000 for each man, woman, and child. Each family of six had just received more than $19,000 from the state as their share of the income from the permanent fund created by the oil boom in the 1980s. In the subsistence village of thirty years ago, this amount would have surpassed most household annual incomes some several times over. But now, there were new uses for the money, including telephone and electric bills to pay.

The presence of a gas station to fuel vehicles and the twelve-foot-wide board "roads" made the use of four wheelers common, carrying whole families to the store, the riverbank, or to "visit." There were even wooden parking spaces built off the boardwalk in front of each house to accommodate the vehicles. Boats had changed as well. At some point, I realized that all the boats I saw were now aluminum and had been bought; three decades before, almost every boat had been homemade from wood. The fund of knowledge Zack had developed building his boat had become unnecessary in this consumer world.

Each of these goods required cash for purchase, far more than arrived in the fat dividend check each year. Some residents traveled to other communities to work, finding paying jobs requiring them to live in other villages—Bethel and even Anchorage. It seemed that many more families now got some sort of support from members working full time in other places.

Others found cash in the growing number of local jobs. There was a second K–12 school in the old village employing many teachers, aides, and maintenance workers. The store, power station, clinic, and new post office had each created jobs. There were even workers now paid to empty the "honey bucket" bunkers located along the boardwalks. With no running water, each house had a metal bucket toilet in a closet or behind a curtain. In the "old days," each of us had carried our own bucket of waste to the end of the boardwalk at "Honey Bucket Lake."

There was a lot of talk about how everything now seemed connected to the price of gasoline. While the wind generators softened the total dependence on fuel oil, the cost of oil and gas has risen to all-time records, starkly accentuating the growing umbilical cord between the village and the outside world.

In the late summer of 2008, energy prices increased considerably as oil prices reached $140 a barrel. The local papers were full of stories about the effects of these events on rural populations in Alaska, and a hearing in Bethel organized by Alaska's lone U.S. representative solicited ideas about how to resolve the "rural energy crisis." The long-term impact of the financial difficulties that high fuel prices put on rural residents was not being underestimated:

> "Out migration," or moving to Alaska's urban areas, was on the lips of everyone concerned about rural residents moving from the Bush to hubs, or into Fairbanks or Anchorage. "This is not only an energy crisis, but a social and cultural crisis that is unacceptable in the 21st century," said Robert Middleton, director of the Office of Indian Energy and Economic Development for the U.S. Department of the Interior. (Stapleton 2008)

The creation of regional boarding schools in the 1970s had been supported by a desire to shift subsistence villages to cash economies. While the growth of rural schools in nearly every village had alleviated the social and cultural disruption of regional boarding programs, the underlying intention to shift Native lifestyles away from a strong dependency on subsistence to a cash basis had—it appeared—been realized. For better or worse, villagers were more closely connected to the national labor and cash economy, linking village lifestyles to oil policies and prices in the "lower forty-eight."

This was not to say that subsistence activities had vanished completely. Buckets of freshly picked blueberries were everywhere, dried fish was served in every house, and moose-hunting season was just getting underway. Boat after boat loaded with young men stopped to gas up before heading upriver to test their luck. However, time to hunt now required young men to take time off from their jobs.

Jobs also took away time from what were common traditional subsistence activities. Some of these, in fact, seemed to have been abandoned. I was told that dipping for white fish, for example, was no longer common. Trapping beaver and mink brought in little cash for the effort and was no longer widely practiced. Subsistence still played an important role in village life, a less essential role, perhaps, but it had not vanished.

But some traditional ways of life had grown more significant as well. When I was a teacher there, the school created a one-week session each semester—once in the fall and again in the spring—where traditional arts and crafts became the academic focus of the students' lives. Whether they were carving ivory and wood or sewing skin and seal gut, students were exposed to traditional skills and guided by elders well-known for their craft. Everyone participated in learning to perform Eskimo dancing, a long-lost art in the village.

On my return visit, I saw that these traditional arts had become solidly integrated into the school and community. The village dance troop now traveled to perform around the state. In school, one day each week was devoted to dance practice, with times set aside so that every student could participate. Some of the student dancers were novices, just learning the first songs and steps; others were experienced performers and led the practices with the help of graduates from the community who returned to beat the drums, sing the songs, and demonstrate the moves. As experienced students graduated and became parents themselves, the popularity and understanding of songs and dances had spread throughout the village.

Although oil, jobs, and food were the major topics of discussions about change, there were other developments as well. When the village had moved to the bluffs, it shifted from a state-affiliated city government to a tribal-council model, a move that had swept through Native Alaska. One of my students was now a tribal judge. The tribal policewoman, another former student, described how kids were beginning to use drugs, brought home by their older siblings at a younger age.

Everyone talked about how the old village was quickly disappearing as the ground seemed to sink away with increasing rapidity. Many people lamented the disconnection between the village youth and the culture and language of their elders. Everyone also talked about getting older. But had the world really changed all that much?

Where Are They Now? Student Stories

Even before arriving in the village, I began to hear about former students. A few had died—from disease, alcohol, and/or violence. Others had moved—some for work, some for marriage. Much was said about how many former students had moved to Bethel or even Anchorage. In all, I was able to locate the whereabouts of thirty-nine of my former students. This represented better than two-thirds of those I taught in my years at the school.

Of the thirty-nine former students, four had died, seven lived in Bethel or other villages in the Delta, and four lived in Anchorage. The remaining twenty-four continued to live in the village. My encounters with five of the thirty-nine are described below. Their names have been changed to protect their anonymity.

Martha. My first morning in Bethel at the bed-and-breakfast, I sat at the table with several people, including some federal "types," a social worker, and a few others. There was one Native woman, sitting alone at the end of the table, who finished and left without speaking. A few minutes later, my former principal arrived to pick me up with my former breakfast companion in tow.

How could I sit there and not recognize Martha? she asked. Martha had been outside waiting for a taxi when Cauline dragged her back inside and laughingly reintroduced us. Martha now teaches in an early-childhood program in another village and was in town for a workshop at the district office.

We used the short ride across town in Cauline's truck to get reacquainted. Martha had not recognized me either, but she had some strong memories of being in my class years before. She remembered that we had taken a field trip to Platinum for marine-science class. I recalled the trip but had been having trouble remembering why we had gone. The next morning, Martha and I lingered talking over breakfast. She wistfully recalled the highlights of our coast trip.

Martha recalled watching the Bering Sea waves lap on the long stone beach, seeing—and smelling!—the dead walrus, hiking forever up what looked to be a nearby mountain, and discovering a whole sand dollar. She also vividly remembered the spaghetti dinner we cooked in the school kitchen. Was it from scratch, she wanted to know. My encounter with Martha was the first of many surprises: could I really have forgotten so much? Memories began to stir from deep storage.

My conversation with Martha was repeated numerous times with other former students. Stories about their school days drew on a significant body of knowledge not required by the formal educational curriculum but instead derived from memorable life experiences and events. Even thirty years later, these experiences continued to have strong personal significance.

Johnny. One morning, as I waited at the gas station on the river for a boat ride to the older village, Johnny was filling up his boat. His wife and five kids were on their way into Bethel for the weekend to visit their oldest daughter, waiting there to have a baby. Johnny's wife worked as the janitor at the school, and I recognized several of his older boys from classes I had visited. Johnny had been a good student, always cheerful and ready to help.

Johnny later recounted his favorite memory of my time in the village, when he had helped me get fuel oil from the old storage tanks. My small snow machine did not have a stiff hitch, so I had used a twenty-foot rope to haul the heavy freight sled with two fifty-five-gallon drums down to the tank and back. With little recent snow, the ice on the river was smooth and slick. Johnny rode the sled to steer.

We got down to the tanks all right, filled up, and I slowly and carefully headed back up river with the two heavy drums of oil and Johnny in tow. But when it came time to turn at the bend in the river, the sled—with Johnny helplessly laughing—kept going straight. When the heavy sled came to the end of the rope, it continued on in a straight line, spinning the lighter snow machine around; gracefully we began to rotate in lazy 360s.

The staying power of these informal interactions was becoming apparent. Though I had taught Johnny day in and day out for four years, he most vividly remembered something that had happened completely outside of the context of school and our formal teacher-student connection. Through shared experiences, we compared our growing understandings of the world as well. Again, what legacies did we, as teachers, leave with our students?

Alice. Returning from a walk the first afternoon in the village, I found four former students waiting for me at the school. One of the four, Alice, was a nine-year member and former chair of the advisory school board. We had a good talk, the first of many over the next few days. We met again while I was down in the old village the following afternoon. Her small cozy house was very warm inside and packed with pictures and mementos.

Alice started up a laptop computer and shared the most recent newsletter to parents she had written as school board member. She was neither shy nor subtle in her call for parents to support the school. Over tea, she told me about a research project she was participating in, collecting data for a study on "story knife" symbols and string stories. Both mediums for local storytelling had still been commonly practiced when she was in school but were now rare and quickly disappearing.

On Sunday afternoon, Alice arranged a gathering for me at the school, inviting all the former students she could locate. She also supplied the salmon casserole, dry fish, juice, and *aquduk*, Eskimo "ice cream." She sought me out my last evening in the village, and we walked for more than an hour around the boardwalks, deep in conversation.

Alice explained that she had been chair of the advisory school board when there was a push by some in the village to remove the principal. This was not a positive experience for anyone and one that had been very difficult for her. In her role as chair, she had been required to both listen to the complaints of the people who were dissatisfied and to translate the discussion for the principal. Ultimately, the principal had been allowed to stay, but as a result, Alice now felt somewhat alienated from both sides.

Alice was not diminished from this experience—far from it. She was now considering a run at the district school board seat but wasn't sure she was ready. "See," she said several times, "we *are* doing something," as if to counter an unspoken criticism from me. Alice had taken significant personal risks to make the most of her opportunities and found that the village—far from limiting—continued to offer her room to grow and prosper.

Frank. One spring, I had traveled with seven older students on a three-week trip to California and Hawaii to see the outside world. Frank had gone along as one of the group. An older student who had returned from Bethel to attend the village school when it opened, Frank was now the maintenance man at the new school in the old village. He could not make the gathering that Alice had arranged because he had to work, so I decided to hitch a boat ride up to the other school to look for him.

As I walked into the store, I saw someone who looked a lot like him and said hello. But it wasn't Frank; it was his little brother James, whom I didn't remember at all. "Wow, you look a lot like your brother," I said and asked him about where Frank was. "Working at the school. Are you interested in going to visit?" "Sure," was my reply. So I waited while James cashed a check at the store, and then we went down to his boat.

After I was seated, James sat on the bow of the boat and looked me in the eye. "Are you sure you don't know who I am?" he said. I suddenly realized that in fact I was talking to Frank, and in true village humor, he had just played a joke on me! "James" did not exist after all! "Well, no wonder you look so much like your brother!" I said to Frank. We laughed and headed up the river.

Frank lived with his family in the same house his mother and father had lived in when I was a teacher. I had lunch with him, his wife, and their fifth child. They had had four girls in a row, the youngest now in high school. But now they had a two-year-old boy. Frank spoke about how happy he would be taking his son hunting and teaching him how to trap.

As we ate and talked, Frank told me that in his job he used a lot of the math he had learned in high school. It made a difference that he felt confident figuring out the amount of chemicals to add to the water to make it drinkable. He also spoke of long-term plans to run a sewage line through the village and sighed, saying he was tired of honey buckets.

Like the other students I encountered, Frank had succeeded in finding life in the changing village productive and fulfilling. He understood and accepted the benefits that came with village life, but he also knew what he might do to improve on the experience when it came time to do so.

Katrina. When I flew back to Anchorage, I was surprised to find two former students—now living in different villages—on the flight, each escorting their parents into the hospital for treatment. As we visited in the waiting room at the Bethel airport, I clearly recollected how it felt to be connected to nearly everyone all the time, wherever you went.

This feeling was further reinforced when I checked in to leave Anchorage at the end of my trip. Behind the ticket counter sat Katrina, a former student who had moved into Anchorage full time and now worked for the airlines. Since Katrina's shift was just ending, we met for a coffee while I waited for my red-eye. She spoke about her life in Anchorage and her frequent opportunities to visit the village through her airline connections. Before I boarded my plane, I shared some photos taken in the old days and while in the village on my just completed trip. In those brief thirty minutes, it was as if the thirty years between had never happened. When you know a whole village, it becomes very difficult to get lost.

Do You Remember Me?

Before I left the village, there was a feast of remembrance held for a former student who had died in Anchorage one year before. People—I can't say how many—traveled from villages around to participate in the traditional memorial feast. Every square inch of the five-room house where it was held was packed, sometimes in double density as children sat in the laps of parents and older siblings.

Large numbers of people could not even get into the house and hung out on the stairs and boardwalk outside. After the memorial service, the feast began. Plate after plate of food emerged from the kitchen, served around the room in what appeared at first to be a quite random fashion but actually driven by an underlying order based on social rank and relationship. Children ate candy and left; then men moved to the table for soup, tea, and bread. Finally, the women moved to the table to linger over tea and fry bread—a delicacy savored in Native communities throughout the North American continent.

I was late in coming to the table, joining the last of the youngest men and the first of the women elders. As I sat down, the younger sister of the former student being honored passed me a plate of dried fish and asked if I remembered her. "Yes," I said, "I do," and called her name. She smiled and turned to get more plates of food. And then the eldest woman of the community sat down across from me, the mother of a good friend. I had known her well when I had been a teacher. "Do you remember me?" I asked. She scrutinized me carefully, but the years had taken her vision and my youth. "No," she said. "No, are you a teacher at the school?"

Village Life Today

The very familiarity of this ritual provided me with an important insight into living on the tundra. On returning, I found village life to be much as it had been thirty years before: complicated and difficult but neither undesirable nor unbearable. Family and social relationships remained strong as ever. While some had chosen to leave for work or marriage, they not only remained connected but also returned regularly to visit family and friends. This was not to say that life stands still, for there were significant differences. Most importantly, the circle of influence the village cast on people's lives had expanded rather than diminished.

Many things in village life had become more dependable (healthcare, telephones, employment), others less dangerous (travel, illness), and still others had disappeared completely (mud and log houses, dip netting). The village inhabitants had not only managed to survive very well alongside the dominant culture—pressuring them now for over a century—without surrendering what they held most important, but they had also found new ways to thrive. Village life carried on, continuing to provide a strong center of support and refuge to members.

True, globalization—with its growing interdependence and connectivity—had tied the fate of the tundra villages more closely to the world's future. But the village appeared to be in no danger of being overrun by the Outside world and its cultures. In many ways, the village—with its own power plant, health clinic, government, and Native Corporation support systems—had emerged into the present far stronger than it had been thirty years earlier. Its population had not only grown but now also included members who lived far away for much of the year.

Culturally Responsive Education

I also realized that, over the years, the school had become integrated into everyday life in practical and useful ways. Like snow machines, satellite telephones, and wind power, the school and its resources had become essential components of the widening circle of village life. Though always posing the threat of external cultural domination, the school also played a central role in the continuing life of the village by providing jobs, opportunities, and information.

Each of the former students whose stories are presented here had a life enhanced by the experiences encountered in the course of his or her secondary education. Not all or even most of these experiences came through the channels of formal schooling, but all occurred in the context of the village because that was where the school was located. Many of these experiences had been outside these students' reach prior to the establishment of village schools and had added to their cultural capital and widened their worlds. Most importantly, these experiences had occurred in the village—not far away from home and friends at a boarding school promoting the dominant culture. The local community had negotiated a school that served its needs—not the needs of external testing companies, curricular experts, and policymakers.

For All Practitioners of Culturally Responsive Education

Ironically, the challenges that confronted those coming to teach in village schools from outside have changed very little. Each new arrival must learn how to navigate the contradictions between working as a change agent and respecting the social practices that together compose a culture. To successfully live between cultural identities means living not just as a teacher—flat, one-dimensional, occasional—but also living as a person: well-rounded, multidimensional, full-time. And—I realized as my visit ended—my story was less about how I had changed the village and more about how the village had changed me.

I have come to think of teaching as like swimming in the sea. Though the swimmer knows strokes and kicks, each wave presents a new relationship between the swimmer and the water, an original problem to solve. Indeed, our lives can be considered as immersed in the ocean of knowledge described by the Nunavik elder in Rasmussen (2002). Learning to swim is not just required to live but also to be alive. As swimmers must constantly adapt and modify their bodies in relationship to the waves, so, too, teachers must learn to relate to each student, classroom, and school day as original, unique compositions of possibilities: never repeating and ever unfolding into new experiences.

As cross-cultural teachers, we must continually question our roles in Native communities. At the same time, it is imperative for us to realize that because of whom we represent as teachers, we may be viewed initially with suspicion. Acknowledging this, we must strive to maintain a style of teaching that supports Native students' intellectual, emotional, and social growth. To do so requires making the linkages between local bodies of knowledge, respecting Native peoples and practices, and exploring ways of enhancing rather than deprecating Native communities and their resources.

Cross-cultural teaching also requires that we make changes within ourselves. We have to become willing to explore and appreciate the new communities into which we are immersed. To teach to the students, we have to connect with them emotionally. And though we, as Outsiders, may never become fully invested members of Native communities—inherently privileged to certain knowledge and ways of being—we will be changed in ways we cannot anticipate. Indeed, teaching is not a value-free profession.

Returning to the village had not provided answers to all my questions. It offered neither closure to the past nor openings to the future. But it did enable me to see the possibilities of the present from new perspectives. I would never again be a member of the village community in the same way I once had been, but in returning, I had become a participant in a new community, with new connections and relationships.

The present and the past had been folded to touch like opposite edges of a blanket, offering new experiences in familiar contexts. The solutions were different, but the problems were familiar, just as wooden boats had become wooden roads. I realized that the village and the school were not in some tectonic competition for cultural supremacy. Indeed, it had never been an either/or choice. A productive future requires access to many options. The school and the community now each need the other in important ways. And together they would not only survive but also thrive by finding solutions to problems yet to come.

REFERENCES

Cotton, S. (1984). "Alaska's Molly Hootch case: High schools and the village voice." *Educational Research Quarterly* 8 (4): 30–43.

Kleinfeld, J., and J. Bloom. (1973). *A Long Way from Home: Effects of Public High Schools on Village Children Away from Home.* Fairbanks: Center of Northern Educational Research and Institute of Social, Economic and Government Research, University of Alaska.

No Child Left Behind Act of 2001: Reauthorization of the Elementary and Secondary Education Act of 1965. (2001). *U.S. code.* Title 20, sec. 6301 et seq.

Rasmussen, D. (2002). "Qallunology, a pedagogy for the oppressor." *Philosophy of Education Yearbook*, 85–94.

Stapleton, R. 2008. "Senate hearing in Bethel paints bleak economic picture." *Anchorage Daily News*, September 15. Retrieved from http://www.gopalaska.com/2008/09/senate-hearing-in-bethel-paints-bleak.html.

Tobeluk v. Lind. (1979). 589 P.2d 873 (Supreme Court of Alaska, January 26).

NOTE

1. *Note from editor*: The Indigenous peoples of Alaska are the Inuit (Eskimo), Aleut, Athapaskans, and Tlingit, together known as "Alaskan Natives" rather than "American Indians." Alaskan Native education is grouped with American Indian education. This chapter centers on Alaskan Native education, focusing on an Inuit village school.

Part II

Integration of Culturally Relevant Pedagogy in an Era of High-Stakes Accountability

Beverly J. Klug

In this section of our book, we focus on what is occurring in our contemporary society with American Indian education and legislation, including the Reauthorization of the Elementary and Secondary Education Act of 1965 known as the No Child Left Behind Act (NCLB) of 2001 and its impacts (National Indian Education Association, 2005; 2012). This act has represented the latest hegemonic effort to remold the education of all students in the United States into a one-size-fits-all model.

In chapter 5, Haynes Writer links NCLB (2001) and past efforts to annihilate American Indian identity through the forced assimilation and physical elimination of tribal peoples. She explores the oppressive measures of the act and provides ample evidence from a Native point of view of how it undermines abilities of Native peoples to provide the type(s) of education they feel are most appropriate for their children.

Klug, in chapter 6, focuses on the effects of NCLB (2001) on one public school located on a reservation in the Intermountain West serving almost all American Indian students, including the frustrations experienced by faculty members in light of the sanctions of the act. The principal at the time had been committed to enhancing the education for the students by providing culturally relevant/responsive pedagogy. However, with the demands of NCLB and teacher fears, doing so involved many challenges, and opportunities became more limited as resources were shifted to prescribed programs and student assessment.

Knowing the importance of languages to cultural integrity, maintenance, and links to educational success, we include information about current efforts to retain and revitalize Native languages. Bowles, in chapter 7, describes the process of revitalizing the Choctaw language from the earliest dreams to present realities. She explores the process from the viewpoint of those intimately involved, language teachers themselves, and how high schools have provided venues for students to learn the language as well as other technology dedicated to this effort. The results of these efforts are made available to readers as a model for others.

Since NCLB (2001), providing opportunities for the integration of Native languages and cultures in schools has largely been dismissed in spite of George W. Bush's Executive Order no. 13336 (2004, 25295) to assist American Indians and Alaska Natives in meeting achievement standards "in a manner that is consistent with tribal traditions, languages, and cultures." This is due in large part to the insistence on "scientific research" and success as measured by high-stakes testing in the order itself (Lee 2012).

Nevertheless, a few programs have continued in this vein. In chapter 8, McCarty provides empirical information about the key roles of language and cultural curricula in promoting the academic success of American Indian students. She concludes with evidence from program models centered on these elements and the positive results in the educational experiences of the students involved, thus reinforcing the arguments for culturally responsive education for Native students.

Throughout all of these chapters, the theme of social justice in education for American Indian students is readily apparent. While laws made by the dominant culture may make sense to citizens, as educators it is important that we continue to advocate for practices that are most effective for the achievement of American Indian students. It is imperative that we provide information to others about what constitutes effective practice and provide insights to others about the need to stipulate educational programs that are more suited to Native populations.

As you read through these chapters, you will learn more about the challenges faced in our current educational system and why differentiation of the approaches available in our schools is not only important but also essential for the maximal growth and achievement levels of our Native students.

REFERENCES

Executive Order no. 13336. (2004). "American Indian and Alaska Native education." *Federal Register* 69 (87): 25295–7.

Elementary and Secondary Education Act of 1965. (2000). *U.S. code*. Title 20, sec. 6301 et seq.

Lee, T. (2012). "No Child Left Behind Act: A bust in Indian country." *Indian Country Today Media Network*, March 7. Retrieved from http://indiancountrytodaymedianetwork.com/2012/03/07/101597-101597.

National Indian Education Association. (2005). *Preliminary Report on No Child Left Behind in Indian Country*. Washington, DC. Retrieved from http://www.niea.org/policy/policy-resources.aspx.

National Indian Education Association. (2012). "The failure of NCLB in Indian Country." *Preliminary Report on No Child Left Behind in Indian Country*. Washington, DC. Retrieved from http://www.niea.org/policy/policy-resources.aspx.

No Child Left Behind Act of 2001: Reauthorization of the Elementary and Secondary Education Act of 1965 (NCLB). (2001). *U.S. code*. Title 20, sec. 6301 et seq.

Chapter 5

The Savage Within

No Child Left Behind—Again, and Again, and Again

Jeanette Haynes Writer: New Mexico State University

ABSTRACT

Utilizing critical race theory and tribal critical race theory, the examination of the "no child left behind" phrase is interrogated in its historical practice and fulfillment manifested in the value of whiteness and practices of colonization within educationally imposed oppressions that have long been a part of the educational terrain for Native Peoples.

In this chapter, snapshots are provided of historical savage initiatives of "no child left behind" (early colonization, Cherokee Removal, Sand Creek Massacre, and the boarding schools), followed by enduring contemporary threads of oppression (English-only, the written word as literacy, assimilative knowledge, and "high-quality" teachers). I explore the present oppressions of the No Child Left Behind Act (NCLB 2001) and identify specific recommendations that could potentially end or mediate NCLB's negative effects on Native students and communities.

Keywords: No Child Left Behind, colonization, oppression, tribal critical race theory, critical race theory

THE SAVAGE WITHIN: NO CHILD LEFT BEHIND—AGAIN, AND AGAIN, AND AGAIN

They should be educated, not as Indians, but as Americans. In short, the public school should do for them what it is so successfully doing for all the other races in this country, assimilate them.
—Commissioner of Indian Affairs, Thomas Jefferson Morgan (1889)

The model of No Child Left Behind was created somewhere far away from Indian reservations and where Indian children live so the whole model—the model that they have created—is totally different than who we are.
—testimony from the Preliminary Report on No Child Left Behind in Indian Country (National Indian Education Association 2005)

The lens that I use to read the world is one of an Indigenous person, a Cherokee woman with a specific historical, social, and cultural experience within the context of a colonized country and a colonizing federal government, and one of a developing tribal critical race theorist. As I have interrogated and decoded the No Child Left Behind Act (NCLB 2001), the phrase "no child left behind" keeps resonating with me but in historical echoes that are most likely not apparent to most.

As Native Americans[1]—as members of hundreds of sovereign and distinct nations—we have heard the phrase "no child left behind" before. We have *lived through* this phrase. In this chapter, I provide snapshots of the United States federal government's savage initiatives of "no child left behind." I then identify enduring threads of oppression as I explore the implications and advancement of dominant and deeply oppressive political positions manifested in NCLB (2001) as related to that history.

Although this history is not inclusive and I make leaps through time, it highlights particular patterns of anguish for Native Peoples and challenges to tribal sovereignty. This investigation results in valid suspicion of the purposes of the act not only from Indigenous communities but also from teacher educators and social justice advocates insisting on a need for a continued resistance to the oppressive directives of the act.

Even though we are past the George W. Bush administration's reign, under which NCLB (2001) was designed, implemented, and enforced as the Reauthorization of the Elementary and Secondary Education Act of 1965, NCLB has yet to be left behind by the Obama administration. As the Democratic presidential candidate, Barack Obama (Haggerty and Raskin 2008) discussed his plan for reform of NCLB by fully funding the law; providing "high-quality" teachers to all students through recruitment, preparation, retention, and reward; and supporting schools in need of improvement rather than punishing them.

President Obama's secretary of education, Arne Duncan (2010), speaks of preparing students for competition in the United States or global economy. What is not adequately addressed is how *schools* will be prepared for the cultural lives and lived realities of the students they serve.

What I present here provides evidence that educationally imposed oppressions, the value of whiteness, and practices of colonization have long been a part of the educational terrain. They will most likely remain in U.S. schools even though NCLB (2001) may be overhauled with the reauthorization of the Elementary and Secondary Education Act unless educators take action within a social justice framework.

For educators, this chapter argues for a critical interrogation of NCLB (2001) so that we may take a political and culturally informed stance on the act and/or continue to resist its oppressive directives. Through storytelling, this examination provides a Native perspective of a phrase habitually used today, excavated in its historical practice and fulfillment. In doing so, I identify historical threads of oppression that assist us to read between the lines and become active in the movement toward social justice for Native students. I also discuss plausible recommendations for resolving continued inequities and oppressions of NCLB.

Theoretical Framework

Critical race theory (CRT) developed out of the field of legal studies in the mid-1970s as a means to examine the relationships among race, racism, and power—assuming that racism encompasses not merely individual acts of discrimination but rather historical, systemic, ideological manifestations of power to serve, maintain, and protect white privilege (Delgado 1989; Harris 1993). CRT adds the dimension of activism to this examination so that future change is possible (Delgado and Stefanic 2001).

The goal of CRT is to construct an alternative reality through the naming of one's reality by utilizing storytelling. This process allows for the contestation, deconstruction, and reshaping of the master narrative[2] by enlisting multiple perspectives and experiences as sources of valid knowledge that can then serve as a catalyst for transformation. Thus serving as a catalyst for transformation, CRT provides a space for the voices of people of color.

For members of the dominating society, CRT produces a "cognitive conflict to jar white dysconscious racism" (Ladson-Billings 1998, 16), disrupting particular beliefs about the world, helping white people to "understand what life is like for others, and [inviting] the reader into a new and unfamiliar world" (Delgado and Stefanic 2001, 41).

Indigenous scholars (Brayboy 2005; Haynes Writer 2002; Haynes Writer 2008; Hermes 1999; Rains 2003; Williams 1997) began utilizing CRT to examine the effects of race, racism, and power in our communities and on ourselves. Bryan Brayboy (2005) used the foundational ideas and concepts of CRT to ground and introduce tribal critical race theory (TribalCrit) to examine the issues of Indigenous Peoples in relation to the United States and its laws and policies.

Although a significant role is played by racism, a primary tenet within TribalCrit is the endemic nature of colonization and its processes in society. In this chapter, I draw upon both CRT and TribalCrit to construct the "story" of NCLB (2001), exposing the continued colonization of Native Americans.

Historical Context

Understanding the historical contexts of racism and the creation of negative attitudes toward Native Peoples is an essential element in our discussion. Without this knowledge, eliminated from the master narrative by those in power, one cannot appreciate the lengths to which colonizing forces went to destroy Native Peoples occupying the continent.

"Civilized" versus "Savage"—Imposing Colonization

As Europeans immigrated to this continent and continued to arrive, interactions with Indigenous communities became more confrontational. Native Peoples were viewed as obstacles to civilization—what was regarded as "progress" in a European-based society.

Our occupancy of land was not appropriate according to European standards. That is, we had use of too much land and were not improving it by clearing trees for farming and building permanent structures. Sacred spaces and places that brought forth stories of our origins and defined our existence were reconfigured into parcels of real estate, acreages in which titles and ownership of the land replaced relationships with the land.

As Europeans, and later, European Americans, encroached on Native lands farther and farther, it became imperative to condemn Indigenous Peoples to the realm of the Other. This Other had to be feared, to be held as less than Europeans—savages to be exterminated. Native Peoples were the "savage" juxtaposed against the European and European Americans' "civilized."

As the power dynamic shifted with the influx of Europeans, the outsiders developed strategies to deal with the Indigenous populace. Those options included genocide (Stannard 1992; Thornton 1987), removal to westward territories, and later, confinement to reservations (Kvasnicka and Viola 1979; Prucha 2000), followed by forced assimilation through civilizing methodologies (Adams 1995; Hoxie 1984).

Even though sovereign-nation status was established for Indigenous Peoples through the formulation of treaties between Tribal nations and the U.S. government, that status was not respected or upheld. In 1819, the Congress passed the Civilization Fund Act and set aside funds for "benevolent" or religious societies to use education as a means to civilize Native Americans.

The instruction for children included reading, writing, arithmetic, and mechanical or domestic arts (Prucha 2000, 33).[3] Families and communities were educated through what Joel Spring (1996, 32) refers to as "ideological management": the attempt to deculturalize Native people whereby tribal epistemologies were silenced and replaced; extended and matrilineal families were reshaped into nuclear patriarchal systems; Native spiritual practices were replaced with Christianity; and diverse techniques of generating sustenance and maintaining life were supplanted with European-based farming techniques and an associated capitalistic economy.

Within the machinery of colonization, Native families were reshaped into something "acceptable," something likened to European forms—no child was left behind in this assimilative transformation. The sovereign-nation status of tribes and tribal peoples was reduced or disregarded within the paternalistic relationships imposed by the U.S. government. Native people were told what was good for them—the outsiders were the experts.

Indian Removal Policies and the Removal of the Cherokee—Early to Mid-1800s

While many tribal nations and individuals resisted the civilizing process, others began to embrace it due to want or necessity of survival in a quickly changing world. The Cherokee, along with the Choctaw, Chickasaw, Creek, and Seminole tribes, obtained the label of the "Five Civilized Tribes."[4] This description was given for the capacity of tribal members to emulate European life ways as a means of surviving and remaining in their Southeast homelands when the threat of removal to the West emerged in the United States federal government's discourse.

Within my tribe, those who inherited land and businesses from their white fathers and those Cherokee people in the lowlands in close proximity to whites adapted to or were raised with the worldview of the white intruders and aspired to fit themselves into white society (Conley 2005).[5] Missionaries, with their European-based schools, were eager to assist in this remolding and used the Cherokee as a model of civilizing success. To other tribes, it was stated, "Why can't *you* be like them?" What follows is a letter written by Methodist missionaries that appeared in the *Cherokee Phoenix*, the newspaper of the Cherokee people, on October 1, 1830.

> When we say that the Cherokee are rapidly advancing in civilization, we speak of them as a body. There are very different degrees of improvement; some families having risen to a level with the white people of the nation, while the progress of others has but commenced. (Kilpatrick and Kilpatrick 1968, 85)

While many Cherokees attempted to meld themselves into the white model, their efforts never removed the imposed label of Other. During his Second Annual Message to Congress, on December 6, 1830, President Andrew Jackson maintained the "us and them" division:

What good man would prefer a country covered with forests and ranged by a few thousand savages to our extensive Republic, studded with cities, towns, and prosperous farms, embellished with all the improvements which art can devise or industry execute, occupied by more than 12,000,000 happy people, and filled with all the blessings of liberty, civilization, and religion? (Jackson 1830, para. 3)

Even though the Cherokee attempted to adapt to and live within the confines of the colonizer, they were still constructed as "savage" within the context of the increasing greed for the rich land and particularly after the discovery of gold in Dahlonega, Georgia (Williams 1993). In December 1835, the Treaty of New Echota was signed by a few Cherokees who were courted and protected by the state of Georgia and the U.S. government, agreeing to the total removal of The People west.

Official Cherokee Nation leaders quickly began a fight through the United States' courts to stop the removal (Conley 2005). Whereas the tribe won in the Supreme Court, Andrew Jackson is said to have defiantly stated, "John Marshall has rendered his decision; now let him enforce it," in response to the Supreme Court Justice's ruling (Woodward 1963, 171).

And so the great tragedy of the Removal, the Trail of Tears, began. As reported by Mooney (1982, 130), "Men were seized in their fields or going along the road, women were taken from their wheels and children from their play." The Cherokee were hunted down for the movement west—it was intended that no man, woman, or child was to be left behind.

Sand Creek Massacre—1864

"I have come to kill Indians. . . ."
—Colonel John M. Chivington (U.S. Congress 1867, 47)

Many other atrocities were experienced by Indigenous nations during the same period as the Removal and in subsequent years. As the hunger for land crept west, so did the violence waged against the Plains tribes in what is referred to as the *Indian Wars*. The Sand Creek Massacre serves as one of the most brutal acts of terrorism[6] against this country's Native citizens. This is also one of the most vicious examples of no child left behind.

On the freezing dawn of November 29, 1864, Colonel John M. Chivington and the Colorado Volunteers brutally attacked a Cheyenne and Arapaho village along Sand Creek in southeastern Colorado. Chivington, with approximately seven hundred well-armed soldiers and with the aid of four howitzers cannons (Hoig 1961), attacked the village of six hundred peaceful people (Brown 1970).

Women and children comprised two-thirds of the village; many others were in their elder years. The younger men had been suspiciously given permission by Major Scott J. Anthony, a subordinate of Chivington's, to leave the area to hunt buffalo. Consequently, they were not present during the planned massacre to assist with protecting their people (Brown 1970).

Having met with Major Anthony at Fort Lyon only a short time before the massacre, Black Kettle, the headman of the Cheyenne, was assured that he and his people would be protected by the soldiers at the fort. However, chaos erupted in the sleepy village on the morning of the 29th as soldiers assembled on two sides of the encampment, readying for the attack.

Calling to his people and reminding them of the agreement of their protection by the U.S. soldiers, Black Kettle told them not to be afraid as they were being surrounded by men in military uniforms. As he tried to establish calm, Black Kettle stood in front of his lodge waving the American flag and a white flag of surrender from a long lodge pole. Women and children were gathering around him as the soldiers began firing howitzers and guns.

As a witness to the massacre, Anthony (as cited in Hoig 1961, 188) testifies concerning this especially brutal scenario:

> There was a little child, probably three years old, just big enough to walk through the sand. The Indians had gone ahead, and this little child was behind following after them. The little fellow was perfectly naked, travelling on the sand. I saw one man get off his horse, at a distance of about seventy-five yards, and draw up his rifle and fire—he missed the child. Another man came up and said, "Let me try the son of a bitch; I can hit him." He got down off his horse, kneeled down and fired at the little child, but he missed him. A third man came up and made a similar remark, and fired, and the little fellow dropped.

Chivington's goal was total extermination of the Native people even though he was confronted with protests from some of the officers (Cramer 1864; Soule 1864). Nonetheless, this church elder and former Methodist minister reacted with, "I have come to kill Indians, and believe it is right and honorable to use any means under God's heaven to kill Indians" (U.S. Congress 1867, 47).

The symbolic phrase "nits make lice" is attributed to Chivington, purportedly stated in a speech he delivered in Denver a short time before the massacre (as cited in Brown 1970, 90). This phrase symbolized his actions to forward the extermination of Native people, including the killing of children and infants. No child was to be spared—no child left behind.

Shortly after the massacre, Chivington and his men returned to Denver to tell their contrived tales of battle and show off their plunder. Hyde (1968, 162) reports they were

> received as heroes and the town went wild over the great "victory" over Black Kettle's "hostiles." One evening at a Denver theater a band of these heroes stepped upon the stage during an intermission and exhibited fully a hundred Cheyenne scalps, mostly those of women and children, while the audience cheered and the orchestra rendered patriotic airs. A few of the men had still more ghastly souvenirs: tobacco bags made of pieces of skin cut from the bodies of dead Cheyenne women.

In this macabre venue, the men were viewed as esteemed patriots in the war against the savage Other. Before the massacre, the *Daily Rocky Mountain News* spun white readers into a frenzy of fear with printed words of Indian depredations against settlers on the frontier; after the attack, the paper's editor manufactured a story of Chivington and the volunteers' bravery and military savvy and lauded them as being glorious patriots (Coward 1999).

In his official reports and during the investigations following the massacre, Chivington maintained being embattled with approximately seven hundred warriors and killing five hundred to six hundred of them (Berthrong 1963, 217). However, later investigations exposed the slaughter of 28 men and 105 women and children by Chivington and his troops (Brown 1970, 89). The intent of Chivington's attack was for no child to be left behind.

Forced Attendance at Boarding Schools—Late 1800s

After the close of the Indian Wars, Native people could no longer collectively resist white aggression; therefore, education was used to further wage the culture war. Children and grandchildren of those who participated in the Indian Wars became wards of a controlling federal education system and victims of assimilationist ideologies through boarding schools—the new weapon of choice to employ against Indigenous Peoples.

The boarding school, a creation of U.S. Army Officer Richard Henry Pratt through the development of the Carlisle Indian School in Pennsylvania, was based on a military model (Adams 1995). Carlisle, opened in 1879 and in operation until 1918, ushered in the era of off-reservation boarding schools across the nation. Children were housed in barracks-like structures and marched to and fro in military-style uniforms (Adams 1995; Lomawaima 1994; Utley 1964).

The boarding schools included prisons or guardhouses for solitary confinement (Utley 1964; Putney 1980). Even the youngest of children faced harsh, military-style punishment for the slightest infractions. Close confinement, unsanitary conditions, and substandard nutrition turned the boarding schools into incubators for disease and epidemics (Putney 1980). Due to the unwarranted deaths of the children, the schools hosted cemeteries on campus for the children who would never again return home (Adams 1995; Archuleta, Child, and Lomawaima 2000).

The curriculum taught in the schools purposefully emphasized all that was valued in white society. Tribal epistemologies and languages were degraded, silenced, and replaced with what was admired and privileged in the dominating white society as a means of "miseducation" (Pewewardy 2005). The children, like their curriculum, were standardized to move them toward the objective of civilization—to move American Indians into the standard of European Americans. The purpose of education was clear: to have Native Peoples "look with feelings of repugnance on their native state" (Wilson 1882, 604). No child was to be left behind in this comprehensive reform.

Psychological conditioning occurred at the boarding schools to make the children forget who they were and where they came from. The following is but one example of this psychological torment, the result of an early "English-only" and "English for the Children"[7] perspective. Captured in an 1881 letter to Captain Richard Pratt from a Lakota child attending Carlisle Boarding School, Nellie Robertson lamented,

> Dear Sir Capt. Pratt: I write this letter with much sorrow to tell you that I have spoken one Indian word. I will tell you how it happened: yesterday evening in the dining-hall Alice Winn talked to me in Sioux and before I knew what I was saying I found that I had spoken one word, and I felt so sorry that I could not eat my supper, and I could not forget that Indian word, and while I was sitting at the table the tears rolled down my cheeks. I tried very hard to speak only English. (cited in Adams 1995, 141)

Imagine what this child was taught in order to have such regret in speaking her language. English acquisition and "English-only" became the policy within the boarding schools. J. D. C. Atkins, in his 1887 Report of the Commissioner of Indian Affairs, mandated instruction of Native students only in English and taught only from English-language texts.

According to Atkins, "teaching an Indian youth in his own barbarous dialect is a positive detriment to him" (Prucha 2000, 174). In July of that year, he wrote to Indian agents that "the instruction of the Indians in the vernacular is not only of no use to them, but is detrimental to the cause of their education and civilization" (Prucha 2000, 174).

Students' home languages were not maintained because Indigenous languages were viewed as obsolete and uncivilized, not the language of intelligent or sophisticated people. Further, as part of his push for the exclusive use of English in boarding schools, Atkins declared that "nothing so surely and perfectly stamps upon an individual a national characteristic as language" (Prucha 2000, 173).

A curriculum of patriotism inculcating allegiance to the United States was enforced in the boarding schools as well. In his December 1889 *Supplemental Report on Indian Education*, Commissioner of Indian Affairs Thomas J. Morgan (1889, 96) maintained that "education should seek the disintegration of the tribes." He further stated,

The Indian youth should be instructed in their rights, privileges, and duties as American citizens; should be taught to love the American flag; should be imbued with a genuine patriotism, and made to feel that the United States, and not some paltry reservation, is their home. (Morgan 1889, 96)

Education for assimilation was the course of action in what was viewed as a superior, high-quality education. According to the 1901 *Annual Report of the Commissioner of Indian Affairs*, the attendance of Indigenous children at the boarding schools occurred "partly by cajolery and partly by threats; partly by bribery and partly by fraud; partly by persuasion and partly by force" (Prucha 2000, 198). Coercion extended back to home communities; the children were considered "hostages for tribal good behavior" (Utley 1964, 202).

Accountability for Indigenous Peoples' progress toward civilization and assimilation was placed squarely on the boarding schools. Commissioner of Indian Affairs Morgan, in his 1889 *Supplemental Report on Indian Education to the Secretary of the Interior*, went so far as to state that the removal of Native children from their familial and tribal influences should be mandated.

Whatever steps are necessary should be taken to place these children under proper educational influences. If, under any circumstances, compulsory education is justifiable, it certainly is in this case. Education, in the broad sense in which it is here used, is the Indians [sic] only salvation. With it they will become honorable, useful, happy citizens of a great republic, sharing on equal terms all of its blessings. Without it they are doomed either to destruction or to hopeless degradation. (Morgan 1889, 95)

Children were kidnapped from their families and often transported hundreds of miles from home (Adams 1995). Because of death from homesickness, epidemics, poor nutrition, and living conditions, as well as because of the ideological management that removed their identities as Indigenous persons, many children never came home again. No child was left behind in this all-encompassing educational master plan.

Present Context

I now move to the present context and the harmful directives of the NCLB Act of 2001. Although I have discussed—through the previous historic events—the role of education and schools in the assimilation and standardization of Native children, I find that NCLB (2001) contains those same threads of savage oppression.

"Stamping Out Their 'Barbarous Dialects'" — Foundations of English-Only

The development and maintenance of Native languages and cultures have received little attention and even less funding in NCLB (2001; Beaulieu 2008; National Indian Education Association [NIEA] 2005). This is of great concern for Native Peoples (NIEA 2010; Reyhner et al. 2003). Of the two hundred or more surviving Indigenous languages, it is estimated that only 34 of those tribal languages are being acquired by children; 155 languages may die out in the near future (McCarty and Romero 2005, 15).

James Mountain, San Ildefonso Pueblo governor and chairman of the Eight Northern Indian Pueblos Council in New Mexico, in his testimony at the August 10, 2007, federal hearing on how to improve NCLB (2001), warned that "once we lose our language, we lose our culture. . . . It's genocide. It's killing our people" (Salazar 2007).

In Oklahoma, tribal communities, in collaboration with local schools and universities, foster activities that encourage young people to learn and maintain their language. However, the imposition of English-only continues to threaten Native languages within the state (Wolgamott and Bair 2010).

At the 2010 eighth annual Oklahoma Native American Youth Language Fair in Norman, Oklahoma, six hundred pre-K through twelfth grade students from seventy schools gathered to exhibit their skills in their tribal languages (Toney 2010). The number of participating students grows each year, yet tribal languages are under attack. In November 2010, with over 75 percent of the vote, Oklahoma voters passed State Question 751, which made English Oklahoma's official language (Oklahoma State Election Board 2010).

Although the question stated that "Native American languages could also be used" (Wolgamott and Bair 2010, 3)—seemingly protecting tribal peoples' rights to language—this "protection" is simply a divide-and-conquer strategy and does not confront assimilationist ideology. Threats of English-only legislation are not limited to the state of Oklahoma; the English-only ideology—couched within the anti-immigrant fervor—has expanded across the nation, threatening both Native-language speakers and speakers of languages other than English.

NCLB and Literacy—Colonization through the Written Word

I strongly challenge the concept of literacy defined in NCLB (2001): that literacy occurs only by means of the written word. At the 2002 National Indian Education Association (NIEA) Convention, Dr. Manu Aluli Meyer, a Hawaiian Native, stated in her keynote address that educators must consider oral traditions as part of what is meant by being *literate* (Meyer 2002).

Drawing from Indigenous scholar Donald L. Fixico (2003), the oral tradition is a valid way of "reading the world" (Freire and Macedo 1987). NCLB's 2001 definition of *literacy* continues the colonization of Native people by forcing the use of only the written word—the written words of non-Natives—extinguishing tribal epistemologies and perspectives.

Being forced to utilize the written words of others serves to silence Native histories and counterstories and operates to establish and maintain the master narrative. This, then, institutes what I term the *privilege of non-knowledge*,[8] the belief that no other story or history—*or ways of teaching and learning*—exists than what is written on the printed page.

Employing the mantra of *scientifically based research,* the privilege of non-knowledge is the very foundation of NCLB's 2001 conceptualization of literacy, curriculum, pedagogy, and standardized tests—not just for Native peoples but also for many diverse communities. However, as taken up by Bowman (2005), Beaulieu (2008), and the National Indian Education Association (2005), very little scientifically based research has been conducted that includes American Indian/Alaska Native students in the research studies or is culturally relevant to Native students.

Approximately 500,000 students comprise the American Indian/Alaska Native school-aged population (NIEA 2004). Of these students, 90 percent attend public schools (NIEA 2010). As compared to the total population of students in U.S. schools, this number is very small and poses a significant problem in collecting data sets to accurately examine the progress and achievement of Native American students.

Testing the "Truth" — Privileging Assimilative Knowledge

Whereas NCLB's 2001 mandate to disaggregate test scores by subgroups has the potential to expose inequities in the schooling of Native students (National Education Association 2005), I assert that today's concept of *accountability* in obtaining higher student test scores becomes a carefully crafted replacement for yesterday's concept of *assimilation* of Native children into the European American society. Assimilation continues through the heavy reliance on standardized testing (Forbes 2000) required by NCLB (2001).

Test content is not based upon the knowledges and lived realities of local communities and families. Therefore, silencing, negation, and replacement occur of the rich knowledges students bring from home. Lomawaima and McCarty (2006, 150) maintain that standardized tests "not only gauge student knowledge but [act] as a surveillance and gate-keeping device, enabling or curtailing educational opportunity as never before."

As Indigenous People, we again experience assimilation as described by Spring's (1996, 32) "ideological management" and prescribed in the boarding schools. Within this "*banking concept of education*" (Freire 1986), what is advanced through standardized tests are those knowledges of the test makers, individuals in far away and privileged places. Teachers, as well, are standardized into what knowledge and pedagogy they may bring into the classroom. Consequently, no teacher is left behind as each is deskilled of his or her professional capabilities (National Education Association 2005).

We must move beyond the colonizing forces of the act couched within the assimilative press of the United States. Tribal officials, educators, and community people stress that NCLB (2001) must embrace and support tribal knowledges, concepts, values, traditions, languages, and histories (Beaulieu 2008; Demmert and Towner 2003; NIEA 2010).

"Proper Educational Influences" — Interrogating "Quality"

NCLB (2001) maintains that all students will be provided a quality education; however, "quality" is a social construct capable of many forms of definition. What is valued or judged as quality in one community may not be in another. At issue as well is the concept of a "highly qualified teacher." Under the auspices of NCLB, this is an individual who possesses content knowledge and required credentials.

At an NCLB (2001) symposium I attended in Albuquerque, New Mexico, a community member made the statement that a high-quality teacher also meant someone who knew the Native community, its children, and was responsive to those needs. The comment was essentially brushed aside by the federal representative attending the meeting (Vasques 2004).

However, this issue was highlighted in the NIEA's *Preliminary Report on No Child Left Behind in Indian Country* (2005) and was embedded in the testimonies to U.S. governmental committees by NIEA President Patricia Whitefoot (NIEA 2010). It is imperative that those who are stakeholders in the educational process—parents, students, tribal communities, and tribal officials, not just federal officials—define *quality education* and *high-quality teacher*.

Recommendations for Change

NCLB (2001)—as is—is defective for diverse students, specifically Native students. Secretary of education, Arne Duncan (2010), in a testimony before the Senate asserted that:

NCLB's accountability system needs to be fixed—now. It allows—even encourages—states to lower standards. It doesn't measure growth or reward excellence. It prescribes the same interventions for schools with very different needs. It encourages a narrowing of the curriculum and focuses on test preparation. It labels too many schools with the same "failing" label regardless of their challenges.

While NCLB's disaggregation of test scores by subgroups (2001) has revealed gaps in the Westernized academic achievement of Native students as compared with their non-Native peers, the *critical issue* is identifying and enacting *effective* and *culturally appropriate strategies and actions* to resolve the inequities needed to close the achievement gap (read: opportunity gap). Tribal officials, community people, Native educators, and advocates have provided formal and informal critique of NCLB (2001) as revisions are considered for the reauthorization of the Elementary and Secondary Education Act.

Recommendations for resolving continued inequities and oppressions include establishing collaborations and cooperation between the federal government, state governments, and tribal governments; increasing support for language immersion programs; recognizing and utilizing tribal culture within the schooling context; and increasing the number of Native American teachers and better preparation of teachers who teach Native children (Klug and Whitfield 2003; Lee and Quijada Cerecer 2010; National Congress of American Indians 2010; National Education Association 2005; NIEA 2010).

Tribes and Native organizations have continually requested federal and state cooperation and collaboration in the effort to educate Native children as a means of respecting and supporting tribal sovereignty and self-determination. Such recommendations include tribes identifying their wants and needs instead of the U.S. government doing that for them; having tribal input into AYP (adequate yearly progress) standards and teacher credentialing, especially for tribal language instruction; advancing culturally based education; and allowing for alternative measurement assessments of Native students (National Congress of American Indians 2010; NIEA 2010).

In the fervor of allotting more instructional time on reading and math, as well as readying students for taking the standardized tests, time for tribal-language instruction and instruction on cultural content has been sacrificed. Tribal leaders, educational organizations, community people, and educational allies continuously advocate for the promotion and maintenance of Native languages (NIEA 2010).

Tribal communities, scholars, and researchers have also recommended including Native culture in curriculum content and pedagogy, thus providing culturally based education for Native students (Ah Nee-Benham 2008; Demmert and Towner 2003; Ho'omanawanui 2010; Klug and Whitfield 2003; Lee and Quijada Cerecer 2010) and exposing non-Natives to Native culture and history (Carjuzaa et al. 2010).

Increasing the number of Native teachers is also a plausible solution in assisting students to negotiate and mediate the schooling context (National Education Association 2005). Preparing teachers from the community provides a sense of stability to counteract the high turnover of non-Native teachers in many tribal community schools. Individuals who are teachers from the community have access to community and family networks in ways that teachers from the outside do not have and/or of which they do not understand adequately.

Teachers from the community may offer the advantage of bridging Westernized curriculum content with tribal and community knowledge and could provide culturally relevant pedagogy. It is also imperative to prepare non-Native teachers to understand the tribal community context in which they teach so they may become high quality in terms of the relationships they form with students and their families (NIEA 2010).

Conclusion

Drawing upon TribalCrit as my theoretical framework to tell the story of "no child left behind," I have provided readers with "a new and more culturally nuanced way of examining the lives and experiences of tribal peoples" (Brayboy 2005, 430). I have done this to "expose the inconsistencies in structural systems and institutions . . . [to] make the situation better for Indigenous students" (Brayboy 2005, 441).

I find that most individuals do not know of these historical events due to the white middle-class-oriented standardized curriculum based within the context of colonization. This curriculum is concerned with the agenda of inculcating patriotism, developing an obedience of not questioning information, and limiting one's exposure to diverse histories, multiple perspectives, and experiences of marginalized and colonized peoples.

Miseducation has happened not only to Native people (Pewewardy 2005) but has also happened and continues to happen to all of us. My hope is for educators to interrogate the history as I presented it here, to critique NCLB (2001), and to take action, thus realizing the transformative quality of TribalCrit.

By doing this, "we . . . expose structural inequalities and assimilatory processes and work toward debunking and deconstructing them" (Brayboy 2005, 440). A critical interrogation sparks critical and political consciousness, resulting in the advancement of social justice for students and communities oppressed by NCLB (2001).

Information presented here can assist in making connections to the past, interrogating what it means to be American, deconstructing formal and informal curricula with particular stances that accommodate or privilege whiteness, and problematizing the conception of quality education. I encourage and expect educators to question the politics of NCLB (2001) and to interrogate and form resistance to its harmful and costly directives, which operate to create Native-language loss and disconnection from or destruction of tribal epistemologies.

Individual tribes are politically sovereign nations. They are independent nations located within the United States as established by the many treaties created between the governments of the various Indigenous nations and the government of the United States. Thus, Native Peoples and nations have the right to self-determination—this includes determining educational destinies.

NCLB (2001) has reformulated the trust relationship that tribes have with the federal government by giving states more power in the education of Native students (NIEA 2005; National Education Association 2005). Thereby, NCLB has challenged tribal sovereignty and self-determination.

As part of the testimony collected for the NIEA *Preliminary Report on No Child Left Behind in Indian Country*, it was stated, "Tribal sovereignty and our children's cultural identity become undermined unless tribes are directly involved in all efforts to develop policy, set standards, guide curriculum, develop a pallet of assessment and lead in the development of culturally appropriate pedagogy" (2005, 20). Students and communities should not be *worked on*; they must be *worked with*.

Barack Obama, as a presidential candidate addressing the Crow Nation in May 2008 and upon being adopted by the Black Eagle family, stated:

> We will never be able to undo the wrongs that were committed against Native Americans, but what we can do is make sure that we have a president who's committed to doing what's right with Native Americans, being full partners, respecting, honoring, working with you. That's the commitment I'm making to you, and since now I'm a member of the family, you know that I won't break my commitment to my own brothers, and my own sisters. (Gavrilovic 2008)

Time will tell if Native American students, families, and communities are heard in their concerns over NCLB (2001) and if the commitment for change occurs.

I have identified and connected the threads of oppression from Indigenous historical events to the implications and advancement of dominant—and deeply oppressive—political positions within NCLB (2001). Education researchers and scholars—Native and non-Native—as well as community people have voiced their concerns and frustrations with NCLB after over ten years of education under the act's mandates. Directives of the act and results from the implementation of NCLB have greatly challenged the cultural continuance of Indigenous communities by further standardizing the curriculum through the enforcement of standardized tests.

I ask the reader to put the pieces together, make historical connections, read between the lines, and become active in the movement toward social justice in education for our Native American students. The act must be overhauled or left behind to ensure the realization of educational opportunities for Native students and communities.

REFERENCES

Adams, D. W. (1995). *Education for Extinction: American Indians and the Boarding School Experience, 1875–1928*. Lawrence: University Press of Kansas.

Ah Nee-Benham, M. K. P. (2008). *Indigenous Educational Models for Contemporary Practice: In Our Mother's Voice*. Vol. 2. New York: Routledge.

Archuleta, M. L., B. J. Child, and K. T. Lomawaima, eds. (2000). *Away from Home: American Indian Boarding School Experiences, 1879–2000*. Phoenix, AZ: Heard Museum.

Beaulieu, D. (2008). "Native American research and policy development in an era of No Child Left Behind: Native language and culture during the administrations of Presidents Clinton and Bush." *Journal of American Indian Education* 47 (1): 10–45.

Berthrong, D. J. (1963). *The Southern Cheyennes*. Norman: University of Oklahoma Press.

Bowman, N. R. (2005). *A Critical, Cultural, and Contextual Analysis of NCLB's Impact on Early Childhood and Elementary Students*. Commissioned paper for the Rural Early Childhood Forum on American Indian and Alaska Native Early Learning, William J. Clinton Presidential Center, Little Rock, AR.

Brayboy, B. M. J. (2005). "Toward a tribal critical race theory in education." *Urban Review* 37 (5): 425–46.

Brown, D. (1970). *Bury My Heart at Wounded Knee: An Indian history of the American West*. New York: Bantam Books.

Carjuzaa, J., M. Jetty, M. Munson, and T. Veltkamp. (2010). "Montana's Indian Education for All: Applying multicultural education theory." *Multicultural Perspectives* 12 (4): 192–8.

Conley, R. J. (2005). *The Cherokee Nation: A History*. Albuquerque: University of New Mexico Press.

Coward, J. M. (1999). "The *Daily Rocky Mountain News* and the scandal of Sand Creek." In *The newspaper Indian: Native American identity in the press, 1820–90*, 98–124. Champaign: University of Illinois Press.

Cramer, J. A. (1864). "The Sand Creek Massacre—Lieutenant Joseph A. Cramer letter to Major Edward Wynkoop regarding the massacre." *Lone Wolf* (web site). Retrieved from http://www.kclonewolf.com/History/SandCreek/sc-documents/sc-cramer-to-wynkoop-12-19-64.html.

Delgado, R. (1989). "Storytelling for oppositionists and others: A plea for narrative." *Michigan Law Review* 87: 2,411–441.

Delgado, R., and J. Stefanic. (2001). *Critical Race Theory: An Introduction*. New York: New York University Press.

Demmert, W. G., and J. C. Towner. (2003). *A Review of the Research Literature on the Influences of Culturally Based Education on the Academic Performance of Native American Students*. Portland, OR: Northwest Regional Educational Laboratory. Retrieved from http://educationnorthwest.org/webfm_send/196.

Duncan, A. (2010). Secretary Arne Duncan's testimony before the Senate Health, Education, Labor, and Pensions Committee and the House Education and Labor Committee on the Obama administration's Blueprint for Reauthorizing the Elementary and Secondary Education Act (ESEA). Washington, DC: U.S. Department of Education. Retrieved from http://www2.ed.gov/news/speeches. Web cast available at http://help.senate.gov/hearings/hearing/?id=45361c35-5056-9502-5deb-a3d743977e08.

Fixico, D. L. (2003). *The American Indian Mind in a Linear World: American Indian Studies and Traditional Knowledge*. New York: Routledge.

Forbes, J. D. (2000). "The new assimilation movement: Standards, tests, and Anglo-American supremacy." *Journal of American Indian Education* 39 (2): 1–35. Retrieved from http://jaie.asu.edu/v39/V39I2A2.pdf.

Freire, P. (1986). *Pedagogy of the Oppressed*. Trans. M. Bergman Ramos. New York: Continuum. Orig. pub. 1970.

Freire, P., and D. Macedo. (1987). *Literacy: Reading the Word and the World*. New York: Bergin and Garvey.

Gavrilovic, M. (2008). "Obama reaches out to Native Americans." *CBSNews.com*, May 19. Retrieved from http://www.cbsnews.com/8301-502443_162-4109427-502443.html.

Haggerty, R., and M. K. Raskin. (2008). "The 2008 presidential candidates: Where do they stand?" *Where we stand: America's schools in the 21st century with Judy Woodruff*. (PBS broadcast). *THIRTEEN* (web site), September 8. New York: Educational Resources Center at THIRTEEN/WNET, New York's Kravis Multimedia Center in New York City. Retrieved from http://www.pbs.org/wnet/wherewestand/featured/the-2008-presidential-candidates-where-do-they-stand/140/.

Harris, C. (1993). "Whiteness as property." *Harvard Law Review* 106: 1701–91.

Haynes Writer, J. (2002). "Terrorism in Native America: Interrogating the past, examining the present, and constructing a liberatory future." *Anthropology and Education Quarterly* 33 (3): 317–30.

———. (2008). "Unmasking, exposing, and confronting: Critical race theory, tribal critical race theory and multicultural education." *International Journal of Multicultural Education* 10 (2): 1–15.

Hermes, M. (1999). "Research methods as a situated response: Toward a First Nations' methodology." In *Race is . . . race isnt: Critical race theory and qualitative studies in education*, ed. L. Parker, D. Deyhle, and S. Villenas, 83–100. Boulder, CO: Westview.

Hoig, S. (1961). *The Sand Creek Massacre*. Norman: University of Oklahoma Press.

Ho'omanawanui, K. (2010). "Mana wahine, education and nation-building: Lessons from the epic of Pele and Hi'iaka for kanaka maoli today." *Multicultural Perspectives* 12 (4): 206–12.

Hoxie, F. E. (1984). *A Final Promise: The Campaign to Assimilate the Indians, 1880–1920*. Lincoln: University of Nebraska Press.

Hyde, G. E. (1968). *Life of George Bent: Written from His Letters*. Ed. S. Lottinville. Norman: University of Oklahoma Press.

Jackson, A. (1830). President Andrew Jackson's message to Congress "On Indian Removal." *Our Documents: A National Initiative on American History, Civics, and Service* (web site). Washington, DC: National Archives and Records Administration. http://www.ourdocuments.gov/doc.php.?flash=oldanddoc=25andpage=transcript.

Kilpatrick, J. F., and A. G. Kilpatrick, eds. (1968). *New Echota Letters*. Dallas, TX: Southern Methodist University Press.

Klug, B. J., and P. T. Whitfield, P. T. (2003). *Widening the Circle: Culturally Relevant Pedagogy for American Indian Children*. New York: Routledge.

Kvasnicka, R. M., and H. J. Viola, eds. (1979). *The Commissioners of Indian Affairs: 1824–1977*. Lincoln: University of Nebraska Press.

Ladson-Billings, G. (1998). "Just what is critical race theory and what's it doing in a nice field like education? *International Journal of Qualitative Studies in Education* 11 (1): 7–24."

Lee, T., and P. D. Quijada Cerecer. (2010). "(Re)claiming Native youth knowledge: Engaging in socio-culturally responsive teaching and relationships." *Multicultural Perspectives* 12 (4): 199–205.

Lomawaima, K. T. (1994). *They Called it Prairie Light: The Story of the Chilocco Indian School*. Lincoln: University of Nebraska Press.

Lomawaima, K. T., and T. L. McCarty. (2006). "Testing tribal sovereignty: Self-determination and high-stakes tests." In *To Remain an Indian: Lessons in Democracy from a Century of Native American Education*, 150–66. New York: Teachers College Press.

Lyotard, J. F. (1984). *The Postmodern Condition: A Report on Knowledge*. Minneapolis: University of Minnesota Press.

McCarty, T. L., and M. E. Romero. (2005). "What does it mean to lose a language? Investigating heritage language loss and revitalization among American Indians." *Show and Tell: A Magazine from ASU's College of Education*, Fall. Retrieved from http://www.u.arizona.edu/~aildi/Useful_Links/McCarty_Romero_article.pdf.

Meyer, M. A. (2002). Keynote address. 33rd Annual National Indian Education Association Convention, Albuquerque, NM, November.

Mooney, J. (1982). *Myths of the Cherokee and Sacred Formulas of the Cherokees*. Reprint of material first published in the 7th and 19th *Annual Reports* of the Bureau of American Ethnology. Nashville, TN: Charles and Randy Elder, Booksellers.

Morgan, T. J. (1889). *Annual Report of the Commissioner of Indian Affairs to the Secretary of the Interior for the Year 1889. Supplemental Report on Indian Education*. Washington, DC: Government Printing Office. Retrieved from http://www.archive.org/stream/annualreportofco188900unitrich/annualreportofco188900unitrich_djvu.txt.

National Congress of American Indians. (2010). *Support of the National Tribal Priorities for Indian Education*. Resolution RAP-10-029. 2010 mid-year sess., June 20–23. Rapid City, SD. Retrieved from https://www.ncai.org/fileadmin/resolutions/Midyear_2010/RAP-10-029_w_attach.pdf.

National Education Association. (2005). *A Report on the Status of American Indians and Alaska Natives in Education: Historical Legacy to Cultural Empowerment*. Washington, DC: National Education Association. Retrieved from http://www.nea.org/assets/docs/ HE/mf_aianreport.pdf.

National Indian Education Association (NIEA). (2004). Testimony of Cindy La Marr, President, National Indian Education Association, before the Senate Committee on Indian Affairs on the FY 2005 Budget Request, February 11, 2004. In *Fiscal Year 2005 Budget Hearing before the Committee on Indian Affairs United States Senate One Hundred Eighth Congress, second session on the President's Budget Request for Indian Programs* (pp. 15–19). Retrieved from http://www.gpo.gov/fdsys/pkg/CHRG-108shrg91835/pdf/CHRG-108shrg91835.pdf.

National Indian Education Association (NIEA). (2005). *Preliminary Report on No Child Left Behind in Indian Country*. Washington, DC: National Indian Education Association. Retrieved from http://www.niea.org/data/files/policy/nieanclbpublication.pdf.

National Indian Education Association (NIEA). (2010). *Testimony of Patricia Whitefoot, President, National Indian Education Association, before the Education and Labor Subcommittee on Early Childhood, Elementary and Secondary Education. On the Elementary and Secondary Education Act Reauthorization: Addressing the Needs of Diverse Students*, March 18, 2010. Retrieved from http://www.niea.org/data/files/policy/2010testimonywhitefootesea.pdf.

No Child Left Behind Act of 2001 (NCLB). (2001). *U.S. code*. Title 20, sec. 6301 et seq.

Oklahoma State Election Board. (2010). *Summary Results: General Election*, November 2, 2010. Retrieved from http://www.ok.gov/elections/support/10gen.html.

One Nation/One California. (1997). *English for the Children* (web site). [California Proposition 227]. Retrieved from http://www.onenation.org/index.html.

Pewewardy, C. (2005). "Ideology, power, and the miseducation of Indigenous peoples in the United States." In *For Indigenous Eyes Only: A Decolonization Handbook*, ed. W. A. Wilson and M. Yellow Bird, 139–56. Santa Fe, NM: School of America Research Press.

Prucha, F. P., ed. (2000). *Documents of United States Indian Policy*. 3rd ed. Lincoln: University of Nebraska Press.

Putney, D. T. (1980). *Fighting the Scourge: American Indian Morbidity and Federal Policy, 1897–1928*. PhD diss., Marquette University, Milwaukee, WI.

Rains, F. V. (2003). "To greet the dawn with open eyes: American Indians, white privilege and the power of residual guilt in the social studies." In *Critical Race Theory Perspectives on the Social Studies: The Profession, Policies, and Curriculum*, ed. G. Ladson-Billings, 199–227. Greenwich, CT: Information Age.

Reyhner, J., O. Trujillo, R. L. Carrasco, and L. Lockard, eds. (2003). *Nurturing Native Languages*. Flagstaff: Northern Arizona University.

Salazar, M. (2007). "'No Child' may leave some behind." *Albuquerque Journal*, August 11.

Soule, S. S. (1864). "The Sand Creek Massacre—Captain Silas S. Soule letter to Major Edward Wynkoop regarding the massacre." *Lone Wolf* (web site). Retrieved from http://www.kclonewolf.com/History/SandCreek/sc-documents/sc-soule-to-wynkoop-12-14-64.html.

Spring, J. (1996). *The Cultural Transformation of a Native American Family and its Tribe, 1763–1995: A Basket of Apples*. Sociocultural, Political, and Historical Studies in Education. Mahwah, NJ: Lawrence Erlbaum.

Stannard, D. E. (1992). *American Holocaust: Columbus and the Conquest of the New World*. New York: Oxford University Press.

Thornton, R. (1987). *American Indian Holocaust and Survival: A Population History since 1492*. Norman: University of Oklahoma Press.

Toney, C. (2010). "Language fair celebrates American Indian heritage." *Oklahoma Daily*, April 7. Retrieved from http://oudaily.com/news/2010/apr/07/language-fair-celebrates-american-indian-heritage.

Unz, R. (2000). "The right way for Republicans to handle ethnicity in politics." *American Enterprise*, April/May. Retrieved from http://www.onenation.org/0004/0400.html.

———. (2001). "Rocks falling upward at Harvard University." *National Review Online*, October 26. Retrieved from http://www.onenation.org/0110/102601.htm.

U.S. Congress. Senate. (1867). *Sand Creek Massacre, Report of the Secretary of War, Executive Document 26*. 39th Cong., 2nd sess., S. Rep. 156. Washington, DC: United States Government Printing Office. Retrieved from http://freepages.genealogy.rootsweb.com/~wynkoop/webdocs/scminqry.htm.

Utley, R. M., ed. (1964). *Battlefield and Classroom: Four Decades with the American Indian, 1867–1904*. [The memoirs of Richard Henry Pratt]. New Haven, CT: Yale University Press.

Vasques, V. (2004). *Indian Education Today*. Presentation at No Child Left Behind: Education of American Indian Students. U.S. Department of Education Office of Indian Education Symposium, Albuquerque, NM, April.

Williams, D. (1993). *Georgia Gold Rush: Twenty-Niners, Cherokees, and Gold Fever*. Columbia: University of South Carolina Press.

Williams, R. A., Jr. (1997). "Vampires anonymous and critical race practice." *Michigan Law Review* 95: 741–65.

Wilson, G. S. (1882). "How shall the American savage be civilized?" *Atlantic Monthly* 50 (301): 596–607. Retrieved from http://digital.library.cornell.edu/cgi/t/text /pageviewer-idx?c=atala;cc=atla;rgn=full%20text;idnc.

Wolgamott, B., and L. R. Bair. (2010). *Synopsis of the 2010 State Questions: Current as of August 9th, 2010*. Oklahoma City, OK: Oklahoma House of Representatives. Retrieved from http://www.okhouse.gov/Documents/2010StateQuestions.pdf.

Woodward, G. S. (1963). *The Cherokees*. Norman: University of Oklahoma.

NOTES

1.   Within this chapter, I use the terms *Native American*, *Native*, *Native Peoples*, *Indigenous*, *Indigenous Peoples*, and *American Indian* interchangeably throughout because of the lack of an agreed-upon universal term. Most Native Peoples prefer to use their specific tribal group name rather than these collective terms. I use the term *Indian* only when it is reflected in historical documents because it is a non-accurate term imposed by European immigrants.

2.   The master narrative encompasses the large-scale or grand theories, philosophies, or stories about the world and acts as the only explanation for knowledge or historical experience. See Jean-Francois Lyotard (1984) in *The Postmodern Condition: A Report on Knowledge*.

3.   It is interesting that the areas of reading, writing, and mathematics are the very same emphasized content areas of NCLB (2001). The Bush administration also advocated a reintroduction of religious organizations receiving governmental funds for societal or charitable work.

4.   The term *Five Civilized Tribes* has been critiqued by Native people and is seldom used due to the connection to the Westernized and colonizing concept of "civilized." Thus, the term *Five Tribes* has been favored in recent years.

5.   Another faction was comprised of the conservatives who were often from the middle and upper towns who fought to maintain the traditional value system and life ways of The People (Conley 2005). See Conley's (2005) book *The Cherokee Nation: A History* for a comprehensive history of the Cherokee people. The book was written by a tribal member and commissioned by Cherokee Nation.

6.   For a discussion of the Sand Creek Massacre as a terrorist event, please see my article (Haynes Writer 2002) "Terrorism in Native America: Interrogating the Past, Examining the Present, and Constructing a Liberatory Future."

7.   In a similar ideological attack on heritage languages, in 1997, wealthy Silicon Valley entrepreneur Ron Unz began the "English for the Children" campaign to end bilingual education in public schools (One Nation/One California 1997). He referred to bilingual educators as "educational terrorists" (Unz 2001, para. 10) and asserted that "our public schools and educational institutions must be restored as the engines of assimilation they once were" (Unz 2000, para. 14).

8.   I coined the term *privilege of non-knowledge* to describe my experience in school. Instances occurred in which I relayed information in the classroom setting about Native history or my Cherokee tribal history. Teachers, because they were not aware of this history, often denied or ignored the information being shared or reacted to me as if I concocted the information I shared.

   Due to the power and authority that the teachers carried over me or other students, these teachers carried privilege and could utilize that privilege when issuing grades, recommending students for various opportunities, or evaluating students' academic intelligence. As such, the teachers' ignorance or lack of awareness—their privilege of non-knowledge—could be utilized as power over students who speak back to historical master narratives, biased perspectives, or misinformation in textbooks or while conveying their family histories that differ from those of their teachers.

Chapter 6

Falling from Grace

How the Latest Government Policies Undermine American Indian Education

Beverly J. Klug: Idaho State University

ABSTRACT

Throughout the history of American Indian education, conflicts have occurred between the government and Native peoples concerning perceptions of the best way to educate Indigenous students. Extreme measures were taken in the past to ensure that Native children would perform like their dominant culture peers in a system emphasizing student competition and measurement of achievement.

The latest legislation affecting the education of American Indian students is the No Child Left Behind Act (2001), which overrides promises made to Native nations to provide culturally relevant/responsive pedagogy for their children in favor of hegemonic models of education for all children. Case study findings concerning one Intermountain West school serving Native students shed light on the negative impacts of this legislation on education for the students and how it undermines the earlier promises made to Native peoples.

Low achievement test results of American Indian students validate the need to return to providing education that is culturally responsive for American Indian students. Recommendations are made for a return to culturally relevant/responsive pedagogy and the use of multiple measures of school achievement over decision making employing high-stakes achievement tests alone.

Keywords: Culturally responsive pedagogy, culturally relevant pedagogy, American Indian students, NCLB

FALLING FROM GRACE: HOW THE LATEST GOVERNMENT POLICIES UNDERMINE AMERICAN INDIAN EDUCATION

> In so many hollowed [sic] buildings we call public schools, the spirits and souls of poor and working-class . . . youth of color, and their educators, are assaulted in ways that bear academic, psychological, social, economic and perhaps, also, criminal justice consequence. (Fine et al. 2004, 2193)

The above criticism of public education and schools in this country for poor and working-class youth has been extremely accurate, as investigated and reported by authors such as Jonathan Kozol (2005) and others. These same conditions have existed in many rural areas throughout the country where children from families of lower socioeconomic status (SES) attend schools, including American Indian students living on reservations.

The stated goals of the Reauthorization of the Elementary and Secondary Education Act of 1965, referred to as the No Child Left Behind Act (2001), have included ensuring equal access to educational opportunities for students of all ethnicities and SES levels in the United States. However, these good intentions toward closing the achievement gap have been overshadowed by the way high-stakes testing has been embraced to accomplish this goal, forcing all schools to conform to teaching to each state's standards, which have traditionally differed across the country (Diamond and Spillane 2004).

Meanwhile, the promise that every child will perform at average or above-average levels remains elusive as standardized achievement measures rely on the bell curve for norming the tests. As Padilla (2005, 250) notes, this culture of measurement versus a culture of engagement reinforces assimilationist and cultural-deficit views:

> High-stakes testing and educational accountability, two anchor points of recent educational reform efforts, so far are strictly framed within the culture of measurement. The chief goals here are the identification of merit and the distribution of material and social rewards based on that merit. . . . The epistemological perspective of the culture of measurement is objectivist knowing. . . . Such knowledge is presumed to be universally valid and free from "subjectivist" influences or local perturbations.

Padilla (2005) reiterated the importance of creating a culture of engagement in schools, emphasizing active involvement in the social construction of knowledge by learners, which has not necessarily been a part of the formula for increasing test scores. Instead, evidence suggests that scores may be rising due to the following: teaching to the tests; promoting test-taking strategies; reevaluating how tests are normed from earlier versions and adjusting cut-off scores; and having higher numbers of students drop out as a result of the emphasis on high-stakes testing (Horn 2003).

Information derived from two surveys reported by the National Center for Educational Statistics (2009) indicated that the dropout rates of American Indians/Alaskan Natives increased from 10 percent in 1994 to 20 percent in 2007, in comparison to dropout rates of approximately 7.5 percent of white students in 1994 and 6 percent in 2007, according to the 2007 Current Population Survey. The report of the 2007 American Community Survey, which used different measures, showed dropout rates at 15 percent for American Indians/Alaskan Natives compared to 6 percent of white students.

These numbers appear to be inaccurate in comparison to the graduation rates reported for American Indian students of 54 percent by Barton (2005), 51 percent in 2001 by Martin and Halperin (2006, "Members of Some Demographic Groups," para. 1), and 49.3 percent reported for 2003–2004 by the Editorial Projects in Education Research Center (National Indian Education Association 2008, 5). Clearly, there is a disparity in the numbers reported, though we may conclude that American Indian students are not succeeding at the same rate as their non-Native peers.

The second area of concern for many engaged in teaching American Indian students is the use of a narrow set of texts approved for teaching reading in Title I schools. These materials reflect the "Reading First" preferred model of direct instruction and reading mastery approaches (Manzo 2006). In the main, these text materials focus on teaching word identification through phonetic approaches (phonics) and not on holistic, literature-based, comprehension-oriented approaches.

The texts replicate the transmission model of education, with the expectations that any child will learn to read with this approach regardless of race, ethnicity, sex, or level of SES—a one-size-fits-all approach in a model critically flawed for American Indians/Alaska Natives (Jones and Ongtooguk 2002). Instead of providing culturally relevant[1] teaching and materials (Klug and Whitfield 2003; Skinner 1992; Pewewardy 1994), NCLB (2001) mandates hegemonic replication of the dominant culture in schools.

Standards for American Indian Students

The *Alaska Standards for Culturally Responsive Schools* (Alaska Native Knowledge Network 1998) have provided direction to enable Native Alaskan students to successfully relate to information given in schools. By making connections between the school curricula and local epistemologies, educators have created a system that is mutually respectful to both cultures. Recommendations have been made to provide similar standards for Native students throughout the lower forty-eight and Hawaii after examining these standards (St. Germaine 2000; Lomawaima and McCarty 2002).

Passage of Clinton's Executive Order no. 13096 (1998) guaranteed a focus on research regarding American Indian education and solutions to the difficulties therein. Unfortunately, NCLB (2001) has undermined these very efforts, leaving many Native communities with a sense of betrayal by the dominant culture and its institutions yet again.

A recent study released by the Commission on No Child Left Behind (2007) has concluded that while the legislation has flaws, it will continue despite the suggested seventy-five recommendations for changes to be made (Hoff 2007). To date, the place of high-stakes testing remains paramount with the attendant sanctions for schools and teachers that are considered "failing."

The commission has called for highly qualified teachers and highly qualified principals in every school to reach goals set by NCLB (2001), especially those serving underrepresented populations (Hoff 2007). Nevertheless, these mandates alone will not guarantee high achievement for American Indian students. It is necessary to acknowledge and analyze other factors that may be involved in achieving academic success for Native students.

Influences of Culture, Language, and Means on Educational Opportunities

> The American Indian model of education, an experiential model that my grandfather Jesse Bowman showed me without ever breathing a word about teaching, could not be more different [from Western education]. It is, quite simply, learning by doing. Whenever he did something, he always made sure that I knew he needed my help doing it. It made me wonder, at times, how he had ever gotten as old as he was without knowing how to do such things as straighten a nail or float a line down to a trout or walk quietly in the forest or take the bark off a piece of willow to make a whistle. It was lucky I was there to help him, I used to think. Sometimes, when we were fishing, he'd even forget to say "Thank you" when we caught a fish. But I would remind him. I realize now, years later, just how much he taught me—including that the journey itself is just as important and rewarding as "getting somewhere." (Bruchac 2004, ix–x)

Those in leadership positions must understand the needs of their American Indian school populations and especially how poverty, language, and cultural factors may influence students' abilities to relate to the school curriculum (Rodriguez and Fabionar 2010). One-size-fits-all approaches work directly against what has been learned about the need for the use of multiple strategies and techniques that take into account the diversity of our school populations.

Schools replicate the systems of power in our society, mirroring the workplace with "hierarchical power and authority, lack of control over curriculum and content, use of extrinsic rewards, competition, specialization, and fragmentation" (Rodriguez and Fabionar 2010, 56). Schools act as sorting mechanisms, with "poverty" indicating which students will be less capable and less interested in academic achievement, whether true or not.

Many Native students are English learners with their own American Indian English (AIE) dialects (Leap 1993). Merino (2007) has reported that addressing issues concerning teaching English learners (ELs) has long been a part of the California teaching system at all levels.

However, more recently, schools have varied in their "attention given to issues of language and culture in the standards outlined for EL programs. The emphasis given to instruction and assessment of academic language within disciplines, particularly at the secondary level, also varied" (Merino 2007, 3). Merino concluded that the current focus shift to academic language, due to NCLB (2001), has resulted in fewer acknowledgments of the roles played by the first languages and cultures of students in educational achievement.

There is evidence indicating that schools that incorporate culturally relevant pedagogy in their practices have been more effective in serving Native students (Cleary and Peacock 1998; Klug and Whitfield 2003; National Congress of American Indians and National Indian Education Association 2010). For this to occur, educators at all levels must look beyond the prescribed "needs" of their Native students as evidenced by standardized test scores in order to acquire an understanding of their students' real needs and explore alternate ways of accommodating them in schools.

Doing so requires that teachers develop the professional dispositions allowing them to make these needed changes for American Indian students instead of following a norm prescribed for all. Osguthorpe (2009) has linked accomplishing this goal to the moral character of teachers and, in turn, to that which earlier doyens of education have identified as being necessary for becoming caring and compassionate teachers.

Culturally relevant pedagogy. The call for including Native cultures and languages in education for American Indian students is not new. When Captain Richard Henry Pratt established the first government boarding school at Carlisle, Pennsylvania, in 1867, he developed a model to eliminate American Indian cultures and languages and completely assimilate Native students into Western civilization (Trafzer, Keller, and Sisquoc 2006). This model was followed by all future government boarding schools.

Children were punished for speaking their languages and practicing their cultural rituals/mores. Bounties were awarded for capturing children who would then be sent to the schools without their families' knowledge or permission (Meriam 1928). Children were given Christian names, their hair cut, their jewelry removed, and their clothing substituted with uniforms. In some of the boarding schools, children's Native names were lost, along with information about their origins. Many families never saw their children again or knew their fates.

Schools operated militarily, with only a portion of the school day spent in educational endeavors and the rest in the labor needed to keep schools operating (Meriam 1928). Often, the food on the tables was substandard and scarce, so children's nutrition suffered. Abuses of all types—physical, emotional, and sexual—took place in the boarding schools. Many children died due to outbreaks of disease that swept through schools and were buried on the school grounds rather than returned to their relatives. According to Jacobs (2006), conditions in some schools resembled prison camps.

After graduating, students returned to their homes, if possible, only to find they no longer "fit in" and lacked the cultural/linguistic skills needed to take their places in Native communities. Instead of benefiting Tribal nations, forced assimilation resulted in alienation and poverty for many of the students who attended these schools. Due to the lack of success of the majority of boarding school returnees, an investigation into the causes was finally instituted, which led to the report on the condition of American Indian families and the government actions that contributed to this dismal situation.

The Meriam Report (1928) finally resulted in acknowledgment that forced assimilation was not a viable option for the well-being of American Indians. Its authors contended that the boarding schools created conditions of greater poverty due to language and cultural losses, as well as the reality of the bleak conditions that existed in the majority of these schools themselves. Many of the schools were subsequently closed, and day schools—many run by missionaries—sprang up close to reservations to fill the void.

The report recommended educating Native students to prepare them for twentieth-century living, with the inclusion of Native languages and cultures in curricula. The labor-industrial preparation model in use for Native education was discouraged with more focus placed on academics. Some efforts were made toward this end, but in large part, curricula and pedagogical practices remained the same as for white students in public schools without the attendant pedagogical additions for Native students (Deloria 1974).

The self-determination era for American Indian Nations began in opposition to governmental efforts to eliminate Tribal nation status and abrogate treaty rights and obligations altogether during the 1940s through 1970s—referred to as the "termination" period (Trahant 2010). Many tribal nations lost their recognition. In its wake, the Indian Education Act of 1972 and the Indian Self-Determination and Education Assistance Act of 1975 were passed in order to ensure that the desires of Native peoples for their children's educations would be honored (St. Germaine 2000).

Fruition of these efforts has been limited, as the majority of teachers hired to teach at schools with Native populations have had no knowledge or understanding of Native heritage languages or cultures (Lomawaima and McCarty 2002). In spite of these difficulties, some Tribal nations have taken on the effort of preparing materials about Native peoples that could be utilized in schools in the hopes of encouraging students to complete their K–12 educations and graduate from high school (Strom).

Influences of language and culture in school achievement. There are many reasons that American Indian students may not be able to adequately demonstrate what they have learned in the areas of literacy and mathematics on the state achievement tests required for NCLB (2001). Ami (2004) maintains that there are at least twenty-four different concerns about Native students and testing that contribute to this situation.

Ami (2004) recognizes that the following areas bear much significance on our discussion: (a) the tests are designed according to white middle-class standards, stressing analytic versus holistic thinking; (b) the curriculum required for Reading First reflects the same perspectives as the tests, therefore excluding students who think differently or have little knowledge of white middle-class culture; and (c) many families do not value testing, as this had not traditionally been a part of their Native cultures; rather, children performed what they learned in front of an elder, taking as long as was needed to master a task.

In addition, two other concerns need to be addressed: (d) Native students may not be able to interpret questions in the way they have been designed because students are not yet proficient with their register-switching abilities to comprehend meanings in English well; and finally, (e) students' socioeconomic status may affect their degree of assimilation into the dominant culture's ways of thinking and practicing and how teachers judge American Indian students' degree of competency or their intelligence.

In terms of culture, we must recognize that ways of acting in different settings may be considered appropriate in one culture and inappropriate in another. Different belief systems may influence what takes place in a classroom, such as the Western idea that reading about any topic is appropriate for any time of year, whereas in many Native societies, telling traditional legends only occurs at certain times of the year, and this belief carries over to reading or writing about their legends.

While educators feel it is important that children continue to read during the summer, many Native families use this time for engaging in traditional cultural practices (D. Gould, pers. comm., June 5, 2008). Children are also taught that it is inappropriate to make oneself look better than others in the group. Therefore, even if students know the correct answer, when called upon they may give wrong answers because of this admonishment. Educators need to understand Native students' cultures to create educational environments where students can succeed (Klug and Whitfield 2003).

Learning and the brain. Recent studies of the brain and learning involving neuroimaging show that effective use of both sides of the brain is extremely important in learning a second language—in this case, standard English for Native students. Additionally, there is accumulating evidence that we can no longer talk about "the right side" or "the left side" of the brain as areas of particular strength for different learners.

It appears that more involvement of both sides of the brain occurs in everything we do than we previously understood (Jensen 2005). Unfortunately, most school activities rely on the use of the left analytic hemisphere to the neglect of the right holistic hemisphere, especially with the emphasis on high-stakes accountability.

Zull (2002) investigated how the brain learns from a biological point of view. Zull's (2002) research reflects what is known about Native ways of learning. In his model, engaging students in concrete experiences during the initial stage of learning is paramount. If children only have experiences with abstract labels (words or symbols) and do not have the real experiences needed to develop their conceptual knowledge, many will not be able to relate fully to these concepts and will quickly forget the knowledge they "learned" even if they do well in their formative testing.

For literacy instruction, teachers should use holistic approaches that encourage the development of comprehension, not just word-recognition skills, especially for American Indian students. Teaching approaches need to be utilized that encourage active participation on the part of students as they construct their understandings about literacy and its role in their lives. Reading real literature—not contrived—is required.

Materials should include concrete objects for introducing new concepts; authentic literature, especially stories featuring Native Americans, nature, and what is happening in the world around us, is especially appealing for Native youth. These approaches reflect emphasis on metacognitive thinking and comprehension skills, such as predicting the story line, monitoring, and reevaluating one's reading; authentic literacy activities connect with what students already know, exercising their own cultural capital.

Using holistic and metacognitive thinking skills also applies to mathematics. Providing concrete experiences with manipulatives is important, along with visual representations of concepts and references to experiences in students' own lives instead of just teaching algorithms and formulas or having students memorize facts. In this way, abstract information is connected in a concrete way for students in order to develop their mathematical knowledge. Geometric shapes can be connected to real objects in students' environments as well as to patterns incorporated in beading and other traditional arts.

Inclusion of the arts in pedagogy. Much research has supported the role of the arts in academic learning (Klug and Whitfield 2011). Hetland and Winner (2001) conclude that when arts are integrated within the curriculum, learning is enhanced. Rabkin and Redmond (2006) cite the results of the *National Educational Longitudinal Study of 1988* (NELS:88) as evidence of the importance of the arts in education, as did Eisner (1998) and Donmeyer (1995), especially when used in conjunction with content areas.

Richards (2003) found that the arts integrated with literacy activities benefited children in poverty and enhanced their world understandings. The arts promote motivation and interest in the academic learning in which students are engaged (Wadsworth 1996). Active learning is injected into curricula through the arts (Gangi 2004), providing additional semiotic or symbol systems for knowledge representation that encourage the retention and recall of information (Gardner 1999; Vygotsky 1978).

Poverty and knowledge capital. For many individuals working in schools of high poverty, it is difficult to reconcile their observations of how much children may lack in relation to others' ways of life. Educators may find it especially difficult to acknowledge that American Indian students may come from homes very different from their own. They may make many assumptions concerning the students' knowledge bases, expecting them to have developed the same cultural capital as the dominant culture, simply because in most homes today there is access to mass media through television and the Internet.

These presumptions are usually based on educators' own experiences and not the lived realities of all their Native students. A case in point is that language acquisition requires interactions between children and adults (not passivity, as in the case of watching television) to acquire the vocabulary and grammar necessary to function academically (Chomsky 1986). The same is true with building conceptual knowledge and acquiring labels for these concepts. Without this interaction, children do not develop high vocabularies or knowledge of language use in a variety of situations.

In the majority of cases where children are in poverty, children will be acquiring a form of language common to their own community, not the Standard English practiced in schools and seen in textbooks (Bernol 2002; Smith 2006). They may not be accustomed to the idea that many words can mean different things in different contexts, come to school with the experiences of playing rhyming games, or have had prewriting and coloring experiences within their homes. These pre-literacy experiences contribute to the knowledge base expected today that children utilize for formal schooling instruction.

For Native students, learning nursery rhymes was not usually a part of their cultural heritages, the practice belonging to the realm of European and European American experiences. However, many children learn dances and know about the drum, rhythm, and beat through these experiences. They may have learned important chants and/or been exposed to tribal legends. Instead of coloring, they may be involved with beading and pottery-making activities that could be drawn upon when teaching concepts. Creating poetry, or pictures with words, is an activity enjoyed by many Native students.

Sacred Mountain Elementary School: Case-Study Findings

The following is a report of case study findings focusing on Sacred Mountain Elementary School[2] concerning the effects of NCLB (2001) on the school, students, faculty, and community for the period of 2002–2006. Interviews took place in the spring of 2006 with four members of the ten faculty (N = 4) employed at the school (two female American Indians, one white male, and one white female) using a semi-structured interview schedule. An additional interviewee could not be reached for the study. The findings demonstrate that NCLB (2001) impacted this school in ways not anticipated by those who crafted the act.

Study and school demographics. At the time of the study, this K–5 school enrolled more than 150 students, 99 percent of whom were American Indian and spoke American Indian English (AIE). The school is located within a public school system of fewer than 10,000 students and is within the reservation boundaries of a tribal nation in the Intermountain West. The nation is made up of fewer than 8,000 enrolled members; the reservation itself is a "checkerboard," with non-Natives living on reservation land that was sold in the past.

Tribal members represent all socioeconomic levels and consider themselves to be traditional, bicultural, or assimilated, with overlapping categories dependent upon family beliefs and practices. There had been a boarding school located on this reservation prior to the Meriam Report (Meriam 1928), followed by day schools. Several religious groups are represented on the reservation as well as the Native American church. Other tribal nations and ethnicities are represented on this reservation, which is true throughout the Intermountain region where intermarriage is not uncommon among populations.

Students attending the school are generally classified as low socioeconomic status (SES). The school offers free breakfast and free lunch, with many children not eating regularly on the weekends. Some families continue to raise children with grandparents and/or other relatives in the traditional way, while other families offer a combination of approaches. Wealthier Native students (low-middle through high-middle SES) generally attend different schools in the same district or other districts bordering the reservation.

Case study results. The following points illustrate the multiple impacts of NCLB (2001) on the school, families, and community. With small Native populations in public schools for 2002 through 2006 throughout the Intermountain West—from lows of 1.2 percent in Colorado and 3.5 percent in Wyoming to a high of 11.4 percent in Montana—there has been a relative lack of influence that Native populations have been able to regionally effect on NCLB required programs and practices and the achievement tests administered to their children, as well as analysis of contributing factors to results.

While examining table 6.1, it can be seen that for the years 2002–2006, American Indian students scored the lowest while their white counterparts scored the highest on the achievement tests throughout the Intermountain West. These findings are consistent with test scores for Sacred Mountain Elementary School.

Table 6.1 2002–2006 American Indian and White Students in the Intermountain West

Students	Montana	Utah	Idaho	Wyoming	Colorado
White	123,548	409,633	217,366	71,525	488,092
% age of total	84.2%	81.7%	82.99%	84.53%	62.5%
Test results Ranking	Highest	Highest	Highest	Highest	Highest
American Indian	16,715	7,448	4,173	2,948	9,188
% age of total	11.4%	1.5%	1.6%	3.51%	1.2%
Test results Ranking	Lowest	Lowest	Lowest	Lowest	Lowest

Sources: Colorado 2007; Idaho 2007; Montana 2007; Utah 2006; Wyoming 2006

Semiformal structured interviews (see figure 6.1) were conducted with the faculty members in the spring of 2006 at the school, lasting from approximately sixty minutes to over two-and-a-half hours. From these interviews, four themes emerged that shed light on the difficulties with implementing curricula required by NCLB (2001) and the ability to be able to accurately judge Native student achievement level gains made on the basis of the standardized achievement test designed for this state.

1. Please tell me what grade(s) you teach/have taught.

2. How long have you been teaching/in administration?

3. What is your perception regarding how often the state tests must be administered in accordance with the reporting required by the No Child Left Behind Act?

4. Have you seen changes regarding your students' attitudes toward school and their efforts since this testing began? Can you tell me about those changes?

5. Has the legislation assisted you in working with your students? Could you describe in what ways this has happened?

6. Has the legislation enhanced/negatively impacted relationships with parents and the community? Can you describe in what ways this has occurred?

7. How has the publication of the data on the state department's website affected you as a teacher in this school?

8. If you could do things differently, in what ways would you assess your students?

9. How does the legislation enhance/undermine the attempts to provide culturally relevant pedagogy for American Indian students?

10. Do you have additional concerns/comments you would like to share?

Thank you.

Figure 6.1 Interview Questions for Case Study of the Effects of High-Stakes Testing and the No Child Left Behind Act (2001) on One School Serving American Indian Students/Second Language Learners

The following represent the four identified themes found in analyzing the interview results:

1. Achievement test scores did not accurately reflect what students had learned and were capable of achieving.
2. Too much time and too many resources for meeting NCLB (2001) took away from actual time to teach students in culturally responsive ways.
3. Higher levels of tension evolved between the school and the community as blame was assigned to both groups by the other for low achievement test scores.
4. Without changes to the legislation, Native students' academic needs will not be addressed in the public schools in this state/region.

These themes are explored below.

First, it is important to recognize that NCLB (2001) was initially viewed as a positive way to reveal the state of education for American Indian students in this state/region. Makyla[3] explained this in the following:

> I think [education for diverse students] has improved, because [the state department] was conscientious of having representatives from Hispanic and Native communities [examine the state's achievement tests for cultural bias]. However, socioeconomic class and disabilities representatives were not included [and these factors impact achievement]. The standards have helped ensure that we're doing more with the students and that teachers are now learning more about working with culturally diverse students. In this state, we've never done this. Before, the test score data were never disaggregated. Before, they just didn't care. It's very easy to say, "It's just those Indian kids. They just don't get it." (Makyla, enrolled tribal member, interview, May 2006).

Faculty members were not opposed to accountability for their teaching. However, frustrations continued due to the mismatch between achievement tests and the lack of language knowledge and dialect differences that influenced students' abilities to respond to test items. Additional contributions to students' low scores were

- having different life experiences from those expected of white middle-class families
- negative family attitudes toward the Western educational system
- lack of knowledge of English language use as well as vocabulary, synonyms, and the use of multiple meanings for words when the students' Native language(s) had only one meaning for each word
- holistic thinking vs. analytical thinking by students, which required them to choose only one right answer
- high rates of tardiness/absenteeism of students, which affected their knowledge base of the required curricula

An example provided by Jenny (interview, May 2006) concerned the language used on the tests, which many times did not match that used by teachers to explain concepts to students as they were teaching them. Third-grade students were given the direction to "circle" the correct answer on the achievement test, while they "ringed" the correct answer in the Reading First workbooks. Students had not been taught that the action required was the same, as teachers did not know what would appear in directions on the test, therefore negatively influencing students' final scores on the achievement test.

Jenny also provided an example with the sentence "Mom asked the _____ to trim the fat off the meat." The correct multiple-choice response was "butcher." However, Jenny's students had never been to a butcher store nor seen someone called a "butcher" who cut meat.

The children had many experiences of watching family members dress deer, elk, or moose in the field after hunting, but the label "butcher" was unfamiliar to them. The students in the class chose the response "knife" as correct because this was the only one that made sense to them, as it was an instrument to cut meat.

Lynn, a fourth-grade teacher, shared her students' frustration when they encountered the word "label" in the directions "Label the following items." The only "label" the students knew was that on a soup can or other canned food. If the directions had simply stated, "Name the following items," students would have known what to do. Because she was not permitted to assist them, the students skipped this whole section of the achievement test, negatively affecting their test results (Lynn, enrolled tribal member, interview, May 2006).

In addition to the differences in vocabulary use and understandings of multiple meanings for words, the prior knowledge needed to be able to provide "correct answers" on the tests also made a difference. Teachers were not privy to what was on the tests and could not provide this type of knowledge for their students. Therefore, many of the Native students lacked the conceptual experiences required for knowledge demonstration on the tests, even if they could have correctly answered a similar question that referred to their own cultural-capital experiences stored in their conceptual bases.

Jenny provided an example supporting this that illustrates the mismatch of expectations and the experiences of her Native students. She took her third graders on a field trip to the symphony in a city thirty miles away (the only trip provided for the year) in the spring. They had been discussing the ocean and ocean life in their curriculum in the classroom. In the Intermountain West, there are no oceans. When the school bus crossed a river, the children "were sure they would see whales because this had to be the ocean—[they] had never seen that much water before" (Jenny, interview, May 2006).

Because many of the students were living in poverty, they did not have experience going to the malls, visiting places around the country, engaging in different sporting activities requiring disposable cash, or being able to leave the reservation at all. They may have had experiences with dancing at local powwows, beading, or watching rodeo events, but these were not activities that were reflected in the items on the tests. There were no questions relating to nature at all on the tests.

Baer (interview, May 2006) made a point concerning tardiness/absenteeism and the influences of poverty on achievement test results in the following:

> Attendance [was] a big problem. Fifty tardies [for students were] not unusual. Which part of a lesson can be skipped without harming [students' educations]? Can you skip the beginning, the middle, the end of a lesson? Kids [were] struggling to have basic needs met. . . . They [didn't] have parents sitting down with [them] and asking about homework. Parents [had] their own struggles; not all had good experiences in school.

Secondly, because of the emphasis on achievement testing, a great deal of time was spent on testing and test preparation, with the tests administered more than once during the year in this state. The assessment results did not accurately measure the achievement rate of many students in the school who started out below grade level in the school year but made tremendous progress not reflected in the cut-off scores established by the state. Several children in all grade levels made 30- to 50-point gains over the course of a school year yet did not reach the cut-off scores for "basic" (Baer, interview, May 2006; Lynn, interview, May 2006).

An inordinate amount of time was focused on Reading First and mathematics to the exclusion of all other subjects. The textbooks adopted for Reading First programs were not reflective of Native students' styles of learning. Teacher creativity, integration of the arts, and integration of culturally relevant pedagogy were eliminated from the formal curricula except for what was provided from the outside once a week. Teachers were told they had to be on the same page every day throughout the school district, regardless of where the students were in their comprehension or learning of the materials.

> [The students got] more teacher attention, and the teacher [had] to be accountable for the kids' learning, so that [was] a good thing. However, . . . [the students] definitely [needed] physical education and the arts, and they don't measure those things on the tests. (Makyla, enrolled tribal member, interview, May 2006)

Third, teacher morale was highly impacted, even though the principal tried to focus on the mantra that they were there to "teach kids," not teach to the test. The fear of being labeled as a "failing" teacher led to a high turnover in the school of 50 percent (N = 5) of the faculty between 2002–2006. Part of this was also due to the blame that was being placed on the school staff for failure to make AYP and the tensions that ensued between the school and the community. The other part was the fear of the sanctions that accompany the legislation.

Consequently, those teachers who had previously committed themselves to changing the way they were teaching to become more responsive to the students' culture and language backed away from continuing to do so due to the demands being placed on them by the legislation and the results that were being noted of school failure to quickly increase all scores to higher levels. Interviewees also gave reports of family members who came into their classrooms and blamed them for the lack of achievement gains being made by their children. This blaming of teachers took place on the reservation in general.

"White man's education"—terminology used to indicate the only type of schooling perceived as taking place and which was true with NCLB (2001)—generally had engendered a great deal of antipathy from American Indian families on this reservation, even if no one in the family had gone to boarding schools following the period of reforms in the aftermath of the Meriam Report (1928). Stories of horrific boarding school experiences had been passed down within families for generations, and the idea of going to school because of one's desire to learn was indeed a "foreign" concept.

Expecting that parents and extended family members would be excited about returning back to this type of oppressive educational system for their children was unrealistic and manifested itself in many ways. One of these ways was in terms of the number of absences and tardiness that had been going up since the "reforms" went into place. In the period prior to NCLB's instantiation into the schools, culturally relevant pedagogy had been steadily rising in classrooms while the rates of absenteeism and tardiness had been constantly going down, at one point to a low of only 7 percent absenteeism. With NCLB, this trend again reverted to higher rates of both.

Finally, it is imperative that the legislation be amended to allow for greater flexibility for schools serving Native students in order to meet the academic needs of their students. Achievement tests must be examined for cultural, linguistic, and socioeconomic biases. To be able to discern if students are really learning in schools and teachers are really teaching, the concepts represented in the test items themselves must truly reflect what all learners would have been expected to learn from the curriculum, not just what may have been learned from white middle-class experiences for families.

As an aside, it is interesting to note that the one year that the state writing test focused on "spiders" as a topic for all fifth graders to write about was the year that the American Indian students throughout the state garnered the top writing scores across the board! As usually occurs, that was the first and last time that a topic revolving around concepts central to nature was ever part of this assessment in this state, and subsequent scores of American Indian students fell back to the lower rates of previous test administrations. Cultural capital must be a consideration taken into academic testing.

The achievement tests require children to choose one right answer, which many American Indian children may not pick due to their exposure and experiences "in the world outside of their culture" (Lynn, enrolled tribal member, interview, May 2006). Continuing with NCLB (2001) in whatever form or reincarnation, with its emphasis on one-size-fits-all, will only benefit a portion of the nation's students: those who are already privileged by the nature of their ethnicity, exposure due to higher SES levels, and/or in general having lives and resources that allow for expansion of their conceptual-knowledge bases.

Conclusions and Recommendations for Schools Serving American Indian Students

It is essential for educators at all levels to recognize that all children possess prior experiences that can be utilized to make linkages with their formal school learning to enhance their academic successes. Many American Indian children have acquired experiences with different animals, observed plants growing in the earth, played games with stones or rocks, and know about life in their neighborhoods in spite of SES. Educators need to familiarize themselves with students' environments and incorporate this knowledge to then teach about concepts with which students may not be familiar.

Incorporating culturally relevant/responsive pedagogy includes more than ensuring students have their languages and cultural activities represented in schools. It also means that we teach in such a way that mirrors Native teaching practices. It entails ensuring that American Indian students see positive reflections of themselves in the bulletin boards and decorations of the school, posters on the walls, books in the school library, and models of successful American Indians.

While many Tribal nations do not have a written language, being able to provide materials with legends of students' Tribal nations and other Tribal nations, books focusing on nature, and access to current media about the world is as equally important as having the latest Newbery and Caldecott books on the shelves. Tribal sovereignty and materials that reflect tribal interests must receive emphasis in schools. In doing so, we need to include Native histories, values, and mores, not just information on how to make a trinket representing an Indigenous people.

Teachers who are non-Native will come to realize that they may feel some guilt when they are teaching about some of the horrific events that occurred involving Native peoples, such as the widespread efforts to annihilate or remove ancestors from their land either through wars against them or by other means of forceful removal. This is a natural response. Since many Native children are also in public schools with non-Native classmates, it is only with honesty that all students will be able to reconcile what happened in the past with making peace in the future and learn to respect each other.

As educators, we can refuse to engage in the winner-loser, hegemonic thinking and move forward to a co-constructed knowledge paradigm with our Indigenous and non-Indigenous students. If we do not understand our Native students' cultural, linguistic, and SES backgrounds, we will continue to utilize ineffective teaching practices and pedagogies. We need to examine the research on alternate ways of teaching content and apply additional teaching methods as appropriate for instructing Native students.

This includes integrating the arts with content areas and finding creative ways for involving students in their learning. This is especially important in terms of what we know about learning and the brain, as students can build on the knowledge they acquire through the arts as well as demonstrate what they have learned through these additional semiotic systems. This creates a win-win paradigm in classrooms, moving students and teachers forward in their endeavors.

Finally, it is essential that we measure the success of Native students by more than one norm-referenced achievement test. We need to use measures that are process-oriented, examining whether or not children can apply what they are learning to new situations. Experiential learning provides many opportunities for this type of assessment, as does service learning within Native communities. Portfolio assessment allows students to demonstrate to "elders" that they have mastered particular concepts receiving attention in school, again resembling the traditional ways of showing mastery to others.

Summary

When students fail, act out, or drop out (physically or mentally) from schools, the burden for their lack of achievement is placed on the learners themselves, their families and communities, and their schools. We can avoid this never ending cycle by providing what is culturally appropriate learning and assessment for American Indian students. We also need to reward teachers who show that progress is being made with their students, again by using multiple means to do so. We must realize what *best practices* are for our Native students and be prepared to defend these practices to our detractors.

It is imperative that we realize the cost of the current system enacted by NCLB (2001) is too high: American Indian student dropout rates will continue to increase, and we will be losing the talents of potential scientists, engineers, business executives, artisans, politicians, and yes, even teachers, to name but a few. We will be losing people who can make great contributions to their Tribal nations, the United States, and the world. We can no longer afford the boarding school mentality. We must eliminate this mindset so that Native students will succeed in both worlds.

REFERENCES

Alaska Native Knowledge Network. (1998). *Alaska Standards for Culturally Responsive Schools*. Anchorage, AK: Alaska Native Knowledge Network. Retrieved from http://www.ankn.uaf.edu/publications/standards.html.

Ami, C. (2004). *What Contributes to Native American Low Performance?* Presentation, Race 2004 Conference, Arizona State University, Tempe, AZ.

Barton, P. E. (2005). *One-third of a Nation: Rising Dropout Rates and Declining Opportunities*. Policy Information Report. Princeton, NJ: Educational Testing Service. Retrieved from http://www.ets.org/Media/Research/pdf/PICONETHIRD.pdf.

Bernol, E. M. (2002). "Three ways to achieve a more equitable representation of culturally and linguistically different students in GT programs." *Roper Review* 24 (2): 82–88.

Bruchac, J. (2004). *Encountering Children's Literature: An Arts Approach*, Foreword by J. M. Gangi, ix–x. New York: Pearson.

Chomsky, N. (1986). *Knowledge of Language: Its Nature, Origin, and Use*. Westport, CT: Praeger.

Cleary, L. M., and T. D. Peacock. (1998). *Collected Wisdom: American Indian Education*. Boston: Allyn & Bacon.

Colorado Department of Education. (2007). Colorado Department of Education Report. Denver: Colorado Department of Education. Retrieved from http://www.cde.state.co.us.

Commission on No Child Left Behind. (2007). *Beyond NCLB: Fulfilling the Promise to our Nation's Children*. Washington, DC: Aspen Institute. http://www.aspeninstitute.org/sites/default/files/content/docs/nclb/MediaExec-Summary_FinalPDF020807.pdf.

Deloria, V., Jr., ed. (1974). *Technical Problems in Indian Education*. Vol. 4 of *Indian Education Confronts the Seventies*. Washington, DC: Office of Indian Education. Education Resources Information Center. Retrieved from http://www.eric.ed.gov (accession number ED113084).

Diamond, J. B., and J. P. Spillane. (2004). "High-Stakes accountability in urban elementary schools: Challenging or reproducing inequality?" *Teachers College Record* 106 (6): 1,145–176.

Donmeyer, R. (1995). "The arts as modes of learning and methods of teaching: A (borrowed and adapted) case for integrating the arts across the curriculum." *Arts Education Policy Review* 96 (5): 14–20.

Eisner, E. (1998). "Does experience in the arts boost academic achievement?" *Journal of Art Education* 51 (1): 7–15.

Executive Order no. 13096. (1998). "American Indian and Alaska Native education." *Federal Register* 63 (154): 42,681–684.

Fine, M., A. Burns, Y. A. Payne, and M. E. Torre. (2004). "Civics lessons: The color and class of betrayal." *Teachers College Record* 106 (11): 2,193–223. http://www.tcrecord.org.libpublic3.library.isu.edu/library/Issue.asp?volyear=2004&number=11&volume=106.

Gangi, J. M. (2004). *Encountering Children's Literature: An Arts Approach.* New York: Pearson.

Gardner, H. (1999). *Intelligence Reframed: Multiple Intelligences for the 21st century.* New York: Basic Books.

Hetland, L., and E. Winner. (2001). "The arts and academic achievement: What the evidence shows." *Arts Education Policy Review* 102 (5): 3–6.

Hoff, D. J. (2007). "Panel report is latest Rx for NCLB." *Education Week* 26 (24): 1, 30.

Horn, C. (2003). "High-stakes testing and students: Stopping or perpetuating a cycle of failure?" *Theory into Practice* 42 (1): 30–41.

Idaho State Department of Education. (2007). *Adequate Yearly Progress Report.* Boise: Idaho State Department of Education. Retrieved from http://www.sde.idaho.gov/site/assessment/ISAT/ayp.htm.

Jacobs, M. D. (2006). "Indian boarding schools in comparative perspective: The removal of Indigenous children in the United States and Australia, 1880–1940." In *Boarding School Blues: Revisiting American Indian Educational Experiences*, ed. C. E. Trafzer, J. S. Keller, and L. Sisquoc, 202–31. Lincoln: University of Nebraska.

Jensen, E. (2005). *Teaching with the Brain in Mind.* 2nd ed. New York: Pearson.

Jones, K., and P. Ongtooguk. (2002). "Equity for Alaska natives: Can high-stakes testing bridge the chasm between ideals and realities?" *Phi Delta Kappan* 83 (7): 499–503, 550. http://www.jstor.org.libpublic3.library.isu.edu/stable/20440183.

Klug, B. J., and P. T. Whitfield. (2003). *Widening the Circle: Culturally Relevant Pedagogy for American Indian Children.* New York: RoutledgeFalmer.

———. (2011). "A mind with a view: Education through the kaleidoscopic lenses of the arts." In *Cultivating Curious and Creative Minds: The Role of Teachers and Teacher Educators, Part II.* ATE Yearbook XVIII, ed. C. J. Craig and L. F. Deretchin, 160–78. Lanham, MD: Rowman & Littlefield Education.

Kozol, J. (2005). *The Shame of the Nation: The Restoration of Apartheid Schooling in America.* New York: Three Rivers.

Leap, W. L. (1993). *American Indian English.* Salt Lake City: University of Utah Press.

Lomawaima, K. T., and T. L. McCarty. (2002). "When tribal sovereignty challenges democracy: American Indian education and the democratic ideal." *American Educational Research Journal* 39 (2): 279–305.

Manzo, K. K. (2006). "Scathing report casts cloud over Reading First." *Education Week* 26 (6): 1, 24.

Martin, N., and S. Halperin. (2006). *Whatever it Takes: How Twelve Communities are Reconnecting Out-of-School Youth.* Washington, DC: American Youth Policy Forum. Retrieved from http://www.aypf.org/publications/WhateverItTakes/WITfull.pdf.

Meriam, L. (1928). "The effects of boarding schools on Indian family life: 1928." In *Destruction of American Indian families*, ed. S. Unger. New York: Association on American Indian Affairs, 1977.

Merino, B. (2007). "Identifying critical competencies for teachers of English learners." *UC Linguistic Minority Research Institute Newsletter* 16 (4): 1–7.

Montana Office of Public Instruction. (2007). *Web Report Card.* Helena, MT: Montana Office of Public Instruction. Retrieved from http://opi.mt.gov/Reports&Data/.

National Center for Educational Statistics. (2009). *Student Effort and Educational Progress.* Washington, DC: U.S. Department of Education Institute of Education Sciences. Retrieved from http://nces.ed.gov/pubsearch/pubsinfo.asp?pubid=2009081.

National Congress of American Indians and National Indian Education Association. (2010). *National Tribal Priorities for Indian Education.* Washington, DC: National Congress of American Indians and National Indian Education Association. http://www.niea.org/data/files/policy/ncai_niea_joint_priorities_revised_13july2010.pdf.

National Indian Education Association. (2008). *Native Education 101: Basic Facts about American Indian, Alaska Native, and Native Hawaiian Education.* Washington, DC: National Indian Education Association.

No Child Left Behind Act of 2001: Reauthorization of the Elementary and Secondary Education Act of 1965 (NCLB). (2001). *U.S. code.* Title 20, sec. 6301 et seq.

Osguthorpe, R. D. (2009). "A reconceptualization of teacher manner." In *Affective Teacher Education: Exploring Connections among Knowledge, Skills, and Dispositions*, ed. P. R. LeBlanc and N. P. Gallivant, 81–98. Lanham, MD: Rowman & Littlefield Education.

Padilla, R. V. (2005). "High-stakes testing and educational accountability as social constructions across cultures." In *Leaving Children Behind: How Texas-style Accountability Fails Latino Youth*, ed. A. Valenzuela, 249–62. Albany: State University of New York.

Pewewardy, C. D. (1994). "Culturally responsible pedagogy in action: An American Indian magnet school." In *Teaching Diverse Populations: Formulating a Knowledge Base*, ed. E. R. Hollins, J. E. King, and W. C. Hayman, 77–92. New York: State University of New York.

Rabkin, N., and R. Redmond. (2006). "The arts make a difference." *Educational Leadership* 63 (5): 60–64.

Richards, A. G. 2003. "Arts and academic achievement in reading: Functions and implications." *Art Education* 56 (6): 19–23.

Rodriguez, G. M., and J. O. Fabionar. (2010). "The impact of poverty on students and schools: Exploring the social justice leadership implications." In *Leadership for Social Justice: Making Revolutions in Education*, 2nd ed., ed. C. Marshall and M. Oliva, 55–73. New York: Allyn & Bacon.

Skinner, L. (1992). "Teaching through traditions: Incorporating Native languages and cultures into curricula." In *Indian Nations at Risk: Listening to the People. Summaries of Papers Commissioned by the Indian Nations at Risk Task Force of the U.S. Department of Education*, ed. P. Cahape and C. B. Howley, 54–59. Education Resources Information Center. Retrieved from http://www.eric.ed.gov (accession number ED339588).

Smith, F. (2006). *Reading without Nonsense*. 4th ed. New York: Teachers College Press.

St. Germaine, R. D. (2000). *A Chance to go Full Circle: Building on Reforms to Create Effective Learning*. Paper prepared for the National American Indian and Alaska Native Education Research Agenda Conference, Albuquerque, New Mexico.

Strom, K. M. (2012). WWW Virtual Library—American Indians: Index of Native American resources on the Internet. Retrieved from http://www.hanksville.org/NAresources/.

Trahant, M. N. (2010). *The Last Great Battle of the Indian Wars*. Ft. Hall, ID: Cedars Group.

Utah State Office of Education. (2006). Utah State Office Of Education Criterion-Referenced Test (CRT) Results. Salt Lake City, UT: Author. Retrieved from http://www.schools.utah.gov/data/Educational-Data/Assessments-Student-Achievement/Results_CRT_State_2006-pdf.aspx.

Wadsworth, B. J. (1996). *Piaget's Constructivism Theory of Cognitive and Affective Development: Foundations of Constructivism*. 5th ed. White Plains, NY: Longman.

Wyoming Department of Education. (2007). *Every Student Counts*. Casper, WY: Retrieved from https://wdese-cure.k12.wy.us/stats/wde_public.esc.show_menu.

Zull, J. E. (2002). *The Art of Changing the Brain*. Sterling, VA: Stylus.

NOTES

1. The terms *culturally relevant* and *culturally responsive pedagogy* are used interchangeably.
2. Pseudonym for the school where this study was conducted.
3. Pseudonyms are used for all interviewees.

Chapter 7

Teaching Choctaw as a Foreign Language in a Nontraditional Setting

A Challenge with High Expectations and Possibilities

Freddie A. Bowles: University of Arkansas at Fayetteville

ABSTRACT

Choctaw language is the third most spoken Indigenous heritage language in the United States. According to the Intertribal Wordpath Society (2007), only 4,000 tribal members remain viable speakers of the language in Oklahoma. In the late 1990s, Chief Gregory E. Pyle and the tribal elders of the Choctaw Nation in Oklahoma envisioned a rejuvenation of Choctaw through a concentrated outreach program including community centers, Head Start programs, and Internet classes.

At the present time, Chahta Anumpa Aiikhvna, the School of Choctaw Language, in Durant, Oklahoma, now offers Choctaw as a high school foreign language credit through Interactive Educational Television (IETV) technology, in addition to Internet courses, community courses, and Head Start classes. These efforts are making it possible for Choctaw's road to recovery as a vibrant language and provide a model for other such efforts.

The importance of language and culture for forming students' identities as Native peoples cannot be overstated. This chapter addresses the importance of language preservation and offers a brief overview of American Indian education to provide the setting and context for the School of Choctaw Language as it strives to meet the challenges, expectations, and possibilities for language preservation.

Keywords: Choctaw, language revitalization, language preservation

TEACHING CHOCTAW AS A FOREIGN LANGUAGE IN A NONTRADITIONAL SETTING: A CHALLENGE WITH HIGH EXPECTATIONS AND POSSIBILITIES

According to Reyhner (2001) in *Cultural Survival Quarterly*, most of the speakers of the estimated 154 Indigenous languages still spoken in the United States at this time were over seventy years of age. About twenty of these languages were still spoken by all age groups, thus making them fully vital. However, Krauss (cited in Reyhner 1995) states that fewer children were learning these languages, and the languages were not being taught at home.

Of those remaining twenty languages, Krauss classifies nine of them as "moribund"—languages that were no longer spoken by the children (cited in Reyhner 1995). According to Crawford (2000), 95 percent of Navajo first graders in the previous generation spoke Navajo as their first language. By the early 1990s, only one-third of Navajo first graders were fluent in Navajo. He saw similar evidence in other once secure Indigenous languages such as Crow, Hualapai, Choctaw, and Tohono O'odham. Crawford warns that if the current drop in young fluent speakers continues, virtually all Native languages could be extinct within two or three generations.

Fishman (2001) identifies three types of heritage languages: immigrant, Indigenous, and colonial. Indigenous heritage languages are defined as those tongues spoken by peoples native to the Americas. Fishman (1991) postulates that there are eight stages of language loss. In stage one, languages are actively promoted, while stage eight immediately precedes extinction with just a few elders remaining who speak the language.

In stage one, the language has the greatest chance of survival and is spoken at the highest levels of tribal governments. Fishman (1991) has concluded that the logical key to language preservation is the intergenerational transmission of the language in the home, not through governmental laws and efforts. Fishman tells us, "The road to societal death is paved by language activity that is not focused on intergenerational continuity" (cited in Reyhner 1995). Fishman's system (1991) has been useful in helping scholars identify a language's health and prospects for revitalization and survival.

The Choctaw—or Chahta—language is classified as Western Muskogean, a branch of the Muskogean language family also spoken by Creeks, Seminoles, Chickasaws, and other tribes who have lived in the southeastern United States (Haag and Willis 2001). As of 2009, the Choctaw Nation of Oklahoma had an ethnic population of 111,400 members living in southeastern Oklahoma with 120,400 members throughout the United States (Lewis 2009).

According to the Intertribal Wordpath Society of Oklahoma (2007), an organization that has monitored the use and status of Oklahoma Indian languages, 591,437 people were enrolled in Oklahoma tribes in 2006. However, only 22,979 were fluent in a tribal language, and of that number, only 4,000 were listed as established speakers in Oklahoma in 2006.

In 2008, Choctaw tribal language teachers Curtis and Teresa Billy (personal communication, March 15, 2008) placed the health of the Choctaw language somewhere between stage one—revitalization—and stage eight—extinction—on Fishman's 1991 Graded Intergenerational Disruption Scale (Fishman 1991). Small pockets of intergenerational speakers existed, and although the language was being used in schools (stage four), it was not the language of instruction but was taught as a foreign language. However, according to the Intertribal Wordpath Society of Oklahoma (2007), Choctaw was considered an endangered language (stage eight) because parents no longer taught the language to their children.

Littlebear (2007), a Cheyenne language teacher and advocate for language preservation, has encouraged Indigenous heritage language speakers to just keep speaking their languages all the time. "To help reinforce what the schools are trying to do, Native Americans should just talk their languages everywhere with everyone all the time" (Littlebear 2007, 5).

The Importance of Language Preservation

Loss of languages has separated many Native peoples from their cultures. Reyhner (1995, 279) tells us, "Each language carries with it an unspoken network of cultural values." He maintains that these are absorbed on a subliminal level in children's early years. Languages establish comfort, self-assurance, and success; they help shape self-awareness, identity, and interpersonal relationships. When people lose their languages, they lose their ability to give voice to their cultures and identities. They walk in multiple worlds without the voices to "recognize and cope with cross-cultural values" (Reyhner 1995, 280).

Maintaining one's heritage languages "confers cognitive advantages, enhances self-esteem and cultural well-being, and strengthens community bonds" (Lutz 2007, para. 4). Research shows that bilingual speakers have performed above grade level in school (Lutz 2007). Brandt and Ayoungman (1989, 51) report that "the use of ancestral language[s] in the school or in the community improves rather than hinders the child's performance on measures of achievement." Lutz (2007) reports that children in a Hawaiian immersion school had a zero-percent dropout rate and attended college at a higher rate than their peers.

Crawford (2000) also points out evidence that conserving Indigenous heritage languages is beneficial from the individual level to the national level of economics and world affairs. At the individual level, this includes cognitive and academic growth and help with identity conflicts, supporting family values, and establishing career advantages as well as maintaining cultural vitality.

Shebala, a Navajo tribal council member, reinforces the importance of maintaining cultural vitality by stating, "Once we lose our language, we lose our culture and we're just another brown-skinned American [sic]" (1999, para. 10). Curtis Billy concludes that the loss of language and culture reflect a deeper level of loss when he surmises that tribal members will become "another white person [sic] in brown skin" (personal communication, March 15, 2008).

Maintaining one's heritage language does not mean a rejection of the dominant language. Littlebear, having written extensively about language preservation, views "our native languages as nurturing our spirits and hearts and the English language as sustenance of our bodies" (cited in Reyhner 1995). Children in early childhood programs who are only learning English may experience a language separation from their parents (Fillmore 1991). Fillmore (1991) maintains that separation could also lead to family breakdown as a result of communication problems and identity crises followed by self-abusive behaviors, such as alcoholism and drug use.

The Cost of Assimilation

Reyhner and Eder (2004) identify the period from 1944 to 1969 as the "termination and relocation period." In an effort to offer Native Americans the same rights as other citizens in the United States, Tribal nations were terminated and reservations eliminated in favor of land distribution to tribal members. Day schools were abolished and conservative tribal leaders called for a return to off-reservation boarding schools, encouraging assimilation of languages and cultures. According to Nash, many rural Native Americans were relocated to urban centers, "essentially a one-way bus ticket from rural to urban poverty" (cited in Philp 1986).

Though many Native American children became enrolled in public school education during this time, the dropout rate still hovered at 20 percent in Bureau of Indian Affairs (BIA) schools as late as 1965. Wax describes reservation schools as "almost . . . colonial, or at the least caste-like" (cited in Reyhner and Eder 2004). Parents had limited participation in school management, and curricula were inappropriate or even nonexistent. Teachers were often reprimanded by administrators for allowing students to speak their Native languages.

In moving away from the assimilation model of educating Native Americans, President Lyndon B. Johnson appointed Robert L. Bennett, a member of the Oneida Nation, as Commissioner of Indian Affairs in 1966. He was the first Indian appointed commissioner since Ely Parker in 1869. President Johnson called for Indian self-determination in a special message to Congress in 1968 and stressed the need for their full participation in the American way of life.

In 1969, a United States Senate Special Subcommittee on Indian Education published its report [Senate Report 91-501] *Indian Education: A National Tragedy—A National Challenge*, also known as the Kennedy Report. In the foreword, Senator Edward Kennedy points out four findings concerning American Indian students:

1. Dropout rates [were] twice the national average in both public and federal schools. Some school districts [had] dropout rates approaching 100 percent.
2. Achievement levels of Indian children [were] two to three years behind those of white students; and the Indian child [fell] progressively further behind the longer he [stayed] in school.
3. Only one percent of Indian children in elementary schools [had] Indian teachers or principals.
4. One-fourth of elementary and secondary school teachers—by their own admission—[preferred] not to teach Indian children; and Indian children more than any other minority group, [believed] themselves to be "below average" in intelligence.

In a personal communication with Curtis and Teresa Billy in March 2008, Mr. Billy brought up the point that though these findings were valid, their interpretation has perhaps contributed to the demise of so many Indigenous heritage languages. Educators misinterpreted the statistics to mean that the success of Native American children in school depended on their rapid acquisition of the English language. As Crawford (2000) points out, almost two-thirds of Navajo first graders lost their monolingual fluency in Navajo in one generation, from the 1970s to the 1990s.

In 1972, Congress passed the Indian Education Act and established the Office of Indian Education and the National Advisory Council on Indian Education (Reyhner and Eder 2004). This effort to further support self-determination provided supplemental funding for Indian students in public schools on and off the reservations. Funding focused on the special needs of Indian students, including culturally relevant and bilingual curriculum materials. During these turbulent years of activism, new tribal leadership found both public and BIA schools unresponsive to their demands for greater local control and a local Indian curriculum (Reyhner and Eder 2004).

In 1975, Congress passed the Indian Self-Determination and Education Assistance Act in an effort "to promote maximum Indian participation in the government and education of Indian people" and "to support the right of Indians to control their own educational activities" (cited in Reyhner and Eder 2004). From 1973 to 1988, the number of tribal schools in the United States increased from twelve to sixty (Reyhner and Eder 2004).

During this time, researchers recognized that most schools in the West did not have the faculty or the materials to teach non-English-speaking students. Cantoni-Harvey, as well as Spolsky, as cited in Reyhner (2000), find in their research that "English as a second language" classes proved mostly unsuccessful for Indian students. Spolsky advocates bilingual education as the route to an equitable education, but in order to be successful, a bilingual program should teach both English and the Native language and culture.

Recognizing the social costs of language loss, tribal governments acted to protect and preserve their languages (Reyhner and Eder 2004). Both the Pascua Yaqui Tribal Council and the Navajo Nation passed language policy resolutions in 1984 (Reyhner and Eder 2004). In 1985, the Northern Ute Tribal Business Committee recognized Ute as their first language and English as the foreign language (Reyhner and Eder 2004). The resolution also required Ute instruction from preschool through twelfth grade and required three credits of in-service training in Ute language for first-year teachers.

In 1990, the U.S. government passed the Native American Languages Act, which established a federal policy to preserve, protect, and promote Native American rights to use, practice, and develop Native American languages (Reyhner and Eder 2004). The United Nations (UN) declared 1993 the "International Year for the World's Indigenous People." It also recognized that humans have the right to speak their languages. As the *United Nations Declaration on the Rights of Indigenous Peoples* states: "Indigenous peoples have the right to revitalize, use, develop, and transmit to future generations their . . . languages" (United Nations General Assembly 2007).

Despite the recognition from local to international levels that Indigenous heritage languages remained endangered, tribal governments still grappled with establishing comprehensive and practical approaches for transmitting languages to the next generation. Drowning Bear—Cherokee instructor at the University of Oklahoma—points out this challenge in *Routes*, the university's online magazine: "We're losing speakers every day, but we're not producing speakers every day to replace them. We need another generation of speakers." (Branson 2010).

Current Models of Indigenous Language Preservation and Renewal

Intergenerational transmission has been critical for the preservation of any language. It has been imperative that parents focus on using the target language at home. Mothers have been encouraged to use their Native language both prenatally and postnatally through conversations with others in the domestic and social environments. This has been to ensure that infants will hear their Native languages both before and after birth and therefore develop the sound structure of the languages more fully (Owens 2007).

The Maori model. The Maori of New Zealand have been successful in preserving their language by creating Kohanga Reo—language nests—which are community-based day-care centers, as Reyhner and Eder (2004) describe. Maori elders volunteered to run immersion day-care centers in 1982. By 1988, 521 centers were filled with 8,000 children—15 percent of Maoris under age five. Maori was used as the language of instruction. Children were addressed in Maori and were expected to respond in Maori. Maori culture centers then offered week-long immersion classes for adults (Reyhner and Eder 2004).

The Navajo in Arizona. Rock Point Community School in Arizona has taught reading and writing in Navajo in kindergarten with one-third of the instruction time spent using oral English only (Reyhner and Eder 2004). At the first-, second-, and third-grade levels, half the instruction has been in Navajo and half in English. In the upper grades, one-fourth of the instruction has been in Navajo. At the secondary level, seventh and eighth graders have had a full year of Navajo studies in the Navajo language with one-quarter of the year in Navajo writing. Ninth through twelfth graders have had a half year of Navajo studies and Navajo writing for a quarter of each year (Reyhner and Eder 2004).

Higher Education

The American Indian Higher Education Consortium (2011) listed thirty-three regular members, three associate members, and one international member. Several members offered four-year teacher education programs, including Sinte Gleska University and Oglala Lakota College, which has included teaching Indigenous languages for Native teacher candidates (American Indian Higher Education Consortium 2011).

The Oklahoma School of Choctaw Language and Culture. The Choctaw language and culture have been actively promoted through a combination of delivery systems. Face-to-face instruction has been offered through university courses and community classes. Public school students in the Choctaw Nation of Oklahoma have been able to earn foreign language credits through distance-learning technology. The same technology has been used to broadcast Choctaw language courses to several colleges and universities from Southeastern Oklahoma State University, and anyone with Internet access can enroll in the online Choctaw language classes.

Language learning initiatives. In the 1990s, Choctaw tribal elders became aware of the diminishing population fluent in Choctaw. Most speakers were solidly in their middle years, having been raised as first language speakers of Choctaw, educated in English, and living as bicultural and bilingual citizens of this great land. Most of their own children, however, were not fluent in their mothers' tongue. The children's skills were passive at best and rarely productive. As the elders began to pass away, the language began to disappear. It was no longer the language of government and church (C. Billy, personal communication, March 15, 2008).

Curtis Billy—a Choctaw language instructor at Southeastern Oklahoma State University and faculty member of the School of Choctaw Language—has identified Councilman Charley Jones as the first elder to act on the community's desire to learn the language:

> I think the councilman, Charley Jones, was one individual who pushed language preservation heavily, and other community people have always wanted to learn the language by telling us, "I wish I could learn," so I think the conditions were right. (C. Billy, personal communication, March 15, 2008)

Mr. Billy also said, "I think the fact that the language was dwindling and not as prominently known by the younger folk, and that fluent speakers were dying out, and so forth, showed a need by the constituents of the councilmen" (personal communication, March 15, 2008). Therefore, efforts proceeded in the direction of preserving the language.

In 1997, the present tribal leader, or *miko*, Gregory E. Pyle, and the tribal council authorized the creation of the Choctaw Language Department and hired a language coordinator and a language specialist to develop Choctaw language community classes (Haag and Coston 2002). The community program began with Native speakers of Choctaw going out into Choctaw communities to teach the language. Anyone could sign up for the classes, which were generally offered in the evening.

A committee recommended teachers for the community programs. "They were screened by a committee of Choctaw speakers who would determine the qualifications for them to speak and read the language. The community concept was that anyone, whether a child or an adult, could attend to learn the language" (C. Billy, personal communication, January 3, 2008). For example, Mr. Billy said, if a group in Little Rock, Arkansas, wanted to start a community class, they could call the tribal headquarters to request a teacher. If one were available, the Nation would pay that person to teach the class.

Choctaw community classes have been taught in over thirty-seven sites across the country, including California, Mississippi, Texas, and, of course, Oklahoma (Haag and Coston 2002). In the beginning, the community schools had no official curriculum, so the teachers created their own curriculum and materials based on their understandings of the language and on the needs of their students.

Students received a certificate of completion for each of four sixteen-week courses, identified as phases I through IV. According to Teresa Billy—curriculum specialist and language instructor at the school—many students repeated the four phases to maintain their fluency (personal communication, March 15, 2008). The teachers attended workshops to discuss the community classes and share their ideas. As Ms. Billy stated, "So that was the beginning of the school. It began with community teachers."

In 1998, Chief Pyle and Assistant Chief Mike Bailey recognized the potential of using distance-learning technology to teach Choctaw (Haag and Coston 2002). The Council agreed to finance a series of telecourses via a closed-circuit television system that used the telephone system. Participants in these courses responded enthusiastically, but technical problems and the exorbitant cost made the courses unsustainable.

The telecourses were phased out in December 1999 (C. Billy, personal communication, January 3, 2008). Free Internet classes began in February 2000. The Nation hired a director and an Internet teacher. Plans called for a phase-in process. "The Internet was then coming into being, so it would be another process. We still have the community, but it's gone out nationwide" (C. Billy, personal communication, January 3, 2008).

These classes have provided access to a broader audience of displaced tribal members and language aficionados (C. Billy, personal communication, January 3, 2008). Over one thousand language learners signed up for Internet classes in the first year. Approximately 2,200 students were enrolled in Choctaw I, Choctaw II, or Choctaw History. A certificate of completion was awarded to participants when the language session ended (C. Billy, personal communication, January 3, 2008).

Chief Pyle's next goal was to offer the language in the public schools (Haag and Coston 2002). He wanted to make Choctaw available to public school children in the ten-and-a-half counties of the Choctaw Nation. The visionaries of the tribe asked for a cadre of certified teachers to join the effort by requesting that the language be recognized as a foreign language credit for public school students. The Oklahoma State Department of Education agreed that the school could teach Choctaw as a foreign language beginning with a pilot program in 2001 (Haag and Coston 2002).

Challenges and possibilities. Every school needed a classroom and every classroom needed a teacher who was highly qualified to teach the language. A successful school had to have fluent speakers who were also licensed to teach, which limited the possibilities. In offering language courses to the local community and through informal Internet instruction, the school legitimately overlooked traditional public school standards for language instruction.

However, as soon as the Nation ventured into public education, accountability for meeting the qualifications of the No Child Left Behind Act (2001), also known as NCLB, played a critical role in how the instruction was organized and delivered (T. Billy, personal communication, January 3, 2008). Finding a location for the school and hiring a certified teacher were the first challenges.

The decision was made to locate the school at the tribal headquarters in Durant, Oklahoma. The Oklahoma State Department had already approved the teaching of Native languages in the 1990s by allowing each tribe to certify instructors to teach tribal languages to tribal members, but the public school program presented different certification issues.

Public school teachers needed licensure in the content area for the appropriate levels of instruction—in this case, foreign language. The Nation hired a certified teacher and provided the classroom in a facility at the capitol complex (T. Billy, personal communication, January 3, 2008). The first two challenges were met.

The next most pressing challenge involved curriculum. The only extant curriculum was for community and Internet classes, which did not meet the public school standards for the state (T. Billy, personal communication, January 3, 2008). After some experimentation with consultants, including linguists and education specialists, the Nation hired several Native language speakers who met the NCLB (2001) status of "highly qualified" teachers. They were given the mission to develop the high school and early childhood curricula.

Delivery of Choctaw language to public schools. These early efforts proved successful when the Oklahoma State Department of Education approved Choctaw I, II, and III for delivery to the public school classroom. The department has also accredited several language and culture books for use in public schools (T. Billy, personal communication, January 3, 2008).

The next challenge concerned content delivery (T. Billy, personal communication, January 3, 2008). How would the School of Choctaw Language most effectively present the instruction in a way that would reach the most students? One certified teacher could not travel to the first four public schools on a daily basis. In this case, distance learning seemed the most logical solution.

Most of the schools in Oklahoma used OneNet, the only statewide IP-based network in the nation. The infrastructure was in place to support connectivity statewide through IETV, which most of the schools in southeastern Oklahoma already had. In 2000, the first OneNet H.323 teacher was hired.

The pilot program, initiated in 2001, offered Choctaw I as a foreign language in four public schools. The teacher provided instruction via distance learning using "talkback TV" or Interactive Educational Television (IETV) in the four public school districts. In the teacher's "classroom," a television monitor was connected to OneNet along with a computer and a document camera. A facilitator managed the high school classrooms equipped with television monitors and controls. The two systems communicated through phone lines. The teacher was able to see and hear students, and students were able to see and hear the teacher.

At the end of the pilot year, students received a foreign language credit. Twenty-seven additional public school districts signed up for the program in the second year, 2002. The concept continued to gain participants. Fourteen Choctaw Head Start centers signed on in 2004. The Oklahoma Department of Education approved Choctaw II in 2006 and Choctaw III in 2009 for the secondary curriculum, according to Justin Fite, Choctaw instructor, and Jim Parrish, director of the School of Choctaw Language (2010).

Current status of the school. As of 2011, the School of Choctaw Language has sixteen faculty members in two facilities in Durant. They have begun intensive summer immersion camps for their newest instructors. Choctaw I and II have been accredited by the State of Oklahoma for foreign language credits in thirty-six schools in the Choctaw Nation, serving over 500 language learners on a daily basis, according to Justin Fite, Choctaw instructor, and Jim Parrish, director (2010). Eleven teachers were certified by the State of Oklahoma to teach Choctaw, the first tribal language in Oklahoma to be listed on Oklahoma teaching certificates.

The school recently received an endangered language grant to initially collect twenty hours of oral recordings of the language (T. Billy, personal communication, January 3, 2008). Plans have been designed for a new facility located near the Kiamichi Vo-Tech Center in the southern part of Durant. All Choctaw language learners can access the school's website for resources, including lessons, vocabulary support, and the word of the day.

Conclusion

The challenges for preserving Choctaw appear daunting when viewed from a historical perspective, but when we narrow our focus to the individual, the family, and the community, we begin to realistically consider the possibility of establishing a model for revitalization. The Choctaw Nation is taking that first step and the next step too. They are teaching the language to the community in multiple venues and contexts and are committed to building a model of language teaching and learning that is effective for language preservation.

The Choctaw model has been one that also could be adapted by other tribal nations facing similar challenges. The teachers at Chahta Anumpa Aiikhvna have developed curricula and materials that reflect the linguistic and cultural attributes of speaking and being Choctaw. They have also been involved in preserving the language through recording some of the remaining fluent speakers (T. Billy, personal communication, January 3, 2008). In addition, they have initiated a language program in Head Start as a way to broach the intergenerational divide.

Discussions have also focused on offering language immersion opportunities in the summer for students and families (T. Billy, personal communication, May 21, 2010). As of December 1, 2010, the Nation announced the availability of a new Chahta Anumpa teacher-education scholarship, a full scholarship for a Choctaw tribal member to attend Southeastern Oklahoma State University. The recipient must agree to complete a licensure program in teacher education and to teach Choctaw for five years at the School for Choctaw Language (Southeastern Oklahoma State University, 2011).

It was the vision of Chief Gregory E. Pyle and the tribal council that the language be preserved. Through the tireless efforts of the Language Department and the faculty of Chahta Anumpa Aiikhvna, Choctaw language may once again be heard from the cradle to the courthouse. As Curtis Billy commented in January 3, 2008, "I was just tuned in to the right spirit at the right time." Such a poignant statement captured the sentiment of the dedication, perseverance, and faith underlying the strong will and determination to keep Choctaw language alive for future generations.

REFERENCES

American Indian Higher Education Consortium. (2011). Tribal colleges and universities (TCUs) roster. Retrieved from http://www.aihec.org/colleges/TCUroster.cfm.

Brandt, E., and V. Ayoungman. (1989). "Language renewal and language maintenance: A practical guide." *Canadian Journal of Native Education* 16 (2): 42–77.

Branson, H. (2010). "Legacy of native languages at OU." *Routes*, March 5. Retrieved from http://routes.ou.edu/story.php?storyID=158.

Cantoni-Harvey, G. (1999). "Using TPR-Storytelling to develop fluency and literacy in Native American languages." In *Revitalizing Indigenous Languages*, J. Reyhner, G. Cantoni, R. St. Clair, and E. Parsons Yazzie (Eds.), pp. 53–58. Flagstaff, AZ: Northern Arizona University.

Crawford, J. (2000). "Heritage language learners in America: Tapping a "hidden" resource." Retrieved from http://www.languagepolicy.net/excerpts/heritage.html.

Fillmore, L. W. (1991). "A question for early-childhood programs: English first or families first?" *NABE News* 14 (7): 13–14, 19. (Reprinted from *Education Week*).

Fishman, J. A. (1991). *Reversing Language Shift: Theoretical and Empiric Foundations of Assistance to Threatened Languages*. Clevedon, UK: Multilingual Matters.

———. (2001). "300-plus years of heritage language education in the United States." In *Heritage Languages in America: Preserving a National Resource*, eds. J. K. Peyton, D. A. Ranard, and S. McGinnis, 81–89. McHenry, IL: Center for Applied Linguistics.

Fite, J., and J. Parrish. (2010). *Choctaw Nation's Distance Learning Program*. Presentation at the Annual Language Summit of the Inter-Tribal Council of the Five Civilized Tribes, Muskogee, OK.

Haag, M., and F. W. Coston. (2002). "Early effects of technology on the Oklahoma Choctaw language community." *Language Learning and Technology* 6 (2): 70–82.

Haag, M., and H. Willis. (2001). *Choctaw Language and Culture: Chahta Anumpa*. Norman: University of Oklahoma Press.

Indian Education Act of 1972. (2000). *U.S. code*. Title 20, sec. 3385 et seq.

Indian Self-Determination and Education Assistance Act of 1975. (2000). *U.S. code*. Title 25, sec. 450f.

Intertribal Wordpath Society. (2007). Status of Indian languages in Oklahoma. http://www.ahalenia.com/iws/status.html.

Lewis, M. P. (2009). *Ethnologue: Languages of the World*. 16th ed. Retrieved from http://www.ethnologue.com/.

Littlebear, R. E. (2007). "A model for promoting Native American language preservation and teaching." Retrieved from http://jan.ucc.nau.edu.

Lutz, E. L. (2007). "Saving America's endangered languages." *Cultural Survival Quarterly* 31 (2): 3. Retrieved from http://www.culturalsurvival.org.

Native American Languages Act of 1990. (2000). *U.S. code*. Title 25, sec. 2901 et seq.

Owens, R. E., Jr. (2007). *Language Development: An Introduction*. 7th ed. Upper Saddle River, NJ: Pearson.

Philp, K. (1986). *Indian Self-rule: First-hand Accounts of Indian-white Relations from Roosevelt to Reagan*. Salt Lake City: Howe Brothers.

Reyhner, J. (1995). "Maintaining and renewing native languages." *Bilingual Research Journal* 19 (2): 279–304.

———. (2000). "Teaching English to American Indians." In *Learn in Beauty: Indigenous Education for a New Century*, eds. J. Reyhner, J. Martin, L. Lockard, and W. S. Gilbert, 114–31. Flagstaff: Northern Arizona University.

———. (2001). "Cultural survival vs. forced assimilation: The renewed war on diversity." *Cultural Survival Quarterly* 25 (2): 22–25. Retrieved from http://www.culturalsurvival.org.

Reyhner, J., and J. Eder. (2004). *American Indian Education: A History*. Norman: University of Oklahoma Press.

School of Choctaw Language. (2010). "The heart of the culture." Retrieved from http://www.choctawschool.com/home-side-menu/news/the-heart-of-the-culture.aspx.

Shebala, M. (1999). "Council slams door on 'English Only.'" *Navajo Times*, July 22. Retrieved from http://www.languagepolicy.net/archives/NT1.htm.

Southeastern Oklahoma State University. (2011). "Choctaw language department announces teacher education scholarship." Retrieved from http://www.se.edu/news/2011/choctaw-lang.

United Nations General Assembly. (2007). *United Nations Declaration on the Rights of Indigenous Peoples*. Resolution 61/295. New York: United Nations.

United States Senate Special Subcommittee on Indian Education. (1969). *Indian Education: A National Tragedy—A National Challenge* (Senate Report No. 91-501). Washington, DC: U.S. Government Printing Office.

Chapter 8

Indigenous Languages and Cultures in Native American Student Achievement

Promising Practices and Cautionary Findings

Teresa L. McCarty: Arizona State University

ABSTRACT

In 1998, President William Jefferson Clinton issued Executive Order no. 13096, which calls for a research agenda to investigate the roles of Native languages and cultures in the education of American Indians. This was reiterated in 2004 when President George W. Bush issued Executive Order no. 13336, which calls for an examination of promising educational practices for American Indian youth. Both of these orders acknowledge the failure of educational improvements based on the exclusion of Native languages and cultures in the education of Native youth.

This chapter focuses on the research findings of one component of a national working group that was tasked with finding the most promising educational programs for American Indian youth inclusive of Native languages and cultures. Several programs, including one school case study, are brought forth as a result of this research that support the premise that Native students fare exceptionally well when their languages and cultures are given prominence within the educational system and when teachers, administrators, and communities all support these efforts.

Keywords: American Indian education, language and cultural inclusion, language immersion

INDIGENOUS LANGUAGES AND CULTURES IN NATIVE AMERICAN STUDENT ACHIEVEMENT: PROMISING PRACTICES AND CAUTIONARY FINDINGS

On August 6, 1998, President William Jefferson Clinton issued Executive Order no. 13096, reaffirming the federal government's "special, historic responsibility for the education of American Indian and Alaska Native students" (Executive Order no. 13096 1998, 42681). In it, he calls for a national research agenda to "evaluate the role of native language and culture in the development of educational strategies" for Native American children and youth (Executive Order no. 13096 1998, 42682).

Eight years later, President George W. Bush reiterated that call in Executive Order no. 13336 (2004), amplifying the need for such research to improve Native students' academic achievement. It was a telling statement about the field of American Indian/Alaska Native/ Native Hawaiian education that research on the role and impact of Native languages and cultures in children's academic achievement remained in question.

There has been ample documentation of the failure of education policies and practices that systematically *exclude* Native languages and cultural content, from the 1928 Meriam Report (Meriam et al. 1928) to the Kennedy Report of 1969 (U.S. Congress 1969). The 1976 *Report on Indian Education* (American Indian Policy Review Commission 1976) reiterates these findings as does the 1991 report *Indian Nations at Risk: An Educational Strategy for Action* (Indian Nations at Risk Task Force 1991).

More recently, the 2007, 2009, and 2011 National Indian Education Study (NIES) documents persistent disparities in National Assessment of Education Progress (NAEP) reading and mathematics performance results for Native American students and, simultaneously, limited use (1 to 4 percent of teachers sampled in the 2007 study) of Native language and culture content standards (Grigg, Moran, and Kuang 2010; Mead et al. 2010; Moran et al. 2008; Stancavage et al. 2006). In contrast to the documented failure of exclusionary curricular approaches, a large and growing body of research from diverse cultural-linguistic settings has documented the academic benefits of approaches that systematically *include* home and community language and cultural practices as integral to the school curriculum. These pedagogies—it is important to point out—go unquestioned for mainstream English-speaking children.

In the most comprehensive review to date of the research on improving Native American students' academic performance, William Demmert (2001), the first deputy commissioner for the U.S. Office of Indian Education, notes the importance of Native language and cultural programs. This is especially true "in motivating students, promoting a positive sense of identity and self, stimulating positive attitudes about school and others . . . and supporting improved academic performance" (Demmert 2001, 42; see also Beaulieu 2003; Brayboy and Castagno 2009; Deyhle and Swisher 1997; Ernst, Statzner, and Trueba 1994; Jacob and Jordan 1993; Klug and Whitfield 2003; May 1999; McCarty, Lipka, and Dick 1994; Ah Nee-Benham 2008; Ah Nee-Benham and Cooper 2000; Yazzie-Mintz 2007).

In his more recent analyses, Demmert and his associates find that the preponderance of research evidence demonstrated positive correlations between comprehensive culturally based education programs, including a strong Native language component and improved student academic, social, and cultural development (Demmert, Grissmer, and Towner 2006; Demmert and Towner 2003; McCardle and Demmert 2006a, 2006b; see also Beaulieu 2003; Yap 2004, 2005). The issue, then, is not whether schooling based on Native students' tribal language and culture is beneficial but rather which approaches are most effective and under what conditions.

This chapter grows out of research undertaken in response to the 2004 executive order and specifically my work as a member of the national working group composed under that executive order and tasked with examining promising practices in the education of Native American children and youth (McCarty 2009a).[1] I first provide a definition of promising practices as developed by the national working group, contextualizing those practices in research from Indigenous language and culture programs throughout Native America.

This is followed by a more in-depth case study of promising practices in a trilingual (Navajo-Spanish-English) school. While innovative programs such as these illuminate exciting possibilities in Native American education, they are increasingly threatened by the pressures of high-stakes standardized tests.

The next section offers cautionary findings regarding these policies' impacts on Native American learners. I conclude by considering alternate possibilities to the exclusionary practices these policies evoke, arguing for strong programs that place Indigenous languages, cultures, and knowledges at the center of education planning and policymaking.

What Are Promising Practices? Definitions and Examples

Any definition of promising practices must take into account the complexity and diversity of Indigenous linguistic, cultural, and educational systems. *Language* and *culture* have been commonplace terms in the literature on minoritized schooling, with abundant research showing home/school linguistic and cultural "mismatches" to be a leading cause of educational disparities.

As helpful as these understandings have been for countering fallacious notions of inherited, racialized intelligence, too often language and culture have been conceived of as static and monolithic. This reduces culture to a superficial list of traits or artifacts and learners to one-dimensional proportions, as in the widespread myth that Native American students are "silent," "non-analytical," or "right-brained" learners (for critiques, see Foley 1996; McCarty et al. 1991).

Similarly, when language is conceived as a bounded, homogeneous, and uniformly distributed system, it becomes easy to lose sight of the variability in students' communicative repertoires, even when they share the same primary language. The risk in both cases is that instructional practices lack relevance and perpetuate damaging stereotypes.

Thus, a primary characteristic of promising practices is that they take the heterogeneity of Indigenous cultural systems into account, capitalizing on the distinctive cultural and linguistic resources present within local communities. In so doing, these practices facilitate learners' self-efficacy, critical capacities, and intrinsic motivation as thinkers, readers, writers, and ethical social agents. As defined by the national working group, promising practices:

1. Enable students to achieve full educational parity with their white mainstream peers, with the long-term goal of preparing Indigenous students for full participation in their home communities and as citizens of the world (Thomas and Collier 1997).
2. Contribute substantively to learners' personal well-being and the development of their academic and ethnic identities.
3. Promote positive, trusting relationships between the school and the community, helping to complete the circle of "the whole child, the whole curriculum, the whole community" (Genesee 1994).
4. Support local educators' professionalism.
5. Promote Indigenous self-determination.

Contextualizing Promising Practices

What do promising practices look like "on the ground," and what has research said about their implementation? There are several examples that will be delineated below.

Rock Point, AZ. Our first example comes from the Navajo (Diné) community school at Rock Point, Arizona, which has had a long-standing bilingual-bicultural education program in which "rigorous, ongoing evaluation of student learning" has been a primary concern (Holm and Holm 1990, 178). In the early 1970s, Rock Point began one of the first contemporary Indigenous literacy programs.

Drawing on international research on second language acquisition, Rock Point based its program on the principle that children learn to read only once, most easily in the language they already speak (Rosier and Farella 1976, 380). Using extant Navajo literacy materials and ones developed locally, students learned to read first in Navajo, then in English.

The students learned mathematics in both languages and studied science and social studies in Navajo, including Navajo clanship, history, social problems, government, and economic development. A high school applied literacy program engaged students in locally relevant research that was published in a bilingual school newspaper and broadcast on a school television station (Holm 2006; Holm and Holm 1990, 1995; McLaughlin 1995).

Longitudinal data from Rock Point shows that its students not only outperformed comparable Navajo students in English-only programs, they surpassed their own previous annual growth rates and those of comparison group students in Bureau of Indian Affairs schools—and they did so by a greater margin each year (Holm and Holm 1990, 177–8). In addition to learning English, of course, these students had the benefit of becoming bilingual and biliterate, an approach referred to as *additive bilingualism*, denoting the fact that one or more languages were added to learners' preexisting communicative repertoires (Baker and Jones 1998, 154).

Rough Rock, AZ. A second example comes from nearby Rough Rock, Arizona, home of the first American Indian community-controlled school. In 1983, anthropologists and reading specialists from the Hawai`i-based Kamehameha Early Education Program (KEEP) came to Rough Rock to see whether the culturally compatible reading strategies proven effective with Native Hawaiian children would work with Navajo students (Vogt, Jordan, and Tharp 1993).

The Rough Rock–KEEP collaboration lasted five years, during which it was determined that approaches that had been successful with Native Hawaiian students required significant modification to produce successful outcomes with Navajo learners. Rough Rock elementary teachers subsequently developed a bilingual-bicultural-biliteracy program adapted from KEEP, organizing their classrooms around interdisciplinary units with local themes.

Summer literature camps involved students, teachers, parents, and elders in field-based research on culturally relevant topics using Native storytelling, song, drama, and arts. Key to all of this was a strong professional development component in which bilingual teachers conducted their own classroom research and regularly collaborated to "indigenize" the curriculum (Begay et al. 1995; McCarty 2002, ch. 11; McCarty and Dick 2003).

Longitudinal data from Rough Rock shows that after four years of the program, students' mean scores on criterion-referenced tests of English comprehension increased from 58 percent to 91 percent. When individual and grade cohort data were analyzed over five years, Rough Rock elementary students demonstrated superior English reading, language arts, and mathematics performance compared to a matched peer group who did not participate in the program.

Not surprisingly, students in the bilingual-bicultural program were also assessed as having stronger Navajo oral language and Navajo literacy abilities. They became stronger in both languages and had the benefit of additive bilingualism (McCarty 2002, ch. 11).

Manokotak, AK. We turn now to Alaska, where two or more languages are still spoken in many Native villages: the Native language as spoken by elders, the Native language modified by English, English modified by the Native language ("village English"), and "standard" or "schooled" English (Hartley and Johnson 1995). Situated along the southern coast of the Bering Sea in the Southwest Regional School District, Manokotak is one such village.

In the 1990s, Manokotak remained an almost entirely Yup'ik-speaking community. Systemic problems within the local K–6 school, which was implementing an all-English curriculum, were evident in high levels of student attrition, poor standardized test performance, student disinterest, and strained student-teacher and community-school relations. According to educators who were close to the school, "these stresses affected everyone in the village" (Hartley and Johnson 1995, 574).

Drawing on research on effective bilingual and English-as-a-second-language (ESL) approaches and data from a community survey, Manokotak began a Yup'ik immersion program with a strong ESL component. This approach enabled students to acquire "Western" literacy skills in the context of their culture while retaining literacy in community-valued knowledge and skills. "In this way," Hartley and Johnson state, "students' identity with their community was supported" (1995, 572). Ongoing staff and materials development and parent workshops were additional program components.

By the second year, all student groups exceeded the district's expected means. Moreover, community feedback, student and family self-reports, student writing samples, behavior reports, and teacher observations showed improved student self-esteem and school-community relations. As Hartley and Johnson describe these outcomes "students reported feeling good about going to school and being interested in what they were doing. . . . Parents were able to discuss school with their children because they now had a common language" (Hartley and Johnson 1995, 581–82, 584).

Math in a Cultural Context. Also in Alaska, the Math in a Cultural Context (MCC) curriculum, developed through university-school-community partnerships with Yup'ik elders and teachers, has proven effective for both Native and non-Native students. As Jerry Lipka and his associates on the MCC project described it, the curriculum "is based on Yup'ik cultural knowledge and norms, and . . . seeks to bridge the culture of the community with that of the school" (Lipka et al. 2005, 368; see also Lipka et al. 2007; Webster and Yanez 2007).

In quasi-experimental and qualitative studies, Lipka and others find that MCC not only improved students' academic performance, it altered the classroom social organization in ways that supported high levels of student engagement with mathematics content. "MCC seems to provide students with a more highly contextualized approach to math learning," which students found both challenging and motivating (Nelson-Barber and Lipka 2008, 117).

The Alaska Rural Systemic Initiative. The Alaska Rural Systemic Initiative has consisted of a statewide partnership among the University of Alaska Fairbanks, the Alaska Federation of Natives, and 176 rural schools serving 20,000 Alaska Native students. It has been implementing an education reform strategy focused on integrating Indigenous knowledge and pedagogical practices into all aspects of the education system.

This partnership—which includes the creation of multimedia science materials, parent involvement, an academy of elders, leadership development, and Alaska standards for culturally responsive schools—has, according to Barnhardt and Kawagley (2005, 15), substantially strengthened the quality of education "and consistently [improved] the academic performance of students in participating schools." (For related Alaska Native examples of standards and guidelines for culturally responsive schools, education practices, and teacher-education programs, see Assembly of Alaska Native Educators 1998, 1999, 2001, and 2003.)

*Hawai`i.* Native Hawaiians have faced many of the same educational challenges as American Indians and Alaska Natives. The Hawaiian language is also severely endangered, and until recently was spoken as a first language primarily by elders. In this context, Nāwahīokalani`ōpu`u Laboratory School (Nāwahī), has been making a positive difference for Native Hawaiian students while serving as the most fully developed model of Indigenous-language immersion in the United States (William H. Wilson, pers. comm., July 23, 2008; see also Hinton 2001; Wilson and Kamanā 2006).

Nāwahī is a Hawaiian-medium, early childhood through high school affiliation of programs featuring a college preparatory curriculum rooted in Native Hawaiian language and culture. The school grew out of the `Aha Pūnana Leo (Hawaiian "language nest") movement that began in the 1980s and aimed to cultivate children's fluency and knowledge of Hawaiian language and culture much as occurred in the home in earlier generations (Wilson and Kamanā 2001; see also Warner 2001).

Nāwahī teaches all subjects through Hawaiian language and values. English instruction begins in fifth grade; elementary students also study Japanese, and intermediate students study Latin—which presents opportunities for contrastive linguistic analysis with Hawaiian and for building students' multilingual-multicultural skills.

Although it has emphasized Hawaiian language and culture revitalization over (English-based) academic achievement, Hawaiian-medium schooling has yielded impressive academic results. Nāwahī students, 60 percent of whom come from reduced- and free-lunch backgrounds, not only surpass their non-immersion peers on English standardized tests, they have outperformed the state average for all ethnic groups on high school graduation, college attendance, and academic honors. The school has had a 100 percent high school graduation rate and a college attendance rate of 80 percent.

School leaders Kauanoe Kamanā and William H. Wilson attribute these outcomes to an academically challenging curriculum that applies knowledge to daily life and is rooted in Hawaiian identity and culture. According to Wilson, the school has succeeded through its strong emphasis on achievement in Hawaiian language and culture "and holding Hawaiian language and culture high through the hard work so highly valued by Hawaiian elders" (pers. comm., July 23, 2008; see also Wilson and Kamanā 2001).

Ojibwe immersion. Finally, in an ethnographic study of Waadookodaading, a pre-K–4 Ojibwe immersion school located near the Lac Courte Orielles Reservation in Wisconsin, Hermes (2005) reports that students were learning Ojibwe while keeping up with the standard curriculum. Although the school was in the early stages of collecting quantitative data on student achievement, Hermes notes that Waadookodaading "has been heralded as a success," as measured by (a) its rapid but exemplary start-up process, including "creating a literate tradition for an oral language"; (b) high levels of parent involvement (90 to 100 percent); and (c) enhanced student motivation—the students "are motivated to learn the Objiwe language beyond our dreams," states Hermes (2006, 60).

Promising Practices and Culturally Based Education

All of these programs reflect principles of culturally based education (CBE), also called "culturally responsive schooling" (CRS) or socially, culturally, and linguistically responsive (SCLR) education (Brayboy et al. 2012). Culturally based education (CBE) is premised on the theory that the most influential factor in students' school performance is "how we teach and arrange social activity in schools" (Beaulieu 2006, 52). CBE assumes that a "firm grounding in the heritage language and culture indigenous to a particular tribe is a fundamental prerequisite for the development of culturally healthy students and communities . . . and thus is an essential ingredient for . . . educators, curriculum and schools" (Assembly of Alaska Native Educators 1998, 2; for a full discussion, see Castagno and Brayboy 2008).

Beaulieu (2006, 52) describes CBE as education that is both academically effective and locally meaningful in light of community members' aspirations for their children. In a review of 145 federally funded language-preservation grants and 1,200 Indian Education Act formula grants, Beaulieu (2006) distills five CBE types: (1) culturally based instruction, (2) Native language instruction, (3) Native studies programs, (4) Native cultural enrichment, and (5) culturally relevant materials. Drawing on a meta-analysis of the research literature, Demmert, Grissmer, and Towner (2006) add these six critical elements of CBE:

1. Native language used as the language of instruction, either as a first or second language
2. Pedagogies that stress traditional cultural practices and child-adult interactions
3. Pedagogies that simultaneously incorporate contemporary ways of knowing and learning
4. Curriculum that emphasizes the importance of Native spirituality, placing this in contemporary contexts
5. Strong Native community participation
6. Knowledge and use of community social and political mores

In both Demmert et al.'s and Beaulieu's frameworks, the most effective programs have been those that systematically incorporate the knowledges, resources, and practices present in the local sociocultural context (Beaulieu 2003, 2006; McCardle and Demmert 2006a, 2006b). The next section examines these practices more closely in the context of a Diné (Navajo) language and culture program at a trilingual public school.

The Puente de Hózhǫ́ Case Study

Puente de Hózhǫ́ (PdH) is a K–5 public magnet school in northern Arizona. The school was identified for study by the national working group because of its unique multilingual program, high levels of parent involvement, and steady record of student growth. An additional consideration was the fact that this is a public school in a linguistically and culturally diverse setting similar to those in which an increasing majority of Native American students attend school (DeVoe, Darling-Churchill, and Snyder 2008; Grigg, Moran, and Kuang 2010; Stancavage et al. 2006).

The school's name derives from the Spanish words *puente de* ("bridge of") and the Navajo *hózhǫ́* ("beauty" or "harmony"). The name mirrors the school's vision "to create an educational environment where students from diverse language and cultural backgrounds can harmoniously learn together while pursuing the goals of *ABC*: academic excellence, bilingualism, and cultural enrichment" (Fillerup 2011, 149–50; emphasis in original).

In a school district in which 25 percent of students are American Indian (mostly Diné) and 20 percent are Latino, "local educators were searching for innovative ways to bridge the seemingly unbridgeable gap between the academic achievement of language-minority and language-majority children" (Fillerup 2005, 15). This school provided an ideal situation to examine CBE in action.

A mixed-method case-study design was used for the research at PdH.[2] Quantitative data included student achievement information collected by the district; qualitative data included ethnographic observations of classroom instruction and Diné teachers' monthly curriculum-development meetings, in-depth interviews with key Diné program personnel, artifact collection and document analysis (e.g., the school mission statement, teachers' lesson plans, student writing samples), and photographs to capture how the Diné language and culture are represented in the visual environment of the school.

To ensure the accuracy and cultural integrity of the research process, member checking occurred throughout the period of fieldwork (2009–2011). The principal investigator (Teresa L. McCarty) provided regular updates and solicited feedback on the study from Diné teachers and from school and district administrators.

Background and school philosophy. Puente de Hózhǫ́ began in 2001 with a kindergarten program that was expanded annually (for more on the school's history, see Fillerup 2011). As described by school cofounder Michael Fillerup, the overriding reason for starting the school was to enhance the academic success of minoritized students by "[creating] an environment where language minority students—in our case, Native Americans and Hispanics—would be invaluable resources for and recipients of a unique and symbiotic linguistic and cultural exchange where the focus on language learning and academics would be enrichment rather than remediation" (2011, 149).

At the time of the study, most of the school's 122 Native American students were Diné, although many came from racially and ethnically mixed family backgrounds. Virtually all of these Native students spoke English as a primary language. While many of the Diné students came from nearby reservation border areas, Diné teachers noted that some also came from the "heart of the [Navajo] reservation" to obtain the kind of "language-rich Navajo-English instruction" provided at the school (interview, November 3, 2009). All the Diné teachers (n = 4) had strong Diné cultural backgrounds and spoke Navajo as a first language.

PdH offers two parallel bilingual programs: a conventional dual-immersion model, in which native Spanish-speaking and native English-speaking students are taught jointly for a half-day in each language, and one-way Navajo immersion, in which English-dominant Navajo students are taught in Navajo. In the latter program, kindergartners receive 80 percent of their instruction in Navajo, with English instructional time gradually increased until a 50/50 balance is attained in grades 3 through 5 (see table 8.1). All state standards are taught in Navajo and English or Spanish and English.

Table 8.1 Distribution of Instructional Time in Navajo and English, Puente de Hózhǫ́ School

Grade	% Time in Navajo (Diné)	% Time in English
Kindergarten	80%	20%
1st grade	80%	20%
2nd grade	70%	30%
3rd grade	60%	40%
4th grade	50%	50%

Language and culture revitalization in practice. PdH is premised on "the Power of Two"—"the ability to speak, read, and write proficiently in two languages" (Fillerup 2011, 150). In and of themselves, however, bilingualism, biculturalism, and biliteracy were not deemed to be sufficient justification for the school; as teachers and administrators stated: "The goals of this school are high academic standards plus Navajo language and culture. If it was just Native language and culture, we would not be successful" (field notes, January 13, 2009).

To understand how the Diné language and culture program works in practice, we asked Diné teachers to describe a "typical day." The kindergarten teacher provided this account:

> When the children come in, in the morning, they follow a routine. I take roll and they answer . . . in Navajo. And then they say the Pledge of Allegiance in Navajo. I do a meal count in Navajo and . . . then we do the calendar activity. The calendar activity itself has a lot embedded into it. They learn counting, . . . shapes, . . . colors, . . . patterns with the shapes and colors; they learn their days of the week and they also learn how to speak the language by saying, "Today is Monday, tomorrow is Tuesday, yesterday was Sunday." Speaking in sentences, they also . . . are learning to count and to recognize numbers. (interview, January 12, 2010)

Everything, the teacher continued, takes place in Navajo; students learn Diné terms for gender by lining up in gender-defined groups for bathroom breaks; they learn color terms by lining up according to the color of their shirts.

> And then they come back in [from their break] and we either do a math lesson, a language lesson, a science lesson—you know, whatever is on the agenda for that day—and [those subjects] are taught in Navajo as well. . . . The only time they have English is when they go to their specials like art, PE, and music. (interview, January 12, 2010)

For the Diné second- and third-grade teacher has second grade in the morning or third in the afternoon or vice versa; we [she and the English classroom teacher] switch every month." A typical day in this Diné classroom begins with the teacher's greeting, "You know, '*Yá'át'ééh abíní*' [Good morning]." Then the teacher and students work with student- and teacher-made books.

> We make . . . at least one or two little books a week, . . . and we work on comprehension throughout the week on those books, so this just kind of reinforces a lot of the skills that they are going to learn [in] reading and writing. . . . And I read the [lunch] menu in Navajo. . . . They are learning different types of foods every day. [After attendance] they go to their [reading] groups. . . . Every week [they] are learning new words. . . . And we keep [the words] in journals and we use [the journal] throughout the whole week. . . . So they have a word bank that they can refer to. (interview, November 3, 2009)

In math and science, this teacher added, "[I use] lots of TPR [Total Physical Response method], lots of stories, lots of modeling, lots of moving around. . . . Because if they are not familiar with [the concepts], then in a second language it is going to be a little tougher (interview, November 3, 2009).

A major thrust of the Diné program has been the development of a viable assessment system for Diné language and literacy. During the period of study, Diné teachers spent much of their time working together, with the bilingual/ESL director facilitating, to adapt the Six Traits writing assessment (Peha 1995–2003) to fit an off-reservation public school context. In this assessment system, writing competencies are keyed to six rubrics considered to be essential aspects of the writing process:

1. Ideas and content: *Hane' hadilyaa'igii ei bóhoneedli*
2. Organization: *Hane' bil'ahoonįįłigií éí nizhónigo bee hozin*
3. Voice: *Shí éí hane' hait'zo yaníse keesígíí shił bee hozin*
4. Word choice: *Saad bidzílgo choo'į*
5. Sentence fluency: *Hane' yázhi éí hazho'ó ałkéé' sinil*
6. Conventions: *Hane' nizhónigo hadilyaa* (field notes, January 13, 2009)

The Diné Six Traits assessment includes a yearlong capstone project that integrates reading, writing, research, oral presentation, and technology. The capstone project represents "a major promising practice," the bilingual/ESL director emphasized. Further, the Diné teachers re-worked the linear model of the Six Traits assessment to fit with a Diné pedagogy and world-view. As documented at one Diné teachers' meeting:

> Rather than teaching writing separately, the teachers had integrated writing with social studies, which includes the Diné cultural component. For example, in kindergarten, pre-writing includes: (1) self-portrait, (2) two-clan (mother's/father's clan) chart, (3) first name, and (4) body parts. This also becomes part of their capstone project. (field notes, January 12, 2010)

As this data excerpt suggests, Diné knowledge has been integrated throughout the curriculum in a Diné-specific design. "At Puente," an administrator noted, "culture is just a daily experi-ence integrated throughout the day—we don't even have to think about it" (interview, May 18, 2010). Four "macro themes" have been used to organize content: earth and sky, health, living things, and family and community (Fillerup 2011, 152). A Diné teacher described how this works in her classroom:

> We have monthly themes, we incorporate science, we incorporate social studies, we incorporate math. . . . So our first month will be about the self. . . . Self-esteem—it is more of your clanship, your kinship, who you are, where you come from: "You are of the Diné people, you should be proud of who you are and how you present yourself as a Navajo person." So that's all intertwined with some stories as well. (interview, November 3, 2009)

Due to the limited number of Navajo curriculum materials for all subject areas, Diné teachers are constantly developing materials. As a teacher explained, "I think we got to the point where the majority of Navajo teachers here can take [an English] lesson and tweak it in Navajo. . . . And a lot of things we still do translate, but we translate it where it is culturally relevant for students" (interview, November 3, 2009).

The Diné language and culture program is part of an overall instructional design that includes the Spanish-English dual-language program. While the two programs enroll different groups of students, each program enriches the other, and both are essential elements of a *multi*lingual, *multi*cultural emphasis. At PdH, "cultural competence" is defined as "You know and are comfortable with people of different races, ethnic backgrounds, and cultures. You're also comfortable with your own cultural identity." Throughout the school, bulletin boards display Navajo, Spanish, and English print.

Indeed, the value placed on multilingualism and multiculturalism is evident before one even passes through the front door. On each side of the entryway, murals created by PdH students and renowned Diné artist Shonto Begay depict the dawn run in the Navajo girl's puberty ceremony (*Kinaaldá*; see figure 8.1), and the multihued topography of Diné Bikeyah, Navajoland.

Figure 8.1 Exterior Wall Mural Depicting Navajo Girl's Puberty Ceremony (Kinaaldá), Puente de Hózhǫ School

Interview and observational data attest to the fact that PdH's success has been centered on a shared vision of the school's mission—*both* academic rigor *and* language and culture revitalization and maintenance. Coupled with this has been what an administrator described as a "passionate commitment on the part of teachers and parents" to make that vision a reality (interview, May 18, 2010). A Diné teacher described these qualities:

> The key element, number one, is that you have to have parents that want to support the program, first and foremost. And . . . number two, you need to have a faculty and administrators who support the intent of the program and the philosophy of the program. (interview, November 3, 2009)

"Passionate commitment" is embedded in the school's very mission, an administrator noted. "[W]e've got to save our language. . . . We want to instill a love of language in the kids" (interview, May 18, 2010).

At PdH, Diné language and culture share equal status with English and the English-speaking world. "This school is predicated on [the assumption] that learning more than one language is a *good thing*," an administrator emphasized; "there is a belief in this school that all three languages should be treated equally" (field notes, January 12, 2010). "We have to tell the parents this is not what they were used to in their own schooling," a Diné teacher pointed out, "and just for the parents to see 'Wow, this is how much my child knows' instead of 'This is what your child *doesn't* know'" (field notes, January 12, 2010).

"I think once we can instill that [students] can be *proud* of who they are," another Diné teacher reflected, "they're going to feel honored to share [their heritage language and culture] and learn it and want to be motivated to learn and to continue teaching their kids or their parents" (interview, November 3, 2009). An explicit part of this has been "shedding the remedial label that has dogged American Indian . . . children for over a century," Fillerup notes in an early report on the school (2005, 16).

Students in the Navajo immersion program are viewed not as problems to be solved but as an educational elite—the ones who are learning Navajo, that most difficult language [used by the Code Talkers] during World War II. These students travel throughout our district performing traditional songs and dances. . . . It is their language, program, school, culture, and heritage.

As a result, this . . . program tends to keep students more interested in their education. And if there is a compelling reason for them to go to school each day, they tend to stay in school longer. (Fillerup 2005, 16)

A central value at PdH is collaboration among all faculty members at the school. Throughout the period of study, Diné teachers collaborated regularly with English language teachers, beginning with kindergarten: "The Diné program is not just an isolated program," an English language teacher stressed (field notes, January 13, 2009). Students also participate in daily "specials"—music, PE, and art—and the Spanish language teachers and their students interact regularly with those in the Diné program. Each spring, both programs put on a cultural program that has been well attended by the local community.

Supporting student success. How well have students done in PdH's Diné language and culture program? With the exception of one year early in the program, PdH has consistently met or exceeded federal and state benchmarks for adequate yearly progress (AYP). In 2008, Native students at PdH surpassed their Native American peers in English-only programs by 14 percent and 21 percent in grades 3 and 4, respectively (see table 8.2).

Table 8.2 Percent of PdH Native Students Meeting or Exceeding State Standards in Reading, 2008 Academic Year

Grade	District Percentage	Puente de Hózhǫ
3	57%	71%
4	54%	75%
5	48%	43%
6	53%	44%

Source: Fillerup 2011, 161

In mathematics, 8 percent and 2 percent more Native PdH students met or exceeded state mathematics standards than Native students in English-only classes (see table 8.3).

Table 8.3 Percent of PdH Native Students Meeting or Exceeding State Standards in Mathematics, 2008 Academic Year

Grade	District Percentage	Puente de Hózhǫ
3	68%	76%
4	61%	63%
5	60%	43%
6	55%	44%

Source: Fillerup 2011, 161

In 2009, fifth-grade Native students outperformed their English-only peers in reading by 11 percent and in math by 12 percent. In math, sixth-grade Native students outperformed their English-only peers by 17 percent. "Finally," Fillerup (2011, 163) writes of these outcomes, "it should be noted that Native Americans at Puente de Hózhǫ outperformed their English-only peers across all grade levels in writing: by 3 percent in grade 3, by 8 percent in grade 4, by 4 percent in grade 5, and by 21 percent in grade 6." Importantly—and reflective of the research reviewed in the previous section of this chapter—the students who performed the best had the longest experience in the Diné language and culture program (i.e., those who began in kindergarten).

But the program's impacts have extended beyond test scores. As one teacher noted, "Hearing parents comment on how much their kids have learned, or that their child may be the only one of all the cousins who is speaking to their grandparents—this tells us that we are doing something [important and meaningful]" (interview, November 3, 2009). These represent the unquantifiable yet very consequential program effects: bridging the generations through the heritage language and, as Fillerup writes, the "smiles on the faces of parents, grandparents, and students as they communicate in the language of their ancestors" (2005, 16).

Synthesis: Promising Practices and Transformative School Cultures

The PdH case study strongly indicates that promising practices in Indigenous education can thrive when they are seeded in a transformative school culture that emphasizes high academic expectations and a robust content-rich curriculum, while also tangibly demonstrating the value of children's heritage language and culture as resources for learning. This is the essence of "strong" Indigenous language and culture programs—those in which the Indigenous language and culture are core curricular elements, "the very heart and soul of the school itself" (Fillerup 2008, para. 3).

As shown in table 8.4, strong programs include Indigenous language and culture immersion (e.g., Manokotak, Nāwahī, PdH, Waadookodaading) or maintenance (e.g., early programs at Rock Point and Rough Rock). Both approaches lead to additive bilingualism. In contrast, weaker transitional pull-out and add-on programs lead to subtractive bilingualism and have not been found to be correlated with high levels of academic achievement.

Table 8.4 Typology of Language and Culture Education Programs for Native American Learners*

Program Type	Strong (Additive or Full Bilingualism/Biculturalism)			Weak (Subtractive or Limited Bilingualism/Biculturalism)		
	Child's Language Status	Language of Classroom	Program Goals	Child's Language Status	Language of Classroom	Program Goals
Indigenous-Language and Culture Immersion	Indigenous/minority	Indigenous language	Indigenous-language maintenance/revitalization; full bilingualism, biculturalism, biliteracy**	N/A	N/A	N/A
Indigenous-Language and Culture Maintenance ("Language Shelter")	Indigenous/minority	Bilingual with emphasis on Indigenous language	Indigenous-language maintenance/revitalization; bilingualism, biculturalism, biliteracy	N/A	N/A	N/A
Two-Way Bilingual/Dual	Language Indigenous/minority and majority (50/50; 60/40, etc.)	Mixed Indigenous language/English (90%/10%; 50%/50%, etc.)	Indigenous-language maintenance/revitalization; bilingualism, biculturalism, biliteracy	N/A	N/A	N/A
Transitional	N/A	N/A	N/A	Indigenous/minority	Indigenous language used for first years of schooling, then replaced with English	Strong English dominance/monolingualism; may include some Native-language and culture enrichment
Mainstream with Indigenous-Language and Culture Pull-Out Classes	N/A	N/A	N/A	Indigenous/minority	Indigenous language and English	Strong English dominance/monolingualism, with some Native-language and culture enrichment

			Indigenous minority and majority	Indigenous language taught as a "foreign" language	Strong English dominance; limited bilingualism; little or no cultural emphasis
Mainstream with Foreign Language Instruction	N/A	N/A	N/A		
Structured English Immersion***	N/A	N/A	N/A	Indigenous/ minority	English only	English monolingualism/ monoculturalism (assimilation)

*This table is taken from McCarty (2011, 77–78) with categories adapted from Baker (2006).

**A primary goal of many Indigenous-language programs is oral proficiency (not Native-language literacy).

***Structured English immersion programs are best characterized as "non-forms" of bilingual/multicultural education, also known as "sink or swim" (Skutnabb-Kangas & McCarty, 2008, 12).

The research reported here also shows that regardless of students' Indigenous-language fluency upon entering school, time spent learning the Indigenous language is not time lost in developing academic English. When provided with sustained cumulative Indigenous-language instruction in the context of a transformative school culture, such as that at PdH, students performed as well as or better than their peers in mainstream classes on academically challenging tasks. Meanwhile, they had the benefit of developing oralcy and literacy in a second language (i.e., additive bilingualism).

In keeping with international research on second language acquisition, the promising-practices study shows that it is critical to ensure an adequate period (four to seven years) for students to develop academic proficiency in a second language. "I have learned that in order to have a program like ours, . . . it takes time," a PdH teacher reflected in an interview. "You cannot start up a program and have it for three or four years and be done with it. . . . You have to wait for the results" (interview, January 12, 2010). Thus, long-term programs that begin with a solid foundation (80 to 100 percent of instructional time) in the Native language and provide four to seven years of high-quality English instruction by the end of the program (which may entail as little as 20 percent of instructional time, as the Hawaiian data show), promote high levels of English achievement while also supporting learning in and of the Native/heritage language and culture.[3]

These approaches share all the qualities of promising practices described earlier in this chapter. They enhance student motivation, self-esteem, and ethnic pride, as evidenced by improved attendance and college-going rates (e.g., Nāwahī), lower attrition (e.g., Manokotak, Nāwahī, PdH), and simultaneously enhance teacher-student and school-community relations (e.g., Manokotak, PdH, Rock Point, Rough Rock). Strong programs also offer rich and varied opportunities to involve parents and elders in children's learning—a positive factor universally associated with improved student achievement.

Strong programs are characterized by equally strong investments in teachers' professional development and local intellectual resources, as evidenced by "grow your own" approaches to Native teacher preparation and curriculum development (e.g., Nāwahī, Rock Point, Rough Rock, Waadookodaading). Finally, this research suggests that the ability to implement strong Indigenous language and culture programs rests on the ability of Native nations and Indigenous communities to exercise self-determination in the content, process, and medium of instruction. Culturally based leadership and decision making are thus integral components of effective CBE/CRS.

The challenges of program implementation. None of these outcomes has been achieved without challenges and setbacks. A major challenge has been the lack of certified Native language teachers and of linguistically and culturally appropriate teaching materials. At PdH, one teacher noted, "We don't have [handy] resources—we can't go to the store and buy a book on a certain topic; we have to create our own" (interview, January 12, 2010).

In addition, although they may be fluent speakers of the Indigenous language, Indigenous language teachers often need to learn to read and write their language "on the job." "I didn't have that practice of writing in my language," a PdH teacher acknowledged. Like other Diné teachers at PdH, this teacher learned Navajo literacy alongside her students in her first years of teaching at the school.

Further, given the fragile state of most Native American languages, students are likely to lack Native language models at home. Their primary exposure to the language is during school hours, a situation that is exacerbated over the summer months when school is in recess. PdH has addressed this with outreach to parents, providing resources such as the Rosetta Stone

Endangered Language Program in Navajo (Bittinger 2011) to assist parents in (re)learning the Diné language and encouraging their efforts to spend family time with elders who are the keepers of Diné language and traditions.

There are also the dual challenges of dialect differences and teaching academic content in children's second language. Although it is essential to provide consistent comprehensible input in the Indigenous language, it is equally important "not to just overwhelm kids and start speaking to them in Navajo, [expecting that they are] going to understand it," a PdH teacher pointed out (interview, November 3, 2009).

Perhaps the greatest challenge, however, is maintaining focus on the Indigenous language and culture in the face of withering pressures from high-stakes school accountability regimes. In particular, the 2001 No Child Left Behind Act (NCLB) has become a de facto language policy (Menken 2008; Wyman et al. 2010, 2011). As Fillerup (2005, 14) asks, "When teachers and administrators are threatened with school closures under NCLB, who has time to teach Navajo, Lakota, or Cheyenne?"

While PdH has been remarkably buoyant in the face of this challenge, not all Native American education programs have been so fortunate. The final sections of this chapter take up these issues, giving an overview of the research on the impact of high-stakes accountability testing on Native American learners and the ways in which those impacts are being addressed by Indigenous educators and their allies.

The Stakes in High-Stakes Testing

NCLB's (2001) stated goal is to eliminate achievement disparities experienced by low-income African American, Latino, and Native American students. A key question in assessing policy impacts, then, is whether those disparities have, in fact, been narrowed. For Native American students, a related question concerns the policy's impacts on educational programs and services, particularly the implementation of promising practices and strong Indigenous language and culture programs in keeping with tribal sovereignty and self-determination.

The recent National Indian Education Study (NIES) provides the largest data set (n = 10,000) within which to examine these issues. In the past two NIES cycles (2005 to 2007 and 2007 to 2009), mean National Assessment of Education Progress (NAEP) reading and mathematics scores for American Indian/Alaska Native fourth and eighth graders did not change significantly and in some cases declined (Grigg, Moran, and Kuang 2010; Moran et al. 2008; for a full discussion, see McCarty 2009b). The NIES data also suggest that the emphasis on high-stakes testing may lead schools to curtail or eliminate Native language and culture instruction.

Part II of the 2007 study (which was undertaken in 2005) surveyed 5,100 students, 1,300 teachers, and 470 principals in 550 schools serving Native students regarding curriculum, standards, and assessment (Stancavage et al. 2006). A key component of the survey was the extent to which the Native culture and language were incorporated into classroom instruction. Only 21 percent of fourth-grade students and 16 percent of eighth-grade students had teachers who reported daily or regular use of an Indigenous perspective in instruction.

At the same time, the large majority of teachers (81 to 90 percent) reported relying almost solely on state content standards for instruction. Of the 5,100 students queried, only 4 percent were learning how to speak and read their heritage language in school (Stancavage et al. 2006).

These findings are reinforced by a 2005 study carried out by the National Indian Education Association (NIEA). While welcoming the renewed emphasis on school accountability represented by NCLB, the NIEA found no evidence of student achievement gains as a result of the law. Further, the report expressed concern that the policy negatively impacts CBE and compromises tribal sovereignty (Beaulieu, Sparks, and Alonzo 2005, 4).

Research on NCLB (2001) implementation at the local school level is limited but growing, with a 2008 special issue of the *Journal of American Indian Education* devoted to this topic (McCarty 2008). Among the research reported in that volume is a study by Robert Patrick, an award-winning teacher-researcher who examined post-NCLB reforms at Warrior Elementary (a pseudonym).

At the time of Patrick's study, Warrior Elementary enrolled 359 K–5 students, the majority of whom were Navajo. Because the school had not met AYP, it faced imminent closure. As a result of personnel and curricular restructuring, Warrior Elementary was able to show test-score gains. Yet, as Patrick (2008) describes, those gains came at the cost of disinvestment in culturally relevant pedagogy, test administration improprieties, and community alienation.

In research among schools serving Yup'ik students in southwestern Alaska, Wyman and others (2010, 2011) document the ways in which high-stakes English-testing pressures "are intersecting with language shift in one of the few areas of the United States . . . where an Indigenous language is still spoken by children" (Wyman et al. 2010, 29). As this team of university- and school-based researchers shows, the majority of the schools in the Lower Kuskokwim School District that are meeting NCLB (2001) progress goals have Native language and culture programs that can be characterized as "strong" according to the criteria in table 8.4.

Yet NCLB (2001) "has created an atmosphere of overhanging anxiety about high-stakes testing," Wyman and others state, leading parents to shift from Yup'ik to English at home, promoting an ideology that "'Yup'ik holds children back from achieving in English,'" and causing reductions in Yup'ik language instruction (Wyman et al. 2010, 40). "Ironically," these subtractive language practices are intensifying "in spite of direct evidence that most . . . schools making AYP . . . have used Yup'ik consistently as a primary language of instruction" (Wyman et al. 2010, 40).

Tribal Sovereignty and the Promise of "Promising Practices"

This chapter has presented findings from empirical research on promising practices that incorporate Native American languages, cultures, and knowledges as core elements of the school curriculum. We have also explored the challenges to those practices emanating from a constellation of factors, most especially the pressures of high-stakes English standardized tests. I close with two additional examples that illustrate the ways in which these challenges are being addressed at the local level.

At Rough Rock, after having been nearly silenced by "school improvement" mandated by NCLB, the Navajo language and culture are being restored in the school's curriculum. According to former Rough Rock school superintendent Monty Roessel, under whose leadership these changes were instituted, while other schools "were focused on AYP, we decided to create a Navajo language immersion program . . . aligning our Navajo curriculum to our traditional ways of thought" (2011, 20). Not unlike the ways in which Diné educators at PdH adapted the Six Traits writing assessment to fit a Diné worldview, Rough Rock educators identified six stages associated with *dzil*, "meaning strength but also translated as sacred mountains" (Roessel 2011, 20). Roessel explains:

With this, as students develop through these six stages, it is believed that they would have a strong foundation of knowledge to plan and live their lives. We went deeper than our roots; we went to the beginnings of what it means to be Navajo. (2011, 20–21)

Although the school has not yet "made AYP," Roessel adds, "we are creating students who know their place in the world—as a Navajo and as an American" (2011, 21).

Similarly, in the Yup'ik villages served by Lower Kuskokwim School District, Yup'ik teacher-researchers have been reclaiming an Indigenous space within their schools, despite NCLB (2001) pressures, by identifying local human and material resources to reverse language loss. Wyman and her colleagues describe those resources:

> All 11 [village] sites . . . have Yup'ik-speaking adults, and vibrant spaces and activities in which most adult members of the community use Yup'ik. Sites have elementary-level Yup'ik language and content materials, and Yup'ik educators trained in language pedagogies and curriculum development. All village sites have at least some Yup'ik speaking children, and . . . an immersion school . . . is additionally demonstrating how strong bilingual education models . . . might foster language revitalization. (2010, 45)

Just as we saw for Puente de Hózhǫ, Wyman and others note the importance of collaboration among local Indigenous educators in marshalling local resources to resist the loss of local language and culture resources. Through their own action research, these educators have been documenting children's language use and proactively "focusing communities on language maintenance, highlighting the local possibilities for bilingualism" (Wyman et al. 2010, 45). In so doing, they have opened new "implementational and ideological spaces" (Hornberger 2006), creating new possibilities for language, culture, and education planning "in challenging times" (Wyman et al. 2010, 46).

These possibilities hinge on the ability of Native American communities to exercise sovereignty—"the inherent right of a people to self-government, self-determination, and self-education," including "the right to linguistic and cultural expression according to local languages and norms" (Lomawaima and McCarty 2006, 9). As Roessel (2011, 20) asserts, Indigenous-controlled education "is about creating the menu and not just selecting items from it. This can only happen if tribes exercise their sovereignty." Moreover, Roessel argues, "Indian education doesn't have to be a one-way choice. . . . Done correctly, it is a BOTH-AND" (2011, 23; emphasis in original).

These have been the lessons of the promising practices examined here: Academic achievement and Indigenous language and culture continuity are not an "either-or" proposition but can and should be an additive "both-and" combination that is eminently doable. The way to accomplish this, as the cases and the research examined here attest, is through policies and practices grounded in the wisdom of local Indigenous communities and intentionally designed to support "strong" language and culture program development.

REFERENCES

Ah Nee-Benham, M. K. P., and J. E. Cooper, eds. (2000). *Indigenous Education Models for Contemporary Practice: In our Mother's Voice*. Mahwah, NJ: Lawrence Erlbaum.

Ah Nee-Benham, M. K. P. (2008). *Indigenous Educational Models for Contemporary Practice: In Our Mother's Voice*. Vol. 2. New York: Routledge.

American Indian Policy Review Commission. (1976). *Report on Indian Education*. Washington, DC: U.S. Government Printing Office.

Assembly of Alaska Native Educators. (1998). *Alaska Standards for Culturally Responsive Schools*. Anchorage, AK: Alaska Native Knowledge Network.

———. (1999). *Guidelines for Preparing Culturally Responsive Teachers for Alaska's Schools*. Anchorage, AK: Alaska Native Knowledge Network.

———. (2001). *Guidelines for Nurturing Culturally Healthy Youth*. Anchorage, AK: Alaska Native Knowledge Network.

———. (2003). *Guidelines for Cross-cultural Orientation Programs*. Anchorage, AK: Alaska Native Knowledge Network.

Baker, C. (2006). *Foundations of Bilingual Education and Bilingualism*. 4th ed. Clevedon, UK: Multilingual Matters.

Baker, C., and S. P. Jones. (1998). *Encyclopedia of Bilingualism and Bilingual Education*. Clevedon, UK: Multilingual Matters.

Barnhardt, R., and A. O. Kawagley. (2005). "Indigenous knowledge systems and Alaska Native ways of knowing." *Anthropology and Education Quarterly* 36 (1): 8–23.

Beaulieu, D. L. (2003). *Descriptive Report of Culturally Based Education Programs*. Portland, OR: Northwest Regional Educational Laboratory.

———. (2006). "A survey and assessment of culturally based education programs for Native American students in the United States." *Journal of American Indian Education* 45 (2): 50–61.

Beaulieu, D., L. Sparks, and M. Alonzo. (2005). *Preliminary Report on No Child Left Behind in Indian Country*. Washington, DC: National Indian Education Association.

Begay, S., G. S. Dick, D. W. Estell, J. Estell, T. L. McCarty, and A. Sells. (1995). "Change from the inside out: A story of transformation in a Navajo community school." *Bilingual Research Journal* 19 (1): 121–39.

Bittinger, M. (2011). "Flutes, facts, and the future of the Navajo language." *Linguavore* (Rosetta Stone blog), January 12. Retrieved from http://blog.rosettastone.com/2011/01/12/flutes-facts-and-the-future-of-the-navajo-language/.

Brayboy, B. M. J., and A. E. Castagno. (2009). "Self-determination through self-education: Culturally responsive schooling for Indigenous students in the USA." *Teaching Education* 20 (1): 31–53.

Brayboy, B. M. J., S. C. Faircloth, T. S. Lee, M. J. Maaka, and T. Richardson. (2012). *Indigenous Education in the 21st Century*. Washington, DC: American Educational Research Association.

Castagno, A. E., and B. M. J. Brayboy. (2008). "Culturally responsive schooling for Indigenous youth: A review of the literature." *Review of Educational Research* 78 (4): 941–93.

Demmert, W. G., Jr. (2001). "Improving academic performance among Native American students: A review of the research literature." Charleston, WV: ERIC Clearinghouse on Rural Education and Small Schools.

Demmert, W. G., D. Grissmer, and J. Towner. (2006). "A review and analysis of the research on Native American students." *Journal of American Indian Education* 45 (3): 5–23.

Demmert, W. G., Jr., and J. Towner. (2003). "A review of the research literature on the influences of culturally based education on the academic performance of Native American students." Portland, OR: Northwest Regional Educational Laboratory. Retrieved from http://educationnorthwest.org/webfm_send/196.

DeVoe, J. F., K. E. Darling-Churchill, and T. D. Snyder. (2008). *Status and Trends in the Education of American Indians and Alaska Natives: 2008*. Washington, DC: National Center for Education Statistics, Institute of Education Sciences, U.S. Department of Education.

Deyhle, D., and K. G. Swisher. (1997). "Research in American Indian and Alaska Native education: From assimilation to self-determination." *Review of Research in Education* 22: 113–94.

Ernst, G., E. Statzner, and H. T. Trueba, guest eds. (1994). "Alternative visions of schooling: Success stories in minority settings." Theme issue, *Anthropology and Education Quarterly* 25 (3).

Executive Order no. 13096. (1998). "American Indian and Alaska Native education." *Federal Register* 63 (154): 42,681–684.

Executive Order no. 13336. (2004). "American Indian and Alaska Native education." *Federal Register* 69 (87): 25,295–297.

Fillerup, M. (2005). "Keeping up with the Yazzies: The impact of high stakes testing on Indigenous language programs." *Language Learner*, September/October: 14–18.

———. (2008). "Building bridges of beauty between the rich languages and cultures of the American Southwest: Puente de Hózhǫ Trilingual Magnet School." Retrieved from http://www.puentedehozho.org/puenteschool.htm.

———. (2011). "Building a 'bridge of beauty': A preliminary report on promising practices in Native language and culture teaching at Puente de Hózhǫ Trilingual Magnet School." In *Indigenous Languages Across the Generations—Strengthening Families and Communities*, ed. M. E. Romero-Little, S. J. Ortiz, T. L. McCarty, and R. Chen, 145–64. Tempe: Arizona State University Center for Indian Education.

Foley, D. E. (1996). "The silent Indian as a cultural production." In *The Cultural Production of the Educated Person: Critical Ethnographies of Schooling and Local Practice*, ed. B. A. Levinson, D. E. Foley, and D. C. Holland, 79–91. Albany: State University of New York Press.

Genesee, F., ed. (1994). *Educating Second Language Children: The Whole Child, the Whole Curriculum, the Whole Community*. Cambridge, UK: Cambridge University Press.

Grigg, W., R. Moran, and M. Kuang. (2010). *National Indian Education Study. Part I: Performance of American Indian and Alaska Native Students at Grades 4 and 8 on NAEP 2009 Reading and Mathematics Assessments* (NCES 2010-462). Washington, DC: National Center for Education Statistics, Institute of Education Sciences, U.S. Department of Education.

Hartley, E., and P. Johnson. (1995). "Toward a community-based transition to a Yup'ik first language (immersion) program with ESL component." *Bilingual Research Journal* 19 (3 and 4): 571–85.

Hermes, M. (2005). "Ma'iingan is just a misspelling of the word wolf: A case for teaching culture through language." *Anthropology and Education Quarterly* 36 (1): 43–56.

———. (2006). "Moving toward the language: Reflections on teaching in an Indigenous-immersion school." *Journal of American Indian Education* 46 (3): 54–71.

Hinton, L. (2001). "An introduction to the Hawaiian language." In *The Green Book of Language Revitalization in Practice*, ed. L. Hinton and K. Hale, 129–31. San Diego: Academic.

Holm, A., and W. Holm. (1990). "Rock Point, a Navajo way to go to school: A valediction." *Annals, AAPSS* 508: 170–84.

———. (1995). "Navajo language education: Retrospect and prospects." *Bilingual Research Journal* 19 (1): 141–67.

Holm, W. (2006). "The 'goodness' of bilingual education for Native American children." In *One Voice, Many Voices—Recreating Indigenous Language Communities*, ed. T. L. McCarty and O. Zepeda, with V. H. Begay, S. Charging Eagle, S. C. Moore, L. Warhol, and T. M. K. Williams, 1–46. Tempe: Arizona State University Center for Indian Education.

Hornberger, N. H. (2006). "*Nichols* to *NCLB*: Local and global perspectives on U.S. language education policy." In *Imagining Multilingual Schools: Languages in Education and Glocalization*, eds. O. Garcia, T. Skutnabb-Kangas, and M. Torres-Guzman, 223–237. Clevedon, UK: Multilingual Matters.

Indian Nations at Risk Task Force. (1991). *Indian Nations at Risk: An Educational Strategy for Action.* Washington, DC: U.S. Department of Education.

Jacob, E., and C. Jordan, eds. (1993). *Minority Education: Anthropological Perspectives.* Norwood, NJ: Ablex.

Klug, B. J., and P. T. Whitfield. (2003). *Widening the Circle: Culturally Relevant Pedagogy for American Indian Children.* New York: RoutledgeFalmer.

Lipka, J., M. P. Hogan, J. P. Webster, E. Yanez, B. Adams, S. Clark, and D. Lacy. (2005). "Math in a Cultural Context: Two case studies of a successful culturally based math project." *Anthropology and Education Quarterly* 36 (4): 367–85.

Lipka, J., N. Sharp, B. Adams, and E. Yanez. (2007). "Creating a third space for authentic biculturalism: Examples from Math in a Cultural Context." *Journal of American Indian Education* 46 (3): 94–115.

Lomawaima, K. T., and T. L. McCarty. (2006). *To Remain an Indian: Lessons in Democracy from a Century of Native American Education.* New York: Teachers College Press.

May, S., ed. (1999). *Indigenous Community-based Education.* Clevedon, UK: Multilingual Matters.

McCardle, P., and W. Demmert, guest eds. (2006a). "Report of a national colloquium, I—programs and practices. Improving academic performance among American Indian, Alaska Native, and Native Hawaiian students." Special issue, *Journal of American Indian Education* 45 (2).

———, guest eds. (2006b). "Report of a national colloquium, I—research. Improving academic performance among American Indian, Alaska Native, and Native Hawaiian students." Special issue, *Journal of American Indian Education* 45 (3).

McCarty, T. L. (2002). *A Place to be Navajo—Rough Rock and the Struggle for Self-determination in Indigenous Schooling.* Mahwah, NJ: Lawrence Erlbaum.

———, guest ed. (2008). "American Indian, Alaska Native, and Native Hawaiian Education in the era of standardization and NCLB." Special issue, *Journal of American Indian Education* 47.

———. (2009a). *State of the Field: The Role of Native Languages and Cultures in American Indian, Alaska Native, and Native Hawaiian Students' Academic Achievement.* Policy paper prepared for the Promising Practices and Partnerships in Indian Education Working Group and the U.S. Department of Education Office of Indian Education Programs, under contract to Kauffman and Associates, Spokane, WA.

———. (2009b). "The impact of high-stakes accountability policies on Native American learners: Evidence from research." *Teaching Education* 20 (1): 7–29.

McCarty, T. L., and G. S. Dick. (2003). "Telling The People's stories: Literacy practices and processes in a Navajo community school." In *Multicultural Issues in Literacy Research and Practice*, ed. A. I. Willis, G. E. García, R. Barrera, and V. J. Harris, 101–12. Mahwah, NJ: Lawrence Erlbaum.

McCarty, T. L., J. Lipka, and G. S. Dick, guest eds. (1994). "Local knowledge in Indigenous schooling: Case studies in American Indian /Alaska Native education." Special issue, *Journal of American Indian Education* 33 (3).

McCarty, T. L., W. Wallace, R. Hadley Lynch, and A. Benally. (1991). "Classroom inquiry and Navajo learning styles: A call for reassessment." *Anthropology and Education Quarterly* 22 (1): 42–59.

McLaughlin, D. (1995). "Strategies for enabling bilingual program development in American Indian schools." *Bilingual Research Journal* 19 (1): 169–78.

Mead, N., W. Grigg, R. Moran, and M. Kuang. (2010). *National Indian Education Study 2009. Part II: The Educational Experiences of American Indian and Alaska Native Students in Grades 4 and 8.* Washington, DC: National Center for Education Statistics, Institute of Education Sciences, U.S. Department of Education.

Menken, K. (2008). *English Learners Left Behind: Standardized Testing as Language Policy.* Clevedon, UK: Multilingual Matters.

Meriam, L., R. A. Brown, H. Roe Cloud, E. E. Dale, E. Duke, H. R. Edwards, F. A. McKenzie, M. L. Mark, W. C. Ryan, and W. J. Spillman. (1928). *The Problem of Indian Administration*. Baltimore: Johns Hopkins Press for the Institute for Government Research.

Moran, R., B. D. Rampey, G. Dion, and P. Donahue. (2008). *National Indian Education Study 2007. Part I: Performance of American Indian and Alaska Native Students at Grades 4 and 8 on NAEP 2007 Reading and Mathematics Assessments* (NCES 2008-457). Washington, DC: National Center for Education Statistics, Institute of Education Sciences, U.S. Department of Education.

Nelson-Barber, S., and J. Lipka. (2008). "Rethinking the case for culture-based curriculum: Conditions that support improved mathematics performance in diverse classrooms." In *Language, Culture, and Community in Teacher Education*, ed. M. E. Brisk, 99–123. Mahwah, NJ: Lawrence Erlbaum.

No Child Left Behind Act of 2001: Reauthorication of the Elementary and Secondary Education Act of 1965 (NCLB). *U.S. code*. Title 20, sec. 6301 et seq.

Patrick, R. (2008). "Perspectives on change: A continued struggle for academic success and cultural relevancy at an American Indian School in the midst of No Child Left Behind." *Journal of American Indian Education* 47 (1): 65–81.

Peha, S. (1995–2003). *Assessing Writers, Assessing Writing*. Retrieved from http://www.ttms.org/PDFs/09%20Writing%20Assessment%20v001%20(Full).pdf.

Roessel, M. (2011). "Preserving the past to secure the future: The Center for Indian Education—the next 50 years." *Journal of American Indian Education* 50 (2): 13–23.

Rosier, P., and M. Farella. (1976). "Bilingual education at Rock Point—some early results." *TESOL Quarterly* 10 (4): 379–88.

Skutnabb-Kangas, T., and T. L. McCarty. (2008). "Key concepts in bilingual education: Ideological, historical, epistemological, and empirical foundations." In *Bilingual Education*. Vol. 5 of *Encyclopedia of Language and Education*, ed. J. Cummins and N. H. Hornberger, 3–17. New York: Springer.

Stancavage, F. B., J. H. Mitchell, V. P. Bandeira de Mello, F. E. Gaertner, A. K. Spain, and M. L. Rahal. (2006). *National Indian Education Study. Part II: The Educational Experiences of Fourth- and Eighth-grade American Indian and Alaska Native Students* (NCES 2007–454). Washington, DC: National Center for Education Statistics, U.S. Department of Education, U.S. Government Printing Office.

Thomas, W. P., and V. Collier. (1997). *School Effectiveness for Language Minority Students*. Washington, DC: National Clearinghouse for Bilingual Education.

U.S. Congress. Senate Committee on Labor and Public Welfare. Special Subcommittee on Indian Education. (1969). *Indian Education: A National Tragedy—A National Challenge*. 91st Cong., 1st sess. S. Rep. 91–501.

Vogt, L. A., C. Jordan, and R. G. Tharp. (1993). "Explaining school failure, producing school success: Two cases." In *Minority Education: Anthropological Perspectives*, ed. E. Jacob and C. Jordan, 53–65. Norwood, NJ: Ablex.

Warner, S. L. N. (2001). "The movement to revitalize Hawaiian language and culture." In *The Green Book of Language Revitalization in Practice*, ed. L. Hinton and K. Hale, 133–44. San Diego: Academic.

Webster, J. P., and E. Yanez. (2007). "*Qanemcikarluni tekitnarqelartuq* [One must arrive with a story to tell]: Traditional Alaska Native Yup'ik Eskimo stories in a culturally based math curriculum." *Journal of American Indian Education* 46 (3): 116–31.

Wilson, W. H. (2008). "Language fluency, accuracy, and revernacularization in different models of immersion." *NIEA News* 39 (2): 40–42.

Wilson, W. H., and K. Kamanā. (2001). "'Mai loko mai o ka 'i 'ini: Proceeding from a dream.' The 'Aha Pūnana Leo connection in Hawaiian language revitalization." In *The Green Book of Language Revitalization in Practice*, ed. L. Hinton and K. Hale, 147–76. San Diego: Academic.

———. (2006). "For the interest of the Hawaiians themselves: Reclaiming the benefits of Hawaiian-medium education." *Hūlili: Multidisciplinary Research on Hawaiian Well-Being* 3 (1): 153–81. Retrieved from http://www.ahapunanaleo.org.

Wyman, L., P. Marlow, F. C. Andrew, G. S. Miller, R. C. Nicholai, and N. Y. Rearden. (2010). "Focusing on long-term language goals in challenging times: A Yup'ik example." *Journal of American Indian Education* 49 (1 and 2): 28–49.

———. (2011). "Focusing communities and schools on Indigenous language maintenance: A Yup'ik example." In *Indigenous Languages Across the Generations—Strengthening Families and Communities*, ed. M. E. Romero-Little, S. J. Ortiz, T. L. McCarty, and R. Chen, 262–80. Tempe: Arizona State University Center for Indian Education.

Yap, K. O. (2004). *Experimental Research in Culturally Based Education: An Assessment of Feasibility*. Final report submitted to the Institute of Education Sciences, U.S. Department of Education. Portland, OR: Northwest Regional Laboratory.

———. (2005). *Preliminary Study for Experimental Research on Culturally Based Education for American Indian / Alaska Native Students*. Research symposium. Report submitted to the Institute of Education Sciences, U.S. Department of Education. Portland, OR: Northwest Regional Educational Laboratory.

Yazzie-Mintz, T. (2007). "From a place deep inside: Culturally appropriate curriculum as the embodiment of Navajo-ness in classroom pedagogy." *Journal of American Indian Education* 46 (3): 72–93.

NOTES

1. The national working group was led by Dr. Bryan McKinley Jones Brayboy of Arizona State University and included (in addition to myself) Dr. Angelina Castagno (Northern Arizona University), Dr. Amy Fann (University of North Texas), Dr. Susan Faircloth (Pennsylvania State University), and Dr. Sharon Nelson-Barber (Pacific Resources for Education and Learning). The group's work was undertaken through a contract from the U.S. Office of Indian Education Programs with Kauffman and Associates, Inc. of Spokane, WA. I thank colleagues on the working group and KAI staff members Susie Amundson and Andy Leija for their support of the research reported here.

2. The research team for the PdH study consisted of myself as principal investigator and Bryan Brayboy as co-PI; Erin Nolan and Kristin Monahan Silver served as the study's graduate research assistants. Although no individual teacher names are used in the reporting of this study, the school and the district gave permission to use the school's actual name.

3. I thank Dr. William H. Wilson (pers. comm., September 8, 2008) for the insights on the percentage of instructional time needed to attain genuine bilingualism, biliteracy, and bi-/multiculturalism. Noting that many people assume that Indigenous language fluency is "fairly easy to maintain with a half-day program," he points out that the Hawaiian experience shows that "English is extremely strong [because of its privileged status in the larger society] and will be learned even under circumstances where a strong academic program is provided through the 'nationally weaker' language"—a finding congruent with students of French-English immersion in Canada and heritage-language immersion in other parts of the world. For more on these points, see Wilson (2008).

Part III

Exploring the Possibilities

Visions of the Future for Indigenous Education

President Barack Obama's recent executive order, "Improving American Indian and Alaska Native Educational Opportunities and Strengthening Tribal Colleges and Universities" (Executive Order no. 13592 2011), again reiterates the necessity of including American Indian languages and cultures in the education of Native students. How this will actually be carried out in public schools across the nation will be important to the future success, or lack of success if this directive is ignored, of all of our American Indian students.

The failure of No Child Left Behind (2001) in schools with high American Indian populations has been well documented (Lee 2012; National Indian Education Association 2005, 2009). As Common Core State Standards proposed by the National Governors Association Center for Best Practices, Council of Chief State School Officers (2010) are adopted by states throughout the country (USC Rossier School of Education 2011), the question remains concerning how to best educate American Indian students without forcing them into the same types of educational experiences that have failed Native students in the past.

In this section, we are introduced to several promising practices and information concerning the needs of American Indian administrators in tribal schools. We also introduce you to the past work of prominent tribal members throughout the country who have been leaders in the movement to precipitate changes in American Indian education at all levels.

In chapter 9, McCarthy and Johnson discuss the groundbreaking work of the Accelerated Schools Project (ASP), which was chosen by those involved with Navajo education for a school district located in Nevada. Some of the challenges, as well as the rewards, of instituting such a system are explored in this chapter with information concerning the effects of this partnership on all the stakeholders involved.

What can we do to ensure that new teachers and those already teaching are prepared to educate American Indian students in ways that allow them to succeed to their highest capabilities? Putney describes an approach that builds on the constructivist philosophies and work of John Dewey, Lev S. Vygotsky, and Paulo Freire to advance educational successes for Native students in chapter 10. Jaime and Rush, in chapter 11, describe a program for teacher preparation designed especially for those who will be working with high American Indian populations.

How does American Indian leadership in tribal schools differ from that in public or private educational settings? Nuby explores this issue in chapter 12, giving readers insights into challenges Native and non-Native administrators may face that are considered relevant as part of their administration-preparation programs.

Who are the American Indian leaders—past and present—who have made impacts in education for Native students, and why do we need American Indian leaders to continue as the voices in education of Native students? In chapter 13, Chavers presents us with a comprehensive list of past and present leaders in education for American Indian students and tells us of their accomplishments and impacts on the field. As educators, what are we doing to ensure that the next generation of leaders is being prepared for their roles in our schools?

The *National Tribal Priorities for Indian Education* issued jointly by the National Congress of American Indians and the National Indian Education Association (2010) details the importance of more involvement from tribes and tribal communities in the education of Native students in order to ensure that they will be receiving an education that is compatible with their needs.

Through this section, we hope to offer information to readers that may be utilized in the course of exploring ways to fill these priorities in order to make education for our Native students as content-rich, challenging, and successful academically and as emotionally, socially, physically, and spiritually appropriate as possible. In other words, we hope to return to the idea of providing education to our youth that is devoted to teaching the "whole child."

REFERENCES

Executive Order no. 13592. (2011). "Improving American Indian and Alaska Native educational opportunities and strengthening tribal colleges and universities." *Federal Register* 76 (236): 76,603–607.

Lee, T. (2012). "No Child Left Behind Act: A Bust in Indian Country." *Indian Country Today Media Network*, March 7. Retrieved from http:// indiancountrytodaymedianetwork.com/2012/03/07/101597-101597.

National Congress of American Indians and National Indian Education Association. (2010). *National Tribal Priorities for Indian Education*. Washington, DC: National Congress of American Indians and National Indian Education Association. http://www.niea.org/data/files/policy/ncai_niea_joint_priorities_revised_13july2010.pdf.

National Governors Association Center for Best Practices, Council of Chief State School Officers. (2010). *Common Core State Standards*. Washington, DC: National Governors Association Center for Best Practices, Council of Chief State School Officers. Retrieved from http://www.corestandards.org/the-standards.

National Indian Education Association. (2005). *Preliminary Report: No Child Left Behind in Indian Country*. Washington, DC: Author. Retrieved from http://www.niea.org/data/files/policy /nieanclbpublication.pdf.

National Indian Education Association. (2009). *Testimony of Robert B. Cook President, National Indian Education Association, before the Senate Committee on Indian Affairs on the President's FY 2010 Budget Request March 12, 2009*. Washington, DC: Author. Retrieved from http://www.indian.senate.gov/public/_files/RobertCooktestimony.pdfhttp://www.niea.org/policy/policy-resources.aspx.

No Child Left Behind Act of 2001 (NCLB). *U.S. code*. Title 20, sec. 6301 et seq.

USC Rossier School of Education. (2011). *Common Core Standards Initiative—Towards a National Curriculum*. Retrieved from http://www.edinformatics.com/curriculum/common_core_standards.htm.

Chapter 9

Who Speaks for the American Indian?

Jane McCarthy: University of Nevada, Las Vegas, and
Helene Johnson: Navajo Nation, Nevada

ABSTRACT

Much has been written about the instructional needs of Indigenous students. We have heard about culturally responsive pedagogy, teaching to Native learning styles, incorporating Indigenous history into curriculum, standards for curriculum design, and so forth. There are many people who know "what should be done" with regard to the education of American Indian students, including the federal government and state legislatures. There are some voices missing from the dialogue, however: Indigenous peoples are *spoken for*, not spoken with, in regard to their dreams for the education of their children.

This chapter centers on the need of a school district located on the Navajo Reservation to answer questions concerning (a) the best educational practices for their students and (b) how to incorporate these practices for their students, staffs, and community. As the authors explore the possibilities of different programmatic approaches and their match to Navajo philosophy, they determine that one program appears to offer the closest match in order to meet these needs.

Jane McCarthy is brought into the community and introduced to Navajo philosophy, lifeways, and traditions and brings with her the expertise needed for the systemic initiative adopted. Written in first person from the eyes of McCarthy, a rich description of the institution of a new program and way of working within the Navajo community emerges. Helene Johnson is behind the scenes as a participant and informant in this journey.

WHO SPEAKS FOR THE AMERICAN INDIAN?

Ten years ago, as I sat in my house in the teacher housing sector of a school district on the Navajo Reservation, it was about 8 pm, and the wind was blowing across the mesa at seventy miles per hour. The lights were flickering, but so far there were no outages. The red sand was coming in around the windows, and a pile had formed on the stove where it had come down the air hood.

I found myself wondering just how securely this modular house was anchored into the ground. Would Rez Babe (my adopted Navajo dog, named by my Navajo friends) and I make a trip to Oz like Dorothy and Toto? One of my neighbors had just told me that this wind was nothing; I should have been here when it was going ninety miles per hour.

Life on the Navajo Reservation is hard. Although the high desert is beautiful, with astonishing geological formations and vistas of reds and golds and whites, the weather is harsh, and the resources are few. While I was snugly tucked away in teacher housing, I wondered about our students and their families living in the hogans on the remote stretches of land.

There are occasional no-school days because of mud—the rain turns the dirt roads into quagmires, and the buses can't get down them to pick up the kids. The school district buses travel 2,200 miles per day, 1,800 of which are on dirt roads.

There are approximately one hundred students who live in the Bureau of Indian Education (BIE) dormitories during the week because they live more than sixty miles out from school, the limit of the bus service. Students can spend upward of two hours each way on buses every day. There are sometimes snow storms so severe that the Navajo Nation must use planes to drop food for people and livestock.

Many of our students live in homes without electricity or running water. Water must be hauled in large tanks from pumping stations several miles away. Although some progress is being made in supplying these utilities, many areas must still do without. Some are turning to solar energy, but it is expensive.

Navajo people do not typically live in villages. They live on large tracts of land in rural areas where clan members live in proximity to each other. The land is sacred to the Navajo, and village living in the funded public-housing developments does not often work out well. In spite of the hardships, the people love the land, and many would not choose to leave for the conveniences of town or city living.

The school district is a public school district affiliated with the state. The residents decided to break away from the BIE (then the Bureau of Indian Affairs) system in the 1970s and form their own district so that they could have more local input into the way the schools were run. It was a brave thing to do at the time, and the transition was successful. Early community leaders were determined that they would be empowered to lead their own way into the future.

This determination exists to this day, as will be discussed in more detail. There is a five-member Navajo governing board for the district, and all members are Navajo. There are currently three schools in the district—elementary, middle, and high school—and slightly more than 1,300 students.

I arrived in teacher housing in June 2002, driving my son's six-year-old four-wheel drive. The dirt road was in such bad shape that my car battery was jolted loose, and all the acid drained out. I experienced how difficult it is to get car repairs on the reservation. Yes, AAA does come out, but it took them three hours, and they broke down on the way as well. The trip to the village takes six-and-a-half hours from Las Vegas if the dirt roads are passable. If not, you must go the long way on roads that are paved but, in many places, not much better than the dirt roads. This trip takes more than eight hours.

There are other difficulties for people living in this area. The nearest medical care for Anglos is two hours away. Care recently became a bit more available for Navajo residents with the building of a new public health clinic in town. However, it is not a twenty-four-hour facility. Navajo Nation helicopters and planes still must provide transportation to larger medical centers. It takes more than two hours for ambulances to reach the area.

Mail delivery (it took two weeks to get a letter from my sister in San Francisco), Internet and telephone access, and shopping are also challenges. The nearest shopping mall is a two-hour drive away. Life in this village is truly remote. As one of the elders told me, "When you come here, you fall off the end of the earth."

Many people have asked me how I came to be in a school district on the Navajo Reservation. In reality, the district found me. In 1998, the middle school was looking for a national school reform project to adopt, and as they reviewed projects on the Internet, they found the Accelerated Schools Project (ASP). I am the regional director of this project, housed at the College of Education at the University of Nevada, Las Vegas (UNLV). Upon further investigation, the team from the middle school determined that our project most closely matched the Navajo philosophy of life and education.

The school contacted me and asked if we would consider working with them. I invited a team of teachers to come visit some of our schools in Las Vegas that were implementing the project. A team of twelve teachers, Navajo and Anglo, came to visit and went home to tell the rest of the school what they had seen and learned. Our project requires at least 90 percent buy-in on the part of the school community before we engage with them, and they received 100 percent buy-in back home.

This was truly an important step in self-determination for this school. The school community was empowered by the district superintendent to do the research and select a project that best met their needs. Many told me that this was the first time they had ever made a decision like this that would impact the future of the school. The school received three years of federal funding to help them start the reform process.

The school district had extremely low test scores and high dropout rates. The teachers and school community were searching for a way to provide their students with a meaningful educational experience that would both honor their culture and traditions and give them opportunities for success in life. Thus we began a process of collaboration and cooperation between a rural Navajo school district and a major urban university that has lasted for fourteen years.

The Accelerated Schools Project

What is the Accelerated Schools Project (ASP), and why did the Navajo school believe it was a match for the Navajo philosophy? The Accelerated Schools model for school reform is designed to facilitate school restructuring that builds on the strengths of every member of the school community. Changes are made in curriculum, instruction, and organization that support increased student academic achievement (Hopfenberg et al. 1993; Levin 1987a, 1987b, 1988).

The mismatch between the knowledge and skills students bring to learning situations and what the school expects them to know and be able to do frequently leads to disastrous results, placing children in at-risk situations (Hopfenberg et al. 1993). The situation of "at-riskness" occurs especially for children who are not from mainstream middle-class society but may occur for any student whose life experiences do not match those depicted in the homogenized curriculum materials adopted by states and school districts.

The definition of "at-riskness" as a situation and not as a personal deficit or characteristic of the learner especially resonated with the teachers from the Navajo school. This was one of the reasons that this particular program was chosen for the school district.

The Accelerated Schools process is a collaborative decision-making model developed by Henry M. Levin at Stanford University in 1986. Levin had done studies of federally funded compensatory education projects around the country and found that, after three years, few were still in existence and fewer still had achieved any significant results in improving the academic achievement of students who were at the time labeled as "disadvantaged."

Levin developed a collaborative decision-making process that utilizes the skills and knowledge of the entire school community to investigate challenges and propose solutions using what he termed the "inquiry process" (Levin 1987b). The development of a shared vision guides the actions of the school.

This collaborative process is similar to the one used by the Navajos in their own personal lives and in their governing structures. In this process, the voice of each participant is heard as decisions are made that are designed to move the school toward its vision. These activities engender a sense of ownership and empowerment at the local level.

Levin believes that all students have the right to an enriched and rigorous educational experience and that for students in at-risk situations, learning needs to be sped up, not slowed down by remedial programs that do not work. Hence the term "Accelerated Schools" was born (Levin 1987a). The notion of providing gifted education strategies for all students and having high expectations was blended with the notion of building on the strengths of all learners and honoring the experiences and knowledge they bring with them to the learning situation. This especially resonated with the teachers from the Navajo school.

The ASP began with two pilot schools in the San Francisco area. The success of these schools brought about a large grant from the Chevron Corporation to expand the project. The senior author, McCarthy, was hired to lead this expansion and worked with universities across the nation that were located in areas of high poverty. In 1991, the project expanded to the University of Nevada, Las Vegas, when it opened as a regional center with myself as director.

Thus, the middle school selected ASP as their school reform model because of the match between the Navajo philosophy and the Accelerated Schools philosophy. The other two schools in the district were excited by the successes of the middle school and joined the project two years later. The district is now an Accelerated Schools district wide project.

Native Students and Dominant-Culture Teachers

When I arrived on the reservation for my sabbatical in 2002, I was placed on the district administrative team. I met with all the principals and administrators, and we discussed the challenges of recruiting and retaining teachers. I shared some of my observations as an outsider; I heard the teachers saying things like, "I just don't understand these kids. They never raise their hands or participate in class; they won't speak." Or "These kids won't look me in the eye when I speak to them."

Others talked about the Navajo teachers in similar ways, saying, "These Navajo teachers never speak up in meetings; they never take the lead; we are forced to run the meetings and make all the decisions." I actually observed this happening at meetings. In Navajo culture, there is a wait time after someone speaks as a sign of respect and to be sure the person is finished speaking. The Anglo teachers are nervous with silence and will rush in to fill it, just as they do with short wait time when asking questions in the classroom.

There was little or no knowledge of the impact of Native culture on behavior in the classroom or at meetings. According to Champagne (2006, 149), it is common for Native student behavior in schools to be misinterpreted because "respect and social interaction, or even modes of learning, are different in Native communities" from the majority culture. Native students are expected to adapt to the mainstream culture while few efforts are made to accommodate their culture.

A lived experience in Navajo life. Since there is a high rate of teacher turnover in the schools, there are always a large number of new teachers coming to the district each fall, mostly Anglo or Asian. More than half of the teachers are non-Native. I suggested that we might create a crash cultural-immersion experience for new teachers that year.

This idea was enthusiastically embraced by the administrators, and of course, I was nominated to head up the adventure. When I protested that I was not Navajo, they reminded me that I had been adopted into several clans and that they would all help me.

The Navajo administrators produced a notebook of cultural materials for new teachers to read. It explained the most important aspects of the culture that might impact the behaviors the teachers would see exhibited in the classrooms and steps they could take to be sure they were not being culturally insensitive.

It was decided that we would take the new teachers on a bus tour of a common bus route so that they could see where the students lived and how difficult it was for students to get to school each day. The Navajo elementary school principal drew up the bus route; we booked a bus and driver; and on the appointed day, twenty-seven new teachers, the Navajo Dean of Students, the Navajo Title III coordinator, and the Anglo university professor set off on our cultural tour.

At first, everything went well. The teachers were eagerly perusing their booklets, our Native guides were pointing out spots of interest, and the new teachers were bonding.

Then the bus driver, a Navajo woman, said "Uh oh!" As a teacher, this is a term I do not like to hear. I asked her what was wrong, and she simply pointed at the distant hills, where dark clouds were forming.

Since it was clear with sunny skies where we were, I did not see the problem. She pointed to the road ahead of the bus where there appeared to be a dry wash. She stopped the bus, and the dry wash was soon filled with a rushing torrent of water—the first flash flood I had ever seen but apparently not uncommon on the reservation. The force of the water was terrifying. If she had not stopped the bus, we would surely have been washed away.

The driver quickly turned the bus around with great difficulty on the narrow dirt road and hurried back the way we had come. She explained that she was trying to get to the other wash before the flood, but unfortunately the road was already engulfed when we got there.

The new teachers thought this was a great adventure and exited the bus to watch the raging water. My two Navajo friends, however, explained that these floods can last for several hours, and even after they subside, the road may be washed out. The driver couldn't reach the district offices because the mountains were in the way of transmission. My cell phone was not in service in this area, either. We were faced with the prospect of sitting by the side of the road for hours with no food or water until someone came looking for us.

My friend Regina, the Title III coordinator, told us that her family hogan and land were up the hill on a side road between the two floods. Although she had no electricity or running water, she had water tanks and some food. She thought that her hogan, only seven years old, was spacious enough to hold all of us if we had to spend the night.

So the big yellow school bus made its way up the hill on a narrow dirt road. We passed Regina's seventy-nine-year-old Aunt Mary out on the land with her sheep and sheep dogs, as she was every day. She looked puzzled to see us but waved as we went by. We passed the one-hundred-year-old hogan where Regina had been married and arrived at her more modern hogan. The teachers got a tour of the property and learned what life is like on family lands for many students. They saw the outhouse, the outdoor cooking facilities, and the horses, sheep, and cattle.

They saw the water tanks that had to be hauled from twenty miles away each week. Regina spoke to them about traditional lifestyle and values. The teachers loved it. They asked lots of questions and learned about the life of their students in a hands-on manner.

Several hours later, we decided to drive back down the hill and see if the floods had let up. They had not. I stood on the seat of the bus and was able to get through on my cell phone. I found out that the superintendent and business manager were on the way with hip boots and shovels and the district grader that would try to pull us out across the flood. I looked at the raging water and washed-out road and decided I would probably not be on the bus if that happened.

A district pickup truck and two men appeared on the other side of the wash, but all they could do was wave at us. Finally, the bus driver said it had let up enough that she thought she could make it across the wash. She gunned it and drove across—almost. The wheels got stuck, and we were being pulled by the current. The men in the truck hooked a chain to the bumper of the bus and pulled us across the rest of the way. Just as we got to the other side, the superintendent showed up with the grader. Everyone cheered, and the bus went on its way.

The culminating activity was to be a meal of Navajo fry bread back at the district, prepared by other teachers. We got there, hot, tired, and hungry, and followed our noses down the hall. We arrived to find the room empty with only dirty pans left. The teachers had given up on our returning any time soon and had eaten our meal! Regina and I just looked at each other. I had passed my fry-bread-maker test last spring, so we got out the supplies and began making some more.

We gave the teachers pieces of dough to shape and let them make and eat their own fry bread. They also learned a bit about the history of fry bread, the Navajo Long Walk, and the change in diet that occurred during the Navajo imprisonment at Bosque Redondo. The experience had ended up being a powerful cultural immersion in more ways than one.

How one experience becomes an opportunity for others. The results of our experience were numerous. Teachers gained an understanding of the culture they would be living and working in and the values of the people. They could now visualize where their students went each day after school and the difficulty of doing homework by kerosene lantern. They understood how difficult it was for their students to get to school in bad weather—even walking from the hogan to the road for the bus could be a huge challenge.

The project was so popular that it has been continued each school year since then. The teachers have taken ownership of the experience and serve as mentors to the new teachers. Unity of purpose is easier to attain when all are seeing through the same lens.

Powerful Learning for All Students

The cornerstone of Levin's dream was that each student would receive a rich and stimulating educational experience in an environment that held high standards for all. The school district, with the collaboration of Accelerated Schools and the district curriculum director, provided professional development in best practices in instruction and assessment.

Cadres worked on challenge areas (n.b., the term "challenge areas" is part of the Accelerated Schools lexicon) and addressed areas of instructional strengths and challenges. Data are constantly analyzed and disaggregated, and instruction is focused. Teachers develop ways to teach that are culturally based and incorporate topics relevant to Navajo students.

Several researchers have written guides to offering instructionally relevant curriculum and instruction for American Indian students (Klug and Whitfield 2003; Reyhner 1992). Most recommend making instruction culturally relevant, providing instruction that matches the learning styles of Indian students, and empowering students as learners. All of these are considered practices that are integral to powerful learning, and our teachers are striving to implement them.

Unfortunately, not all teachers are comfortable teaching in what are new and different ways for them. Not all have high expectations for all learners. Not all know how to differentiate for the diversity of learners in their classrooms. So the process is ongoing. A dissertation by one of my doctoral students at UNLV, William Young (2009), looked at the teaching strategies employed by teachers in classrooms in a large urban school district with a fairly high percentage of American Indian students.

Young (2009) found that there were indeed teachers who did not hold high expectations for Indian students and thus provided a different quality of instruction for them. He also found that there were teachers who held high expectations for all their students and differentiated instruction to enable students to achieve. We find the same diversity of attitudes exist in the reservation schools.

One of the most impressive powerful learning products developed was the unit of study about the Navajo Long Walk, produced by two Navajo middle school teachers, Emma and Laura. The unit was multidisciplinary and included hands-on activities, such as cooking traditional Navajo foods, studying plant life of the area, learning the history of Kit Carson's raids and imprisonment of the Navajo, measuring distances for the walk, and studying the importance of sheep to the life of the Navajo and what the effects were of the slaughter of their sheep and the destruction and burning of their crops.

Parent permission had to be secured for the teaching of the unit because the traditional culture does not encourage talking about history and people who have died. Thus, few students knew much about the event and the bravery and resilience of their people. The parents enthusiastically gave permission and even participated in the unit by giving demonstrations to the students of Native crafts and tools used during that time.

The culminating experience was a trip along the route of the Long Walk—some four hundred miles. The student attendance record was at an all-time high during this unit. They designed T-shirts to commemorate the Long Walk. Teachers like Emma and Laura are helping students become proud of their heritage. The academic achievement of the participating students was the highest among all sixth graders that year, proving that learning can be interactive, culturally relevant, engaging, and rigorous at the same time. Problem-solving activities can lead students to desire to learn needed basic skills.

Teacher Turnover on the Navajo Reservation

One of the challenges of our school district is the high rate of teacher turnover. The schools are in a remote location, and it is a difficult adjustment for some teachers to make. With up to one-third of the teachers being new to the district each year, the challenges of professional development are huge. The district is struggling with finding solutions for retaining teachers. It seems that some of the schools are making progress with action items like mentoring programs and social activities, such as hiking and exploring the scenic wonders of the area, and so forth.

Teachers are being hired based on their willingness to work in an Accelerated School and to teach in powerful ways. The teacher accountability system is becoming more rigorous. The goal is for all students to have access to powerful learning strategies.

Traditional Ways of Knowing and Teaching

Our second author, Helene, says that one of the problems with the instruction utilized in schools is that it does not mirror the traditional Navajo way of education where girls are instructed by females and males are instructed by males, where children learn by doing and imitating the adults, where the culture is transmitted along with the basic skills for living, and where certain things are only taught during certain seasons.

How can these cultural practices be implemented in public schools with accountability measures for teaching and testing state curricular standards? A number of authors in this book and elsewhere have documented the problems that No Child Left Behind (2001) has caused for American Indian children, as well as for children of other minority groups (Patrick 2008).

The district has made some efforts to accommodate the cultural philosophy of education without endangering student academic achievement. Medicine men are invited to tell the seasonal stories. The National Aeronautics and Space Administration (NASA) and the Navajo medicine men have presented programs together to blend the Navajo stories of creation and the stars with the scientific explorations done by NASA.

The elementary school was built with a traditional hogan incorporated into it for ceremonies and celebrations. There are classes in Navajo language and culture. Teachers like Laura and Emma are helping their students take pride in their heritage. This is certainly not a perfect solution, but it is a start. And most importantly, the initiatives are developed by the school community, not imposed from outside.

Respect for Differences of Opinion Regarding "Best" Educational Practices

One challenge has been that not all families favor their children's learning in the traditional way. Some believe that the only way for their children to succeed in life is to adapt to the mainstream model of education and to speak only English. There have also been some studies that question the positive impact of Navajo culture on academic success (Willeto 1999). The majority of the parents in this school district have indicated their desire for the inclusion of culture and language in the curriculum. Parental permission for inclusion of students in these classes can be withheld, thus giving all stakeholders a choice.

Although the Navajo Fundamental Laws decree quite clearly in chapter 4 that the Navajo beliefs and values are to be taught to the children, there is great difficulty in ensuring that this will happen in schools that are controlled by outside non-tribal entities (Lee 2011, 218–19). In fact, as Lee confirms, many families are not teaching their children history, culture, traditions, or language at home either.

There are some charter schools or grant schools on the reservation that are devoted to Navajo language and culture. Students may choose to attend these schools at no cost. In many cases, there is no charge for transportation. There are many challenges in developing, governing, and financing these schools, as documented by McCarty (2002).

Several states have passed legislation either encouraging or requiring the inclusion of culturally responsive standards that address American Indian history and culture (for example, Alaska and Montana). Starnes (2006) has provided a detailed history of the development and implementation of these standards in the schools and classrooms in the state of Montana. There has been little research so far on the influence of cultural studies on the achievement of American Indian children in the state or the extent to which the standards are actually being implemented.

Reaching out to Families and Community

Community and family involvement are key components of the process of making positive changes for education of Navajo children. Traditionally, families were not very involved with the school. It is difficult for parents to travel the long distances to attend meetings at the school. Many parents did not feel comfortable or welcomed at school.

This challenge was addressed at each school. The need for a unified vision for the schools required the cadres to come up with some creative solutions for involvement, including setting up parent resource rooms at the school, having babysitting available during meetings and conferences, and creating special celebrations, entertainment, and award ceremonies at the schools. Food was served at most meetings so families wouldn't have to worry about preparing meals late at night when they got home.

Awareness sessions that were hands-on and interactive were held for community members to familiarize them with Accelerated Schools. Parents and community members were invited to participate as part of the cadres. Their input was critical in addressing the challenges facing the district.

The annual two-day Accelerated Schools retreat held for staff each May on the university campus was expanded to include selected students from the middle and high schools and their parents. School board members were included as was the Indian Education Committee made up of elders in the community.

The Indian Education Committee members presented the results of a survey administered to families and soliciting their opinions about topics of interest to them regarding the schools. This provides important insights into community thoughts and concerns. This year's surveys dealt with topics such as bullying in the schools, safe environment, shared responsibility for student success, commitment to the learning of all students, and so on (Indian Education Committee 2012).

Students and families were provided with tours of the university campus and meetings with the Native American Student Association members, who talked to them about how to get into college and finance a college education. A trip was made to a local charter school where Navajo students were paired with charter school students and engaged in creative activities with each other.

A bond formed between the students that led to yearlong e-mail communication and plans for the Las Vegas students to come out to the reservation for a trip in the fall. These activities broadened the horizons of all involved and engendered mutual understanding and respect.

Limits on Decision Making—It Can Be Messy!

Teachers in most schools are not used to being empowered to make big decisions about the instruction and life of the school. It is something they typically do not receive any training for in their teacher preparation programs, although some universities, such as ours, are now including teacher leadership in the curriculum. So it takes a lot of professional development and practice to learn how to operate using the Accelerated Schools governance system. The cadres form the basis for governance.

After the school as a whole has created its vision and analyzed data (the "taking stock" process) and prioritized the most critical areas of challenge that need to be addressed ("what is getting in the way of academic achievement"), cadres are formed around three to five challenges, depending on the size of the school community.

Cadres then meet at least twice a month to refine the challenge area, hypothesize why the challenge exists, brainstorm solutions, pilot test, assess, implement school wide, and reassess. The Steering Committee, made up of cadre leaders, administrators, parents, and perhaps students, looks at the action plans proposed by the cadres to be sure they have followed the inquiry process and have looked at all the ramifications of the plan and then give approval for the plan to go on to the school as a whole for approval.

Many stakeholders are used to throwing solutions at problems; taking time to go through a thoughtful process before trying solutions is difficult. It takes a lot of coaching to successfully implement the governance process. Training is provided by the university ASP on site and at the university.

The district curriculum director, who has extensive training in the Accelerated Schools process, serves as the internal coach, visiting cadre and steering committee meetings and providing guidance and training as needed. The superintendent, also very knowledgeable about the project, has principals provide monthly reports on how the process is working and also spot-checks cadre and steering-committee minutes for fidelity to the process.

Hope for the Future

The experiences of this school district have demonstrated the commitment to the well-being and success of the youth of the community. The willingness to work hard and to never give up in the face of adversity (including new state or federal initiatives or directives) has been impressive. The energy and enthusiasm with which the stakeholders begin each school year is encouraging. It has certainly not been smooth sailing, and there are still many challenges to address, but the fact that there is a process in place to deal with them seems to keep hope alive.

There is a sense of empowerment within the confines of state and federal regulations, which enables the district to value and pass on its culture and beliefs to the new generation. With the continued support of the superintendent, the school board, the families, the elders, and the community, the students will be able to reach their goals.

Conclusion

Other chapters in this book have recounted the historical trends and issues in American Indian education, looking at the history of forcible removal from tribal lands, the treaties, the laws, the boarding school experiences, the theories of multicultural education, and the challenges among the Indian population.

This chapter has framed the experience of one reservation public school district's journey to self-determination with regard to the education received by the children. The story has been told within the context of the history and current efforts of other Indigenous peoples as they struggle to influence their destiny through education. The struggle goes on, not just for the American Indian, but all other peoples in the nation during a time of standardization of curriculum and testing.

All of our students may soon find themselves in at-risk situations with regard to academic achievement in the current environment. The Accelerated Schools process has provided a tool for decision making and action that is enabling this school district to continuously address its challenges and keep student academic success and respect for culture at the forefront of its vision. The process is truly a journey, not a destination.

REFERENCES

Champagne, D. (2006). "Education, culture and nation building: Development of the tribal learning community and educational exchange." In *Indigenous Education and Empowerment: International Perspectives*, ed. I. Abu-Saad and D. Champagne, 147–68: Lanham, MD: AltaMira.

Hopfenberg, W. S., H. M. Levin, and Associates. (1993). *The Accelerated Schools Resource Guide*. San Francisco: Jossey-Bass.

Indian Education Committee. (2012). *Parent Survey: Standards and Rubrics for School Improvement*. PUSD no. 4. Pinon, AZ: Indian Education Committee.

Klug, B. J., and P. T. Whitfield. (2003). *Widening the Circle: Culturally Relevant Pedagogy for American Indian Children*. New York: RoutledgeFalmer.

Lee, L. (2011). "Indigenous knowledge in transition: The fundamental laws of Diné in an era of change and modernity." In *Indigenous Philosophies and Critical Education: A Reader*, ed. G. J. Sefa Dei, 212–24. New York: Peter Lang.

Levin, H. M. (1987a). "Accelerated schools for disadvantaged students." *Educational Leadership* 44 (6): 19–21.

———. (1987b). "New schools for the disadvantaged." *Teacher Education Quarterly* 14 (4): 60–83.

———. (1988). "Accelerating elementary education for disadvantaged students." In *School Success for Students at Risk*, ed. Chief State School Officers, 209–25. Orlando, FL: Harcourt, Brace, Jovanovich.

McCarty, T. L. (2002). *A Place to be Navajo*. Mahwah, NJ: Lawrence Erlbaum Associates.

No Child Left Behind Act of 2001: Reauthorization of the Elementary and Secondary Education Act 0f 1965 (NCLB). (2001). *U.S. code*. Title 20, sec. 6301 et seq.

Patrick, R. (2008). "Perspectives on change: A continued struggle for academic success and cultural relevancy at an American Indian school in the midst of No Child Left Behind." *Journal of American Indian Education* 37 (1): 65–81.

Reyhner, J. (1992). *Teaching American Indian Students*. Norman: University of Oklahoma Press.

Starnes, B. A. (2006). "Montana's Indian education for all: Toward an education worthy of American ideals." *Phi Delta Kappan* 88 (9): 184–92.

Willeto, A. A. (1999). "Navajo culture and family influences on academic success: Traditionalism is not a significant predictor of achievements among young Navajos." *Journal of American Indian Education* 38 (2): 1–24.

Young, W. M. (2010). *Exemplary Teachers for Native American Students*. PhD diss. University of Nevada, Las Vegas.

Chapter 10

Collectively Transformative Pedagogy

Negotiating Enhanced Educational Opportunities for Native American Students

LeAnn G. Putney: University of Nevada, Las Vegas

ABSTRACT

Collectively transformative pedagogy (CTP) is a theoretical framework that combines the work of three theorists from different backgrounds with complementary orientations: John Dewey, Lev S. Vygotsky, and Paulo Freire. The philosophical underpinning of CTP draws on the premise that classroom participants act together as a unitary culture. The language and actions of participants in such classrooms become a cultural resource for members to access academic content.

Juxtaposing constructs from the above three mentors from our past made visible the complexity of classroom life regarding (a) the dialogic nature of learning and development of the individual within the collective through relational language engagement (Vygotsky 1978, 1987), (b) the construction of progressive and relevant classroom processes (Dewey 1899, 1916), and (c) reading the world of the classroom and beyond as responsible and action-taking citizens (Freire 1970, 1998). This work is particularly critical for Native American students. It draws on relevance, relationship, and responsibility through collaborative problem solving as integral components of classroom activity.

Keywords: American Indian students, collectively transformative pedagogy

COLLECTIVELY TRANSFORMATIVE PEDAGOGY: NEGOTIATING ENHANCED EDUCATIONAL OPPORTUNITIES FOR NATIVE AMERICAN STUDENTS

Much has been written about how to make classroom environments settings of culturally responsive pedagogy or those in which classroom experiences align with students' home cultures. As noted by Young (2010), various labels used to describe this approach include "culturally relevant teaching" (Ladson-Billings 1994, 2005), "culturally appropriate" (Au and Jordan 1981), "culturally congruent" (Mohatt and Erickson 1981), as well as "culturally relevant pedagogy" (Klug and Whitfield 2003).

While many terms have been used to reflect such practices, the overarching concept has been that all students will find educational success in environments in which the following elements are fundamentally represented and continuously operationalized. First, the students' personal values and cultures are respected. Second, students can relate to the classroom participants and curriculum. Third, they become actively reflective and responsive learners.

I have expanded upon the previously stated aspects of culturally responsive teaching by further weaving these aspects with the philosophies and teaching theories of John Dewey (1899, 1916), Lev S. Vygotsky (1978, 1987), and Paulo Freire (1970, 1973, 1998) into a theoretical framework called *collectively transformative pedagogy* (CTP). In this way, I have made visible not only the foundational aspects of learning theories but also have shown how theory and practice are interrelated in best practices (Wink and Putney 2002; see also Shor 1999).

In constructing the CTP theoretical framework, I have combined the work of these three educational theorists from different backgrounds who have espoused complementary orientations (figure 10.1). Juxtaposing constructs from their works has made apparent the complexity of classroom life regarding (a) the construction of progressive and relevant classroom processes (Dewey 1899, 1916), (b) the dialogic nature of learning as well as development of the individual and the collective through relational language engagement (Vygotsky 1978, 1987), and (c) the act of reading the world of the classroom and beyond as responsible and action-taking citizens (Freire 1973, 1998).

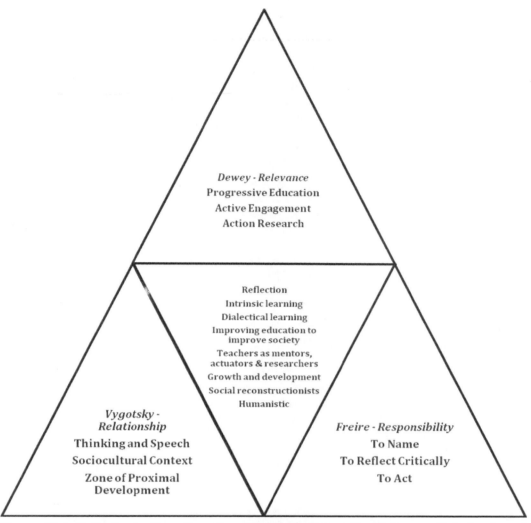

Figure 10.1 Collectively Transformative Pedagogy: Promoting Relevant, Relational, and Responsible Teaching and Learning (Developed with Joan Wink)

This work is particularly critical for Native American students because it draws on dialogic collaboration as an integral component of classroom activity. I relate this pedagogical stance to the situated nature of classroom learning by recognizing that classroom participants act together as a culture to create norms and expectations for student learning.

When this approach has been used, the expected outcome of this perspective is that classrooms would become places in which students take pride in their own learning and become self-regulated and responsible citizens, both in and out of the classroom setting. The classroom is then viewed as a place in which teachers and students negotiate meaning, jointly constructing knowledge that is relevant while serving as a conduit of communication for families.

The philosophical underpinnings of CTP have been underscored by three premises related to classroom interactions. The first premise is that classroom participants act together to construct a classroom culture. An additional premise is that the language and actions of participants in such classrooms become, in effect, cultural resources for members to access academic content. Thirdly the work that students and teachers accomplish together is progressive and consequential to those who participate in the activities (Putney 2007; Putney et al. 2000; Wink 2011; Wink and Putney 2002).

In other words, when classroom teachers and students participate in CTP, the topics of study are interconnected in such ways that work accomplished in one lesson builds toward more complex instruction. At the same time, involvement in such instruction becomes consequential for students who participate, in that the instruction moves them forward in their academic and social development.

In what follows, I first illustrate the different educational contexts from which the three theorists worked. I then discuss what these theorists have in common in terms of how we can come to view teaching and learning. After examining their commonalities, I reflect on the contrastive work of the theorists to make visible how each one has contributed to the whole of CTP. In the final section of this chapter, I underscore how the learning theories relate to what can be accomplished in practice with examples from classrooms with Native American students.

Theoretical Contexts of John Dewey, Lev S. Vygotsky, and Paulo Freire

These three theorists came from different cultures with differing yet compatible views of pedagogical considerations. While illustrating the differences in their contexts, I have also examined how similar their views were in terms of calling for education that is relevant and that values intrinsic motivation and placing the student at the center of learning rather than relying on extrinsic motivation and test scores. Although emanating from the past, their work has offered theoretically based strategies for teaching and learning even in today's educational climate of reliance on test scores alone to measure student achievement.

John Dewey (1859–1952), an American philosopher and psychologist, was known for his philosophy of pragmatism and his work in the progressive education movement (or "progressive movement") in the early 1900s in the United States (Putney and Green 2010). Dewey's work places the child as an active participant at the center of classroom practice through experiential learning.

Dewey (1916) notes that teachers and students were using communication as a way of constructing meaning through experiential learning. Dewey states that "the communication which ensures participation in a common understanding is one which secures similar emotional and intellectual dispositions" (1916, 4).

Supporting this concept, Putney and Floriani (1999, 18) note, "As teachers and students interact they construct a common set of expectations, responsibilities, practices, and language that define ways of learning, living, and being in the classroom." Placing the needs of students at the center of the classroom has ensured that the curriculum related to the needs and experiences of the students and could contribute to the construction of community; and indeed, that a democratic society could be guaranteed (Dewey 1902).

During a similar era in Russia, Lev S. Vygotsky (1896–1934), a psychologist, was promoting a unification of psychology that departed from the more traditional behaviorist movement (Yaroshevsky 1993). Vygotsky (1978, 1987) studied children's learning and development and recognized that children acquired knowledge through interaction with others in an environment that consisted of the socially organized world of culture. Individuals who constructed the culture simultaneously developed knowledge and skills about the culture.

Vygotsky (1978, 1987) observed that children's mastery of skills occurred through activity and interactions with others within the society through internalization. However—as further noted by Vygotsky—the construct of internalization was not a passive one but one in which the child was actively processing information afforded by others and in relational dialogic problem-solving activity with others.

The work of Paulo Freire (1921–1997) was more contemporary than Dewey and Vygotsky. Freire was a Brazilian educator and theorist whose work has undergirded the critical pedagogy movement (Macedo 1987). While both Dewey and Vygotsky taught us about classrooms as zones of activity—and both encouraged interactive learning—Freire (1970, 2000) updated their work and charged educators to view classrooms as zones of potentiality and possibility.

Freire (1970, 2000) was best known for his assertion that classrooms must be moving beyond the "banking" concept of education, in which teachers deposited information into the receptacles that are the students' minds. Freire calls for classrooms in which teachers and students transform knowledge and engage in "the practice of freedom, the means by which men and women deal critically and creatively with reality and discover how to participate in the transformation of their world" (2000, 34).

Each of these distant mentors lived in different sociocultural contexts, which contributed to their stances on education. Dewey (1899, 1916) viewed education in societal and democratic terms, with relevance of curriculum and actively engaged learners as the focus of instruction. His focus on active learning dovetails into Vygotsky's (1978, 1987) work that has become related to activity theory (Shor 1999). While Vygotsky also proposed that student learning be active, he understood education to be historical, social, and cultural.

Through Vygotsky's psychological lens, he focused more on the psychological dynamics of individual learning and change within a classroom collective (Elsasser and John-Steiner 1999). Building from Dewey and Vygotsky, Freire (1970, 2000) concentrated on developing appropriate pedagogical strategies (Elsasser and John-Steiner 1999), while urging us to recognize education as also being political. I have viewed these differences as serving to pull together pedagogical considerations that are even more important in our current educational climate.

Theoretical Commonalities of Dewey, Vygotsky, and Freire

Juxtaposing the theories of Dewey (1899, 1916), Vygotsky (1978, 1987), and Freire (1970, 2000) has uncovered the various pedagogical considerations they have in common. In this section I focus on the variations these theorists noted in relation to some of the common considerations made visible in figure 10.1.

For example, all three theorists saw classrooms as potential places for social reconstruction and improvement in education and society through educational growth and development. All three theorists called for teachers to be reflective about their practice and to encourage their students to be reflective learners so as to provide the best practices for all. Likewise, all three theorists called for educational practice to move away from externally motivated learning to a focus on intrinsic learning.

While Dewey (1899, 1916) focused on learning taking place through active and relevant experiences among the members of the classroom community, Vygotsky's focus was on the relational use of language to construct and negotiate meaning among members of the community (Vygotsky 1978, 1987). Freire's work encourages teachers to use dialogic interactions to create responsible "possibilities for construction and production of knowledge rather than to be engaged simply in a game of transferring knowledge" (1998, 49).

Dewey's (1899, 1916) work is more focused on the individual actively constructing knowledge within an active environment. At the same time, Vygotsky (1978, 1987) takes a more cognitive approach to learning and development of the individual within the collective through the use of language as a tool for problem solving.

Freire's (1970, 2000) more contemporary work focuses not only on problem solving but also on problem posing so that what is being learned in the classroom through inquiry becomes a vehicle for taking responsible action in one's local setting. Together, all three theoretical implications become a compatible and highly applicable framework for current pedagogical considerations for Native American students.

In addition to intrinsic learning, each of these educational theorists was a humanist and regarded education as a means of improving society. Dewey (1916) viewed the progressive movement in the United States as a way of preparing students for success in their lives beyond the school walls.

Dewey's (1916) notion of democracy was that all citizens should be learning from and about each other so as to move the society forward in a cohesive manner. As he notes, "A society which makes provision for participation in its good of all its members on equal terms and which secures flexible readjustment of its institutions through interaction of the different forms of associated life is in so far democratic" (1916, 99).

In his view of development and education, Vygotsky (1997a) places high importance on the role of language as being shaped by historical forces, and as a tool for shaping thought through problem-solving classroom interactions. According to Glassman (2001), Vygotsky viewed education as a means of the society and culture fused together, becoming a change agent for the individual, while Dewey viewed education as a vehicle for individuals to change society.

Throughout his life, Freire (Macedo 1987; Wink 2011) strove to improve the position of people in society, particularly for those who were not in spheres of power. He saw education and literacy as mediators and means for people to understand their own position in life as well as how others position them so that they would be able to find the power of their own voices. Throughout his work, Freire (Wink 2011) encourages people to name the problem, to critically reflect upon the issue at hand, and to act on the issue to promote positive change.

Freire's work (1970, 2000) perhaps bridged the work of Dewey (1899, 1916) and Vygotsky (1978, 1987) and also extended their works by promoting transformative education as a means for individuals to better understand society and culture. As part of this understanding, people must also have viewed their positions and roles in both so as to take responsible action toward improving themselves and their positions within society, and thus societies overall.

In other areas of convergence of these theorists (see figure 10.1), all three theorists viewed classrooms as areas of active learning with the role of the teacher being instrumental in actuating learning. For example, Dewey (1916) believed the school experience should benefit the whole child. In other words, education should approach the child from artistic, intellectual, social, and moral perspectives. He also believed that learning best took place when students were actively engaged and that experience was critical for making ideas clear and available to students.

According to Dewey (1899, 1916), one role of the teacher was that of a researcher who identified an issue, hypothesized a solution, tested the hypothesis, and evaluated the consequences. In this way, the teacher regulated the curriculum according to what was needed by the students rather than allowing the curriculum to dominate the classroom structure.

In turn, Vygotsky (1997a) recognized that the classroom should be an experiential space in which the teacher was actively leading the students' development through learning. As such, the teacher became active, the students became active, and the classroom became an environment of activity for negotiating meaning. Vygotsky notes that the role of teacher is that of mediator and co-constructor of knowledge. As defined by Wink and Putney (2002), the teacher becomes an *actuator of learning*.

Likewise, Freire encourages teachers to take on the role of learners as well, thus reducing the polarity of teaching and learning, "so that both are simultaneously students and teachers" (1973, 72). In other words, teachers must be expected to expand learning beyond ingesting facts and concepts by encouraging problem posing about people in their relations with the world (Freire 2000). Thus, teachers who encouraged students to engage in dialogue and inquiry around a topic participated with the students in the construction of knowledge rather than the dispensing of knowledge.

In understanding how these three mentors viewed classrooms as progressive places for active learning, I now illustrate below some strategic differences in their views that indicate why I have called for bringing their work together. These differences are also illustrated in figure 10.1 as the three *r*'s of *relevance*, *relationship*, and *responsibility*.

Dewey's Emphasis on Relevance

Dewey (1916) epitomized the work of progressive educators who supported making education as lifelike as possible with the educative process being a wholehearted, purposeful activity consistent with the child's goals (Webb, Metha, and Jordan 1996). In addition, Dewey sought to highlight the study of democratic classroom practices.

Dewey (1916) described democracy as being more than a structural form of government but as a way of life. Dewey summarizes his notion of a democratic society as one that "makes provision for participation in its good of all its members on equal terms and which secures flexible readjustment of its institutions through interaction of the different forms of associated life" (1916, 99). A democratic classroom, then, was defined as one in which all members participated, and all voices were considered through active engagement in constructing knowledge.

Dewey (1916) recognized that participating in democratic classroom practices had the potential for promoting the classroom as learner centered. This precipitated the development of "reflective thinking" whereby students acquired the ability to problem solve. Reflective thinking for students had important implications when the result of reflective thinking was students' transformations from having casual curiosity about a subject to actually engaging in thorough inquiry regarding that concept (Doll 1993; Klockow 2003).

While Dewey (1899, 1916) advocated a student-centric approach, the role of the teacher as the guide and facilitator was vital to the success of the classroom. This role as guide was similar to Vygotsky's (1978, 1987) view of a *more knowledgeable other* leading students to negotiate meaning.

Relational Nature of Learning and Development through a Vygotskian Lens

Vygotsky (1978, 1987) proposed the dialogic or relational nature of learning by revealing the importance of the reciprocal relationship of thinking and speech as played out in our experiences with others. Using speech moved us toward building intellectual capacity while our expanded thought paved the way for more speech. He notes that students would become active participants in their learning through the use of language and by having interactions with others. Vygotsky further viewed activity and sustaining interpersonal experiences as key factors impacting the relationship of thinking and speech in lifelong learning.

A construct from Vygotsky's work (1978, 1987) that illustrated the relationship of thinking and speech with student development was the *zone of proximal development* (ZPD). The ZPD indicated the difference between what students were able do by themselves today and what they could come to know by working collaboratively with more experienced others in problem-solving situations (Vygotsky 1978).

Children would have actively transformed the help they received from others through internalization, an active component of the interpersonal action of reciprocating thinking and speech (Vygotsky 1978, 1987). What would have begun as an interpersonal action was transformed into intrapersonal activity as students reflected on what was made available to them through the activities in which they were engaged. Students eventually used the same means of guidance from others as they directed their own subsequent problem-solving behaviors (Díaz, Neal, and Amaya-Williams 1990).

Vygotsky (1978, 1987) notes that the course of development was not a linear one, nor was it totally predictable; rather, it was cultural, historical, dynamic, and interactive, and it was so for both the individual and the collective. Viewed this way, the individual and collective were placed in a reflexive relationship. This relationship of individuals within a collective was recursive, transformational, and produced through the sociocultural context (Vygotsky 1978, 1987).

In other words, in acquiring cultural knowledge the individual also contributed to the shape and resources of the collective. As individuals participated in collective activity, they shared their own personalized meanings that others were then able to access and use to create their own understandings of what was being shared. In this way, individuals showed active agency in processing the information through problem solving with more experienced others. This relationship of individual and collective interactions was similar to the progressive view of Dewey's (1902, 1916) of classrooms as active, problem-solving, and democratic units.

Another aspect of Vygotsky's work (1978, 1987, 1997a) applicable to teaching and learning in diverse classroom settings was to understand the sociocultural context of the classroom within the school, of schools within local communities, and of students within their respective familial homes. In this way, teachers would come to understand the localized situation of their students and families.

This understanding was fundamental for teachers to develop trust among their students and families in terms of educational expectations. It also made a difference for teachers to be able to understand how their pedagogical stance toward the students' learning then positioned the students for academic success.

Taking Responsible Action through Freire's Critical Lens

Combining Vygotsky's (1978, 1987) and Dewey's (1916, 2001) work afforded us foundational premises for researching in classrooms from which we have been able to interpret the individual/collective consequences of learning and development through democratic classroom processes. What Freire (1998) offered us was a way to examine these processes through a critical lens that makes visible for whom these processes are effective, including under what conditions, for what purposes, and with what consequences and outcomes (Putney et al. 2000).

Freire argues that responsibly teaching from a transformative approach meant that the teacher was acquiring new knowledge while engaging students in a "continuous transformation through which they became authentic subjects of the construction and reconstruction of what was being taught, side by side with the teacher" (1998, 33). From this perspective, a transformative approach was one in which teaching and learning were in a dynamic and reciprocal relationship and also one in which learning and development were essential for both teacher and students (Putney and Floriani 1999; Wink 2011; Wink and Putney 2002).

In addition, Freire (1998) addresses the notion of teacher as mentor. From this perspective, mentoring was not being paternalistic—taking control of the life, dreams, and aspirations of the mentee; cloning your mentee; or transforming the mentee into the mentor's worker—as this was exploitative and fundamentally antidemocratic. Mentoring was, however, authentic and challenging to the student's creative freedom while also stimulating to the construction of the student's autonomy. Mentoring then became a liberatory task that transcended the instructive task.

Freire (1987) identifies progressive teachers as those who built coherence and consistency and helped students become literate in content, while also building understandings of the politics in the world. Thus, Freire (1998) gives us another way of examining the sociocultural context of a democratic classroom.

This was done in order to recognize how teachers and students constructed and "read the word and the world" (Macedo 1987) through conscientious understanding of themselves as teachers and learners. As mentors and guides, teachers and students were responsible for jointly constructing and negotiating meaning through their interactions.

What we have found in common in the juxtaposition of these theorists is the importance of intrinsic and dialectical learning, improving education and society, of naturalistic teachers and learners interacting together to construct knowledge, and of human growth and development as lifelong processes. Combining the work of these theorists has resulted in teachers and students engaging in a mutual-learning democratic process. As Shor notes, the "mutual development ethic constructs students as authorities, agents, and unofficial teachers who educate the official teacher while also getting educated by each other and by the teacher" (1999, sec. 5, para. 3).

In addition, we have come to understand observations of learners as a way of assessing what they want to know and what they still require for learning and viewing classrooms as venues for socially reconstructing life through the humanistic juxtaposing of ideas. As Wink and Putney (2002) note,

> Students of today and citizens of tomorrow will need the ability to transfer and transform their knowledge to challenging, unforeseen problems and complex realities. They will need to solve problems that do not yet exist; they will need to be able to find workable solutions, both individually and with others; and they will need to learn dialectically from oppositional thought. (p. 121)

Turning Theory into Practice

I had the privilege of teaching an *action research* course with classroom teachers from a Navajo reservation school district. I also occasionally worked with the classroom teachers as a coach in the Accelerated Schools Project (ASP), which exemplified the type of transformative pedagogy that has been presented here as collectively transformative pedagogy, or CTP. In what follows, I illustrate some examples taken from my observational notes of my work with these teachers over time.

The succeeding examples show how teachers transformed the sociocultural context of their classrooms to better engage students in their learning. By engaging in CTP, these teachers moved from being the distributors and directors of knowledge acquisition to facilitators, mentors, and co-constructors of knowledge with their students.

The Problem of Homework and Other Lessons

In trying to understand why students were not completing their homework assignments, the teachers working at the middle school on a Navajo reservation conducted an action research project to determine what they needed to change in their homework approach. As part of the ASP process, the teachers had already redesigned their homework to make it of interest to the students and to make the homework assignment an integral part of the next day's lesson. However, this had not proved to be enough, and together they brainstormed other potential ways to make homework more accessible for their students.

One idea that they decided to try was to have students work together in small groups at the end of each period to get a start on the homework together. While this was somewhat helpful, it still did not result in students finishing and turning in homework. The teachers then posed the problem to the students to have a better understanding of what was needed to accomplish the task of homework completion. What they discovered was that many of the students rode buses for up to two hours each way to and from school. By the time the students reached their home it was nearly dark, and for some, electricity in the home was not an option.

In coming to understand the sociocultural context of their students, the teachers offered class time at the end of the period in which students worked together in small groups. The students rotated roles in the small groups and had to show their individual contributions to the homework. This strategy worked well for the duration of the research project but took class time to finish the work. After the course was completed with me, the teachers continued to work through the homework issue by attempting to engage a tutor to ride the bus with the students to help them with their homework during the commute time.

This resulted in an even higher engagement with the homework problems: the students were prepared for class the next day, and the work in the classroom was improved due to increased participation on the part of the students. In this particular case, understanding the sociocultural context of the students and families led to improvement in classroom attendance, attention to detail, and improved homework participation.

In other examples of teachers taking relevant, relational, and responsible action with students in their classrooms, the science teachers worked in collaboration with the art teacher so that students drew representations of the science terms they were learning. One teacher noted that students were drawing pictures of cells and labeling them in their lab notebooks. She encouraged them to take the drawings to a larger scale and displayed them about the classroom. As the science lessons grew more complex, so did the drawings and the displays. The students improved their understanding of science by negotiating meaning through their art.

Other teachers from the same Navajo school district engaged elder family members in relating tribal traditions in the classroom, while in the sixth-grade classrooms the teachers team-taught a thematic unit on the "Long Walk," a defining moment in Navajo and U.S. history when the Navajo were forced to leave their land and walk on a journey of four hundred miles. In this study of the students' cultural heritage, the teachers integrated math, history, science, nutrition, culture, reading, and art through project-based learning.

They culminated the unit by taking the students in vans along the four-hundred-mile route. While this unit resulted in higher student engagement, higher attendance, and higher test scores, the teachers remarked that engaging students in a study that was cultural, political, and historical provided the teachers opportunities to learn about and from their students.

What's in a Name?

As part of their work with ASP, teachers and students in the Navajo district take on leadership roles. Near the end of one school year, teachers and student leaders from the middle school and high school located on the Navajo reservation were involved in a leadership training opportunity on a university campus, an eight-hour road trip from the reservation.

As part of their training, the students visited a linguistically and culturally diverse local public K–12 charter school near the university to meet with middle and high school students there who had taken on leadership roles. The thirteen students from the charter school represented the diversity of the school, being Latino, black, biracial, white, and Pacific Islander. The staff and students at the charter school prepared an activity in which the students from the different cultures could meet the Navajo students and work together to get to know each other.

The Navajo students, along with three of their teachers, arrived at the charter school, excited by the prospect of meeting new acquaintances. As they pulled up to the school in their bus, the students from the charter school lined the sidewalk leading to the school so they could greet their counterparts and welcome them into the school.

Once inside the school, the students gathered in the multipurpose room and began chatting with each other. The teacher demonstrated for them an activity in which they could etch a key fob with a drawing, emblem, or name of their choosing. This would be a keepsake for each of the students to take with them to remember their day together. The students began sketching designs they would use to decorate their keychain. The students from both schools admired each other's artistic talent. Soon they were helping each other make designs that could be used on their key fobs and exchanging ideas about what to use for their etchings.

As they continued chatting and sketching, the Navajo students and charter school students began discussing their names. The Navajo students noted that while they had their given names, they often earned additional names acquired in their Native language. The charter school students noted that their names often reflected the names in their families but that they were not given additional names.

This revelation resulted in an exchange: the Navajo students gave names to their charter school counterparts, wrote the names for them, and explained the meaning of the names to their newfound friends. The charter school students took notes so that they would remember the significance of the names given to them by their Navajo friends.

At the end of the morning, all of the students boarded buses and rode to the university where they enjoyed lunch together. As I rode the bus with the students from our charter school, they were abuzz with talk about how much they learned about the Navajo culture from the morning's activity. They all wanted to know if they could take a trip to the Navajo reservation to see the school their new friends attended so that they could learn more about their culture.

Once at lunch, I debriefed with the teachers from the Navajo reservation who were elated with the way the students all got along and worked so well together all morning. They remarked that the Navajo students wondered if the charter school students would be able to come and visit them the following year so that they could return the favor of being treated so well by their counterparts.

We found that involving students and teachers in leadership roles so that they take active part in their schooling was a key part of powerful learning. The students in both schools came together around a simple activity of making a symbolic artifact that was meant to be meaningful to them. However, that action of engaging students in an activity in which they had a choice in expressing themselves led them to share more about their respective cultures than we could have anticipated.

The Navajo students took up the naming of their counterparts and shared a part of their culture that is very personal and meaningful. The charter school students readily took part in their naming process and in doing so learned a part of Navajo culture that might otherwise not have been shared had students just read about this culture in a book. Bringing all of the students together to work and learn from each other was a powerful experience for us all as we realized that the students reinforced for their teachers and administrators the importance of bonding and learning with and from each other.

Looking Toward the Future Education of Our American Indian Students

In each of these classroom cases, the teachers and students were engaged in learning that was relevant, relational, and geared toward their being responsible learners and citizens. The current context for pedagogical considerations becomes a "contested terrain" that "ignores the work that shows that individual students do not live large-scale, replicable lives. They live local and situated ones" (Putney et al. 1999, 375). Consequently, teachers must be able to adjust curriculum to the needs of their students in order to make learning the journey it was meant to be: relevant, relational, and responsible.

The voices of our distant mentors Dewey, Vygotsky, and Freire are extremely relevant in our current educational situation of reliance on testing and accountability as evidence of students' learning and teachers' teaching. A change in pedagogical course is clearly needed. Our clarion call for use of CTP is critical as the political scene in our educational spaces currently continues to call for even more accountability measured only through quantified means that do not reflect the lived experiences our American Indian students.

REFERENCES

Au, K., and C. Jordan. (1981). "Teaching reading to Hawaiian children: Finding a culturally appropriate solution." In *Culture and the Bilingual Classroom: Studies in Classroom Ethnography*, ed. H. Trueba, G. Guthrie, and K. Au, 69–86. Rowley, MA: Newbury House.

Dewey, J. (1899). *The School and Society: Being Three Lectures.* Chicago: University of Chicago Press.

———. (1902). *The Child and the Curriculum.* Repr., Chicago: University of Chicago Press, 1956.

———. (1916). *Democracy and Education.* Repr., New York: Free Press, 1996.

———. (2001). "Education and social change." In *SOURCES: Notable Selections in Education*, ed. F. Schultz, 3rd ed., 333–41. New York: McGraw Hill Dushkin.

Díaz, R. M., C. J. Neal, and M. Amaya-Williams. (1990). "The social origins of self-regulation." In *Vygotsky and Education*, ed. L. C. Moll, 127–54. Cambridge: Cambridge University Press.

Doll, W. E. (1993). *A Post-modern Perspective on Curriculum.* New York: Teachers College Press.

Elsasser, N., and V. John-Steiner. (1999). "An interactionist approach to advancing literacy." In *Freire for the Classroom: A Sourcebook for Liberatory Teaching*, ed. I. Shor, 45–62. Portsmouth, NH: Boynton-Cook.

Freire, P. (1970). *Pedagogy of the Oppressed.* New York: Seabury.

Freire, P. (1973). *Education for Critical Consciousness.* Repr. New York: Seabury, 1998.

———. (1987). "Letter to North-American teachers." In *Freire for the Classroom: A Sourcebook for Liberatory Teaching*, ed. I. Shor, 211–14. Portsmouth, NH: Boynton-Cook.

———. (1998). *Pedagogy of Freedom: Ethics, Democracy, and Civic Courage.* Lanham, MD: Rowman & Little-field.

———. (2000). *Pedagogy of the Oppressed.* New York: Continuum.

Freire, P., and D. Macedo. (1987). *Literacy: Reading the Word and the World.* South Hadley, MA: Bergin and Garvey.

Glassman, M. (2001). "Dewey and Vygotsky: Society, experience, and inquiry in educational practice." *Educational Researcher* 30 (4): 3–14.

Klockow, J. A. (2003). *Examining Democratic Ideals: A Case Study of Dialogic Interactions of Fifth-grade Citizens.* PhD diss., University of Nevada, Las Vegas.

Klug, B. J., and P. T. Whitfield. (2003). *Widening the Circle: Culturally Relevant Pedagogy for American Indian Children.* New York: RoutledgeFalmer.

Ladson-Billings, G. (1994). *The Dreamkeepers: Successful Teaching for African-American Students.* San Francisco: Jossey-Bass.

———. (2005). *Beyond the Big House: African American Educators on Teacher Education*. New York: Teachers College Press.

Macedo, D. (1987). *Reading the Word and the World*. New York: Routledge.

Mohatt, G., and F. Erickson. (1981). "Cultural differences in teaching styles in an Odawa school: A sociolinguistic approach." In *Culture and the Bilingual Classroom: Studies in Classroom Ethnography*, ed. H. Trueba, G. Guthrie, and K. Au, 105–19. Rowley, MA: Newbury House.

Putney, L. G. (2007). "Discursive practices as cultural resources: Formulating identities for individual and collective in an inclusive classroom setting." *International Journal of Educational Research* 46 (3–4): 129–40.

Putney, L. G., and A. Floriani. (1999). "Examining transformative classroom processes and practices: A cross-case analysis of life in two bilingual classrooms." *Journal of Classroom Interaction* 34 (2): 17–29.

Putney, L. G., and J. L. Green. (2010). "The roots and routes of teacher-based action research and curriculum inquiry: A historical perspective." In *International Encyclopedia of Education*, ed. P. Peterson, E. Baker, and B. McGraw, 1: 355–61. New York: Elsevier.

Putney, L. G., J. L. Green, C. N. Dixon, and G. J. Kelly. (1999). "Evolution of qualitative research methodology: Looking beyond defense to possibilities." *Reading Research Quarterly* 34 (3): 368–77.

Putney, L. G., J. L. Green, C. N. Dixon, R. Duran, and B. Yeager. (2000). "Consequential progressions: Exploring collective-individual development in a bilingual classroom." In *Constructing Meaning through Collaborative Inquiry: Vygotskian Perspectives on Literacy Research*, ed. C. D. Lee and P. Smagorinsky, 86–126. New York: Cambridge University Press.

Shor, I. (1999). "What is critical literacy?" *Journal for Pedagogy, Pluralism, and Practice* 1 (4). Retrieved from http://www.lesley.edu/journals/jppp/4/shor.html#intro.

Vygotsky, L. S. (1978). *Mind in Society: The Development of Higher Psychological Processes*. Cambridge, MA: Harvard University Press.

———. (1987). *The Collected Works of L. S. Vygotsky*. Vol. 1. Trans. N. Minick. New York: Plenum.

———. (1997). *Educational Psychology*. Trans. R. Silverman. Boca Raton, FL: St. Lucie.

Webb, L. D., A. Metha, and K. F. Jordan. (1996). *Foundations of American Education*. 2nd ed. Englewood Cliffs, NJ: Prentice-Hall.

Wink, J. (2011). *Critical Pedagogy: Notes from the Real World*. 4th ed. Boston: Pearson.

Wink, J., and L. G. Putney. (2002). *A Vision of Vygotsky*. White Plains, NY: Allyn & Bacon/Longman.

Yaroshevsky, M. G. (1993). *L. S. Vygotsky: V poiskakh novoi psichologii* [L. S. Vygotsky: In search for the new psychology]. St. Petersburg, Russia: Publishing House of International Foundation for History of Science.

Young, W. M. (2010). *An Investigation of Exemplary Teaching Practices of Teachers of Native American Students*. PhD diss., University of Nevada, Las Vegas.

Chapter 11

A Three-Part Strategy for Ensuring Culturally Relevant Pedagogy for American Indian Children

Angela Jaime and R. Timothy Rush: University of Wyoming

ABSTRACT

In this chapter, we argue that American Indian peoples and the schools serving their children require the long-term flexibility to implement, formatively evaluate, and refine culture-based education (CBE) programs for children and teachers without threat of sanctions based on achievement test performance. We review historical evidence and recent opinion that curriculum that is divorced from experience, language, and culture is inappropriate and therefore ineffective with Native children.

We establish the premise that schools have persisted in methods that fail Indian children because the schools are driven by funding and evaluation models determined by federal and state outsiders who do not understand the need for CBE. We propose a solution involving integration of the standard curriculum with CBE curriculum through three related strategies: (1) education of decision makers, (3) education of educators, and (3) place-based teacher preparation.

We then detail implementation of these strategies with reference to examples from the Wind River Indian Reservation and University of Wyoming experiences. We conclude that CBE education can no longer be excluded from the formula for academic success for American Indian children in our schools.

Keywords: American Indian culture-based education (CBE), American Indian curriculum, American Indian pedagogy

A THREE-PART STRATEGY FOR ENSURING CULTURALLY RELEVANT PEDAGOGY

Dollars drive decision making in twenty-first-century U.S. schools. Funding allocations are tied to student performance on standardized achievement tests. One effect of test-driven federal and state funding policies is that standardized curricula follow standardized tests. *Culture-*

based education (CBE) programs for American Indian children are driven out of their schools when decision makers feel they must focus on the basics of a de facto national mainstream program of public education.

There is strong evidence that culture-based curricula have positive effects on school achievement for American Indian students (Stokes 1997). However, in spite of the Esther Martinez Native American Languages Preservation Act (2006) aimed at preserving Indigenous cultures and languages, culturally responsive curriculum and instruction remain secondary priorities in schools serving American Indian children during the testing-craze era of the No Child Left Behind Act of 2001 (NCLB) and the Race to the Top Fund Assessment Program, part of the American Recovery and Reinvestment Act of 2009 (ARRA).

Schools serving American Indian children in the early twenty-first century continue to emphasize conventional mainstream curriculum and instructional methods to the neglect of tribal cultures and languages. Equally ironic is the situation with some governments and universities in states with substantial Indigenous populations that have instituted policies and programs that focus on cultural awareness and appropriate practices for teaching American Indian students. Their schools and school districts continue to adopt instructional programs that undermine and are contrary to these initiatives.

A study conducted by the National Center for Education Evaluation and Regional Assistance (Smiley and Sather 2009) investigated the state educational policies of the Northwest Region (Washington, Oregon, Idaho, Montana, and Alaska) regarding American Indian education. The Smiley and Sather study (2009) found that the states in the region agreed to require (a) teachers to have training in Native American culture and history, (b) Native communities represented on school boards, (c) Native American culture and history offered in curriculum, and (d) academic standards addressing Native American culture and history.

To our knowledge, a follow-up study asking the question as to whether the classrooms in the Northwest Region were addressing these academic standards or if the teachers have, in fact, received this training has not been conducted or reported. Nor does there appear to be a plan for doing so.

These initiatives are addressed within the University of Wyoming's Teachers of American Indian Children (TAIC) certificate/endorsement program (College of Education 2011). The TAIC endorsement was established in the spring of 2008 and is now offered nationwide through online access. Many of our students take courses in the TAIC program to further their own knowledge. Some school districts have contracted delivery of all five of the courses for their own educators in an effort to address the needs of faculty and students.

Unfortunately, 2004 saw the beginning of a trend for highly structured, scripted basal reading programs, which replaced more child-centered, culturally appropriate approaches in the public schools on the Wind River Indian Reservation in Wyoming because of the Reading First initiatives required under NCLB (2001). Direct parallels can be documented between the adoption of so-called scripted instruction and the test-driven adequate yearly progress (AYP) pressures of the federal government with this legislation. Dollars drive decision making.

In addition to funding constraints on school programs imposed through the federal legislation, another reason for ignoring the CBE evidence and current school practices concerns the absence of research on long-term CBE programs. However, there have been good examples of effective CBE schooling, such as the Kameamea Early Education Program (Villegas 1991) in Hawaii.

Problematically, only a few of these CBE programs have been in place for more than three years, and fewer still have been carefully documented with data collection and analysis. School curricula seem to change as frequently as district superintendents, fifty percent of whom are in their positions for less than six years (Alborano 2002).

In these pages, we argue that with respect to the education of American Indian children

1. Child-centered, culturally responsive curriculum and instruction be developed, implemented, refined, and evaluated by tribes and their local education agencies.
2. External pressures to raise scores on conventional, standardized achievement tests must be relaxed. This includes federal pressures on state governments and state government pressures on schools and districts that serve American Indian communities to accomplish this goal.

In both cases, state and federal decision makers must afford tribes and schools time—six to ten years, in our view—to accomplish cultural/curriculum integration and to document its effects on American Indian students' achievement through formative evaluation. A research base for culture-based education cannot be established unless such curricula are implemented and assessed over several years and long-term effects are documented.

We also define, describe, and argue for

3. Implementation of long-standing calls for the special training and certification for teachers of American Indian children, and that this effort begin with those currently serving in classroom roles.
4. Place-based teacher-preparation programs dedicated to the preparation of teachers of American Indian children and employing CBE curriculum methodologies and materials.

Tribes and schools require the long-term flexibility to implement, assess, and refine CBE programs for children and teachers without threat of sanctions based on achievement test performance. We propose integration of the standard curriculum (that assessed through high-stakes achievement tests) with CBE curriculum to accomplish this goal through three related strategies: (1) the education of decision makers, (2) the education of educators, and (3) place-based teacher preparation.

Strategy One: Educate the Decision Makers

Why would the community of educators not press for the culture-based education of American Indian children? Evidence supports that at least 140 years of curriculum—aimed at "Americanization," developing isolated skills, and teaching disconnected knowledge—has failed these children repeatedly (Adams 1995; Prucha 1979).

Pressures to increase standardized achievement test scores influence district- and state-level education leaders to focus on skills-based instruction and curricula aimed at typical mainstream students as a result of NCLB (2001). In the face of budgetary and punitive incentives to implement standardized curricula, administrators have focused on conventional approaches and remained largely ignorant of culture-based education and Native ways of learning and knowing.

This section provides

1. An overview of fundamental knowledge and evidence in support of culture-based curriculum for American Indian children.

2. A description of how we might educate state-level decision makers, including legislators and school district administrators, about the validity of culturally based curriculum and instruction.

Support for culture-centered education. Culture-centered education has the potential to make a tremendous impact on education for American Indian youth. The following information is needed in order to accomplish this goal.

Essential understandings. Teachers have known the value of culture in making studies relevant for Native students since before the *reservation era* of education for American Indian children began around 1890 (Reyhner and Eder 2004; Szasz 1999). Scholars and experts have recognized the importance of family, community, and cultural foundations in connecting American Indian children to school since at least the 1920s. Many have recognized that the learning styles and preferences of Native people vary from those of typical mainstream learners. Decision makers should, at least, be aware of these words from Cornel Pewewardy regarding American Indian children:

> A review of theories, research, and models of the learning styles of American Indian/Alaska Native students reveals that American Indian/Alaska Native students generally learn in ways characterized by factors of social/affective emphasis, harmony, holistic perspectives, expressive creativity, and nonverbal communication. Underlying these approaches are assumptions that American Indian/Alaska Native students have been strongly influenced by their language, culture, and heritage, and that American Indian/Alaska Native children's learning styles are different—but not deficient. (2002, 22)

Deyhle and Swisher (1997) conclude that the evidence of learning-style preferences across and within different tribes was plentiful and caution that there was a strong tendency for educators and others to attribute deficiency, rather than difference, to these characteristics. Authoritative sources of guidelines and recommendations for schools challenging deficiencies as causation include Cummins (1992); Reyhner, Lee, and Gabbard (1993); Reyhner and Jacobs (2002); McCarty and Watahomigie (1998); Doherty and others (2003); Demmert (2001); and Demmert and Towner (2003).

Cummins (1992) addresses factors affecting the school success of American Indian children. He notes that research suggests that American Indian and other minority students succeeded in school when

- Their teachers and school programs incorporated the students' heritage languages and cultures.
- Community participation was encouraged and integrated in the education programs.
- Instruction motivated the use of first languages as tools for learning.
- Assessment focused on ways in which academic difficulties were functions of the school contexts and were not problems located within the student. [1]

Essential content knowledge. Reyhner, Lee, and Gabbard (1993) identify five areas of essential knowledge that specially prepared teachers of American Indian children should share. Foundational knowledge of *American Indian history* must be sought because American history education in public schools omits studies of America's Native peoples.

If the teachers' acquired knowledge of American Indian history is lacking in this area, then their knowledge of *anthropological*, *sociological*, and *psychological* foundations involved in educating Native students, areas fundamental to effective teaching of these students, is nearly entirely absent. Finally, Reyhner, Lee, and Gabbard (1993) identify *pedagogical* (curricular and instructional) knowledge as essential for teachers of American Indian children.

Each of these areas has a broad, general knowledge component, but due to the experiences of each group, the needed knowledge of details for teaching will change for different audiences. These areas are essential to teachers' understandings, and each would merit an introduction in the form of a three-semester-hour course of study.

Essential pedagogical knowledge. In elaborating on the work done earlier by Reyhner, Lee, and Gabbard (1993), Reyhner and Jacobs (2002) articulate specific research-based knowledge that was available to teachers of American Indian children and, more particularly, to the programs that prepared those teachers. Reyhner and Jacobs (2002) emphasize that teaching of Native children could be improved through non-assimilationist approaches that use content and methods that stem from the knowledge brought to school from home and community and that actively engage students.

Reyhner and Jacobs (2002) remind teacher educators to apply the urgings of Richard Littlebear, or to "cross the cattle guard"—to venture into reservation communities—in order to learn more about students, their families, communities, cultures, and challenges. This, it seems to us, is the essence of CBE.

McCarty and Watahomigie (1998) elaborate on the cultural, linguistic, and literacy foundations with which educators should be familiar. From place to place and group to group, Indigenous linguistic and cultural diversity is enormous. Yet this fact was nearly universally misunderstood by mainstream Americans. Likewise, McCarty and Watahomigie (1998) explain, communication patterns vary significantly from people to people.

Beyond the realm of general foundational knowledge, state and local education leaders should also possess local knowledge of tribal communities (McCarty and Watahomigie 1998). They should know about the children, their families, their communities, their heritage language, and their tribal culture, customs, and ceremonies. Leaders and decision makers must be made aware that, contrary to "public opinion," education has been valued as a tool for helping others across all tribes.

Tharp and others at the Center for Research on Education, Diversity and Excellence (CREDE) (Tharp et al. 1999; Doherty et al. 2003) define and document the value of five standards (principles) of effective instruction with American Indian children as follows:

1. Encourage joint productive activity (teachers and students working together to create useful, meaningful products).
2. Develop language and literacy across the curriculum.
3. Contextualize instruction in home and community experience.
4. Teach complex thinking through challenging activities with clear standards and performance feedback.
5. Teach through dialogue—planned, goal-directed instructional conversations between the teacher and a small group of learners.

These principles seem essential tools for educators in all professional roles. The powerful, positive effects of the five standards (Doherty et al. 2003) have been documented with English learners, with Native students, and other students recognized as "at risk" across K–12 grade levels. The five standards seem matched to descriptions of the traditional ways of teaching and learning observed among American Indians.

Data and stories: How to inform decision makers. The "bottom line" is fundamentally important to those who manage organizations. For those responsible for public education, the effects of expenditures on measurable outcomes—test results indicating success or failure— are central. Yet it is also important that decision makers know the stories behind the numbers—effects of dollars, schools, and teachers—on living individual learners.

An example of the impacts of Reading First results from the adoption of a certain highly structured reading program. In this instance, the morning routine of ten kindergarten children has changed from six fifteen-minute periods of active engagement in lessons and games using English and their heritage language to ninety minutes of drill and practice with English letters and sounds while seated at a table with their teacher.

Time and measurement effects. We believe that curricular change must be implemented and effects measured during extended periods—minimally eight years. Continual formative evaluation over extended periods of implementation is essential, but American Indian CBE curricula have rarely been well-documented in this manner. This is because newly adopted curriculum requires at least three years to be fully implemented and, according to the American Association of School Administrators (Alborano 2002), the average tenure of American school superintendents has been about six years.

As James Alborano writes in his report on the longevity of school superintendents, "successful school reforms typically require five years or more of a superintendent's attention to implement" (2002, 132), and—in the abstract of this report—

> One can assume from the study that [six] years is the median length of service. This meant that a number of superintendents survive less than that time, and that stable, long-term standing in a position is necessary to make significant change happen. (2002, 1)

This has resulted in situations that may also be confusing in schools. Because of curriculum changes at the direction of each successive superintendent, we have had decade upon decade of partially implemented and assessed programs in schools serving American Indian children.

During a period of CBE program implementation, decision makers should ensure time for the integration of cultural content and its assessment, in addition to teaching conventional knowledge and skills. This means relaxation of sanctions and penalties based on adequate yearly progress (AYP) as determined by standardized test results.

Strategy Two: Educate the Educators

A second strategy necessary for making culturally responsive pedagogy a reality, a way to elevate the success of American Indian schoolchildren, is to educate their teachers in ways that help them become responsive to the cultural uniqueness of the children they teach. As noted earlier, the call for educators who are specially prepared to teach American Indian children goes back at least to 1928's *The Problem of Indian Administration* (known as the Meriam Report after the project's technical director Lewis Meriam).

The 1969 congressional report of the Special Subcommittee on Indian Education, *Indian Education: A National Tragedy—A National Challenge* (U.S. Congress 1969), known as the Kennedy Report after committee chairmen Senators Robert and Ted Kennedy, echoed the clarion call some forty years after the original Meriam Report (1928). In a real sense, our second strategy is interlaced with the education of the decision makers, and it should not be a difficult goal to achieve.

Model programs of teaching Native students for beginning and veteran teachers, based on sound recommendations for the development of foundational knowledge and competence, could be made available in even the most isolated venues. Other teacher-preparation programs could easily follow an approach, already in existence, of model programs for certification of teachers of American Indian children. To accomplish this goal, we recommend several considerations be followed, which are described below.

Solicit tribal support. Many sovereign tribes (for example, the Northern Arapaho) have created sets of education standards that place traditional language and culture at the center of their children's education (Northern Arapaho Tribe 2006). Even though federal/state-oriented public schools may not have acted to enforce this culture-centered orientation, tribal leaders have demanded elevation of culture and language in the curriculum.

Specify and adopt standards for teachers of American Indian children. Culture-based standards establish tribal expectations for teachers. These standards can be met by higher education institutions through programs of professional development and certification. In fact, standards can be developed to extend to students, parents, and communities, as in *Alaska Native Ways of Knowing* (Barnhardt and Kawagley 2005), which provided this information to readers.

Establish institutional/university support. The first step in this process involves designing and field-testing courses that address expert recommendations about the knowledge and competencies needed for teachers specifically prepared to teach American Indian children. Formal evaluation of the required courses by participating teachers and tribal members establishes the validity of and need for the courses. Required protocols for course and program approvals need to be followed at each level of higher education institutional organizations.

An example of one such program is the University of Wyoming's Teachers of American Indian Children (TAIC) certification and endorsement program (College of Education 2011), conceived in 2005. At first, the vision was to start the program with the teachers on or near the Wind River Reservation in Wyoming. That goal quickly grew to a need for educating teachers across the country.

The classes started with one of this chapter's authors, Rush, teaching seminar courses to cohort groups sponsored by their schools on the reservation. The seminar courses covered topics neglected in teacher-preparation programs, namely those considered to be the foundation areas of American Indian history, education, and sociological and psychological influences on American Indian educational practices. Last, the instructional models and practicum for practicing teachers were introduced for participants in the program.

With much manipulation and discussion, the courses that were piloted became the four courses for the Teachers of American Indian Children certification and endorsement. A fifth course was added to ensure a foundation in multicultural education, which provides a basic knowledge of culturally responsive curriculum and instruction.

Courting support of state certification agencies. Well developed initiatives that promise to improve the success of at-risk children are thoughtfully and appreciatively received by decision makers at all levels. Initiatives that clearly address state and professional standards for teaching and learning are particularly well-received.

Recognition of the program by state licensing officers is important. Adding endorsements to teaching certificates often brings prestige to school districts and salary adjustments to teachers. Standards for teachers of American Indian children should be defined and adopted by state licensure offices.

As part of the state endorsement approval process, the standards for the Teachers of American Indian Children became educational standards in the state of Wyoming in the fall of 2009 (Wyoming Professional Teaching Standards Board 2009). Native educators, who persisted in working with the two tribes on the Wind River Reservation to create and approve state standards for teachers of American Indian children, applied the pressure and persuasion needed to accomplish this. These standards became the basis for the state licensure board to approve the proposal submitted for the University of Wyoming Teachers of American Indian Children certificate program (College of Education 2011).

Specify certification processes. Teacher education program developers may have little influence on district policies, but they can make clear to one and all that professional development in CBE will impact student and school success in very positive ways. Just as it is important for teachers, school officials and others need to understand program benefits. In turn, they should know the procedures for obtaining the certification afforded by these programs to teachers of Indigenous children.

If clear university and state level certification processes are stated, the school district-level policies become more important in motivating teacher interest in pursuing certification. District-level salary and prestige incentives have been persuasive in moving teachers toward more advanced levels of certification. Additionally, educators are recognizing the importance of culturally based education, diversity education, and social justice education. The trend is no longer to ignore the call for curriculum and instruction to address the needs of all students rather than a select few (Ladson-Billings 2001; Nieto and Bode 2007).

Recruit teachers/offer university courses. Professional development programs for teachers of American Indian children will not be attractive to a large segment of the classroom-teaching population. It is therefore important to advertise the existence of programs and their availability to national, if not international, audiences.

By employing distance and Internet technologies, the Teachers of American Indian Children program has been successfully offered as an online program. Threaded discussion, podcasts by the instructors and Native community members, video streaming educational movies relevant to course content, and Internet conferences have all contributed to allow teachers across the country and globe to interactively learn the information needed to understand historical and current issues in Native communities and how to teach American Indian children.

Strategy Three: Place-Based Preparation of Indigenous Teachers

While non-Native teachers seem to compose the majority of faculty in the schools for American Indian children (in reservation schools we frequent, only 15 out of 91 teachers are Native), there is a need to recognize the importance of American Indian teachers as affirmation, role models, and cultural capital support for Native children. Recruitment and retention of American Indian educators has been hampered by the lack of locally delivered programs of teacher preparation.

Many otherwise excellent Native candidates for teaching careers are unable to remove themselves from their home communities to pursue teaching certificates at distant college campuses. In the following, we describe two types of approaches to programs that are locally accessed, culture/language based, and linked to long term education in American Indian communities.

Examples of locally delivered programs. We believe that, in such rural settings as Wyoming for example, permanent place-based teacher preparation programs are essential for the development and support of American Indian teachers. Such programs have been delivered and documented through temporary funding via Teacher Corps (1970–1973).

Additional programs have been delivered through the Extended Degree Program in Elementary Education (1982–1987); the Wind River Teacher Education Project (1998–2001); and the Teacher Quality Enhancement Grant Project (2002–2006) of the University of Wyoming. Combined, these programs prepared nearly forty American Indian teachers. While the programs were successful in meeting their goals, with the expiration of external funding used to develop and support these programs, each had been discontinued. Without instantiation in colleges/universities, programs disappear.

Distance-learning opportunities. Teacher certification programs are typically administered and delivered through accredited colleges and universities. These institutions may be several hours distant from the prospective teachers to be served, but recent developments in electronic learning offer convenience and cost reductions for programs. These amplifications should make preparation of Native teachers in their home communities as viable as enduring university programs operated in concert with tribal organizations, colleges, and schools.

We suggest that the delivery of long term, and possibly permanent, programs of teacher preparation and professional development for those educating American Indian children employ distance-delivery technologies. Online course delivery could fulfill this need. Isolation from college campuses would no longer be prohibitive in providing teacher preparation programs if offered through such programs. Some relatively simple programmatic adjustments must be made to ensure the success of these endeavors.

Collaboration between tribes, local education agencies, and teacher preparation programs could merge Internet delivery with local support for Native teacher candidates. While required course meetings and assignments would be completed online, local facilitators, working in concert with college instructors, could provide student support. This would optimize learning for Native teacher candidates, ensuring that they would receive the needed support for successful program completion.

The Traveled Road

Education for Native children is the right type of education for all children. As such, for American Indian students it should be culturally responsive and incorporate Native languages and literacies across the curriculum. In addition, instruction must be contextualized in home and community experiences. Complex thinking would be taught through challenging activities, with clear standards and performance feedback, and would include teaching through dialogue that is planned involving goal-directed instructional conversations between the teacher and a small group of learners (Doherty et al. 2003).

At the University of Wyoming, these are the tenets we strive to teach our students in the TAIC courses. Our goals include developing understanding, sensitivity, empathy, and compassion for all the children our teachers serve.

As we look back at the road we have traveled, we acknowledge the many individuals who have supported the initiative to create and maintain the Teachers of American Indian Children program. We are also reminded to recognize the role of Native students as contributors to the classroom and curriculum as they are engaged in their learning, including how their involvement influences and enhances the success of all programs designed to create equitable learning opportunities for Native communities.

REFERENCES

Adams, D. (1995). *Education for Extinction: American Indians and the Boarding School Experience, 1875–1928.* Lawrence: University of Kansas Press.

Alborano, J. A. (2002). "American superintendent longevity and time study." *ETD Collection for Fordham University.* Retrieved from http://fordham.bepress.com/dissertations/AAI3040390.

American Recovery and Reinvestment Act of 2009 (ARRA). (2009). Public Law 111-5. Title 14, sec. 14006 [Race to the Top Fund Assessment Program].

Barnhardt, R., and A. O. Kawagley. (2005). "Indigenous knowledge systems and Alaska Native ways of knowing." *Anthropology and Education Quarterly* 36 (1): 8–23.

College of Education. (2011). *Teachers of American Indian Children.* Laramie: University of Wyoming. Retrieved from http://www.uwyo.edu/TAIC/.

Cummins, J. (1992). "The empowerment of Indian students." In *Teaching American Indian Students*, ed. J. Reyhner, 3–12. Norman: University of Oklahoma Press.

Demmert, W. G. (2001). *Improving Academic Performance among Native American Students: A Review of the Research Literature.* Charleston, WV: ERIC Clearinghouse on Rural and Small Schools.

Demmert, W. G., and J. C. Towner. (2003). *A Review of the Research Literature on the Influences of Culturally Based Education on the Academic Performance of Native American Students.* Portland, OR: Northwest Regional Education Laboratory.

Deyhle, D., and K. Swisher. (1997). "Research in American Indian and Alaska Native education: From assimilation to self-determination." In *Review of Research on Education*, ed. M. W. Apple, 22: 113–94. Washington, DC: American Educational Research Association.

Doherty, R., R. Hilberg, A. Pinal, and R. Tharp. (2003). "Five standards and student achievement." *NABE Journal of Research and Practice* 1 (1): 1–24.

Esther Martinez Native American Languages Preservation Act of 2006. (2006). Public Law 109-394. *Statutes at Large* 120: 2,705–707.

Ladson-Billings, G. (2001). *Crossing Over to Canaan: The Journey of New Teachers in Diverse Classrooms.* San Francisco: Jossey-Bass.

McCarty, T., and L. Watahomigie. (1998). "Language and literacy in American Indian and Alaska Native communities." In *Sociocultural Contexts of Language and Literacy*, ed. B. Perez, 69–98. Mahwah, NJ: Lawrence Erlbaum Associates.

Meriam, L. (1928). *The Problem of Indian Administration: Report Made at the Request of Honorable Hubert Work, Secretary of the Interior.* Washington, DC: Institute for Government Research.

Nieto, S., and P. Bode. (2007). *Affirming Diversity: The Sociopolitical Context of Multicultural Education.* 5th ed. New York: Allyn & Bacon.

No Child Left Behind Act of 2001: Reauthorization of the Elementary and Secondary Education Act of 1965 (NCLB). (2001). *U.S. code.* Title 20, sec. 6301 et seq.

Northern Arapaho Tribe. (2006). *Northern Arapaho Code: Title 8, Education.* Ethete, WY: Northern Arapaho Business Council.

Pewewardy, C. (2002). "Learning styles of American Indian/Alaska Native students: A review of the literature and implications for practice." *Journal of American Indian Education* 4 (13): 22–56.

Prucha, F. (1979). *The Churches and the Indian Schools, 1888–1912.* Lincoln: University of Nebraska Press.

Reyhner, J., and J. Eder. (2004). *American Indian Education: A History.* Norman: University of Oklahoma Press.

Reyhner, J., and D. T. Jacobs. (2002). "Preparing teachers of American Indian and Alaska Native students." *Action in Teacher Education* 24 (2): 85–93.

Reyhner, J., H. Lee, and D. Gabbard. (1993). "A specialized knowledge base for teachers of American Indian and Alaska Native students." *Tribal College* 4 (4): 26–32.

Smiley, R., and S. Sather. (2009). *Indian Education Policies in Five Northwest Region States.* Issues & Answers. REL 2009-No. 081. Portland, OR: Northwest Regional Educational Laboratory/National Center for Education Evaluation and Regional Assistance.

Stokes, S. M. (1997). "Curriculum for Native American students: Using Native American values." *Reading Teacher* 50 (7): 576–84.

Szasz, M. (1999). *Education and the American Indian: The Road to Self-determination since 1928.* Albuquerque: University of New Mexico Press.

Tharp, R. G., H. Lewis, R. Hilberg, C. Bird, G. Epaloose, S. S. Dalton, D. G. Youpa, H. Rivera, M. Riding In-Feathers, and W. Eriacho. (1999). "Seven more mountains and a map: Overcoming obstacles to reform in Native American schools." *Journal of Education for Students Placed At Risk* 4 (1): 5–25.

U.S. Congress. Senate. Committee on Labor and Public Welfare. Special Subcommittee on Indian Education. (1969). *Indian Education: A national Tragedy—A National Challenge.* 91st Cong., 1st sess. S. Rep. 91-501.

Villegas, A. M. (1991). "Culturally responsive pedagogy for the 1990s and beyond." Princeton, NJ: Educational Testing Service.

Wyoming Professional Teaching Standards Board. (2009). *Teacher of American Indian Children Endorsement.* Retrieved from http://ptsb.state.wy.us/.

NOTE

1. Note that a degree of institutional racism, or what Cummins (1992) terms "Anglo-conformity," was evident in schools where the cultures of the students were ignored.

Chapter 12

Looking into the Future

Native Americans in Tribal Educational Leadership

Jacqueline F. Nuby: University of Montevallo, With Special Thanks for the Contributions of James Smith: Cherokee High School

ABSTRACT

This chapter concerns the need for Native Americans to look into the future of tribal education as it directly relates to successful educational leadership. Although strides have been made in Native American communities, there are remaining formidable challenges that are often not faced by the dominant culture. There is a great need for educational leaders to maintain a positive relationship with the tribal council, community members, and parents.

To groom such leadership skills, it is imperative that Native students are afforded teachers who realize the necessity of including culturally responsive pedagogy in both academic and vocational learning. Furthermore, institutions of higher learning must realize the importance of providing leadership training that applies not only to members of the dominant culture but also to future Native American leaders.

Native educational leaders must be primed for exceptional leadership and have the fulcrum, or centralized support, necessary to move forward. There is much hope for the future of tribal communities. This chapter will provide information to Native American communities to enable them to create conditions in the preparation and employment of Native American educational leaders necessary for their requisite success.

Keywords: American Indian educational leadership, American Indian education

LOOKING INTO THE FUTURE: NATIVE AMERICANS IN TRIBAL EDUCATIONAL LEADERSHIP

What does the future hold for Native American education? What part must Native American leaders play in the advancement of educational opportunities? These issues have been explored extensively, yet no answers are definitive in terms of the outcome. There will be strides as well as setbacks. Yet the story of Native Americans is one of survival against almost insurmountable odds.

Many Native American educators have made contributions, moving their respective Tribal nations forward in the educational realm (Lynch and Charleston 1990). That said, there is a great need to produce many more Native American leaders for the future to improve education for the youth in Native communities. These much-needed educational leaders must have vision, integrity, a sense of spirituality, a self-deflecting image projection, modesty, and a collectivist decision-making approach (Smith 2008).

Educational Leadership at the Local Level

Educational leaders in tribal communities face more than the typical leadership responsibilities commonly found in mainstream institutions. They are charged with infusing traditional cultural values, languages, and mores into tribal educational systems while providing an education that will equip Native students to succeed in today's world. It is very clear that to do so, tribal educational efforts cannot continue to simply duplicate a system that has historically failed Native American people (Churchill 1994; Cummins 1992; Deyhle and Swisher 1997; Duran and Duran 1995; Guthrie 1998; Smith 2008; Spring 2001; Tierney 1993; Williams 2000).

There are no easy answers, no simple changes that can immediately provide those very much-needed Native American leaders for the future. Individuals aware of the plights of Native Americans are cognizant of the fact that Native Americans have not been afforded access to equal educational opportunities as compared to the dominant culture (Churchill 1994; Pewewardy 1999; Tierney 1993, 1995). The challenge to future potential Native American leaders is to wade through the rhetoric to glean the preeminent research on effective educational practices applicable to Native American students and to follow their own best instincts in improving Native American education (Smith 2008).

There are numerous responsibilities and expectations for successful tribal leadership for tribal schools and/or Bureau of Indian Education (BIE) schools. Among the responsibilities are to ensure the recruitment, employment, training, and retention of proper personnel to conduct the successful operation of the schools; to maintain a positive work environment; to support the development of language, culture, and tradition; and to sustain a high level of ethical conduct and professional integrity (Smith 2008).

In addition, educational leaders in tribal schools or BIE schools must manage financial resources in accordance with tribal finance procedures, with federal agencies, and/or other funding sources. They must also maintain positive relationships with the tribal council, the director of education, the board of education, parents, and community members (Boloz and Foster 1998).

Acquiring Leadership Skills at Institutions of Higher Learning

There are so many theories of leadership that are utilized in programs for certification in educational leadership. To name a few, there are behavioral theories, the trait theory, the Great Man theory, participative leadership, contingency theories, transactional leadership, transformational leadership, motivational theories, management theories, path goal theories, and the Goleman leadership theory. These models are intended to prepare those with a dominant-culture viewpoint to take on leadership roles in schools.

In most non-Native universities, administrators are trained as managers of bureaucracies. Instructors employ pedagogical techniques and curricula geared toward the dominant culture.

The educational background future administrators receive in curriculum, law, finance, budgeting, and leadership techniques enables them to function with a degree of success in a culturally determined environment characterized by likeness and control. In such an environment, the end product is explicit and agreed upon. The process for achieving goals is understood, stable, and uniformly predictable.

How is an educational "leader" defined in American Indian cultures? Many institutions with programs in educational leadership are not designed to prepare Native American administrators for the numerous roles they must assume as leaders. As Nygard (2009) points out, there is a dramatic difference between Anglo leadership and Native leadership. Those in the Anglo world who aspire to leadership seek it out. In the Native American world, leadership is not sought; rather, it is given for a particular period or until a particular result is attained. This cultural construct is central to the debate of Anglo versus Native American leadership.

Many of the theories of leadership and what they expound do not work well in Indian country, nor do they take into account the Native American experience. The conditions upon which successful leadership as proscribed in these programs rest are seldom present in the world of Native American education.

Instead, Indian schools are characterized by a multitude of additional cultural variables that may not exist in other settings (Austin 1982; Barnhardt 1977). Programs for future American Indian leaders must address the differences in the dominant and Native cultures; educational backgrounds of future leaders; attitudes toward life, success, and spirituality; group consensus-making; and many more topics to prepare Native leaders for successful leadership (Smith 2008).

Developing new educational leadership programs for Native Americans. A Native American leader must have the knowledge, courage, and ability to convince the community to hear, believe in, and promote much-needed reforms. This leader must convince the board of education, tribal council, and community that what works for the Anglo community may not work for Native Americans. This is especially true when federal and state governments promise that "no child will be left behind," as in the current educational climate.

It will take a strong educational leader to convince tribal members, parents, and the community that the educational system must be changed to meet the needs of Native American students (Smith 2008). Because the makeup of the majority of Native communities represents a wide range of educational attainment—from those with no high school degree or GED for adults, including elders, to those who have attained doctoral degrees—there will not be a common understanding of what quality education should resemble available as a referent for community members to utilize in examining educational practice.

There is also a dichotomy between Anglo and Native American ways of thinking which may not be acknowledged in many academic leadership programs. However, as a result of this awareness, some universities have responded by developing new, more pertinent courses for administration programs to equip Native American leaders with the knowledge necessary to be successful in these leadership positions. The creation of a new, robust knowledge base for Native administrators includes courses on ethics, social contexts, and critical theory, as well as on school law, finance, and human resources (Mills and Amiotte1996).

Some institutions are including partnerships with Native tribes in Minnesota, South Dakota, and North Dakota. One particular program, the Native American Leadership Program (NALP; Wellstone Action), provides leadership and civic engagement skills training, culturally specific training curricula, highly skilled Native American trainers, and technical support for the creation of community action plans. This program is designed to create a pipeline of Native leaders who are ready to step into key leadership positions in their communities.

Other Native American training programs include the Native American Leadership in Education (NALE) program, in Albuquerque, New Mexico, aligned with Peck Community College and Little Horn Community College; Cardinal Stritch University Center; Southern Illinois University; the University of Pennsylvania; and the Educational Leadership and Policy Studies Program in Denver, Colorado.

In addition, there are colleges dedicated to Native American education, such as the Northwest Indian College in Bellingham, Washington; Little Big Horn College in Crow Agency, Montana; Haskell Indian Nations University in Lawrence, Kansas; College of the Menominee Nation in Keshena, Wisconsin; Oglala Lakota College on the Pine Ridge Reservation, South Dakota; Fort Belknap College in Harlem, Montana; and Sitting Bull College in Fort Yates, North Dakota. These programs are including more focus on coursework tailored to the needs of American Indian leaders in education.

These are only a few of the many examples of programs designed to prepare Native Americans for leadership roles. There are additional tribal colleges not mentioned above that are also well suited to address the educational leadership needs of Native Americans (Austin 1982; LaCounte 1987). Doing so will lead to a richer knowledge base, raising the standards of educational administration and rescuing educational practice in tribal schools. As Smith (2008) points out, the extended argument is that if professors develop better theories of Native leadership, Native educational administrators would be more effective and tribal and other schools stronger.

Tribal Council, Family, and Community Practices

Parents and communities play major roles in providing Native Americans with what they believe are the tools that will help ensure their success, whether it is in the field of academic or vocational-technical education. As with any cultural group, Native American children thrive on strong familial foundations. Based on parental involvement, young children and youth can be given opportunities to learn about and experience their cultures in addition to learning about the required school subject areas.

Working with families. The parents' roles are to instill the value of the children's heritages and to teach children to be proud of who and what they are. This comes along with instilling in their children a love of learning and encouraging an inquisitive nature about learning and their surroundings (Butterfield 1994; Butterfield and Pepper 1991; Coggins, Williams, and Radin 1996; Lewis 1981; Red Horse 1980).

For many Native Americans, there has been resistance to the formal educational system because of the boarding school experience, a lack of appropriate education, and problems associated with poverty (Adams 1995; Choney, Berryhill-Paapke, and Robbins 1995). These factors may have resulted in education not being as valued as it is by the majority in the dominant culture. In the Native American family, happiness is traditionally based on living a peaceful, harmonious, serene life and is not based on one's level of education.

Therefore, Native American educational leaders must seek the support of parents and community members when addressing educational needs for American Indian students. The educational process must be a collectivist effort (Butterfield 1994; Butterfield and Pepper 1991; Coggins, Williams, and Radin 1996; Cotton 1995; Leveque 1994; McInerney, Ardington, and De Rachewiltz 1997). Educational leaders must realize that it is very difficult to overcome historical barriers that have existed regarding education. Overcoming this will take special commitment of all leaders.

Working with tribal councils. In order to improve Native American education and administrator effectiveness in the future, an effective leader in the Native American community must have a strong, positive relationship with the members of the tribal council. It is imperative that school board members receive training for their responsibilities and have a clear understanding of their roles. All must be informed of current curricular thoughts, trends, and practices and be interested in what are considered "best practices" for Native American students (Smith 2008).

Educational leaders, board members, and the tribal council must have the support of the community, especially parents and extended family members. Ideas about education are directly related to what is learned by parents and the community. Parents and community members are the children's first teachers. Education begins at birth, and what is "right" for Native Americans is taught according to beliefs of the community. These belief systems follow future educational leaders throughout their lives; what is taught as "right" for the dominant culture does not always apply in Native communities (Gilliland 1999; Leveque 1994; Lewis 1981; Spring 2001).

Working with parents and communities on curriculum. Parental and community involvement in the design and implementation of school programs is strongly associated with improved student achievement, school achievement, and higher completion rates (Mason 1998; Tippeconnic 1983). With more involvement with family and community members, the proper ground will be laid to prepare Native American children as the educational leaders of tomorrow.

If Native stakeholders are kept informed about what is being done and why it is being done, they will understand the need for changes. Some Native Americans may be unsure about how to help their children achieve academically and hesitate to take the first step in contacting school leaders. Educational leaders, therefore, must be involved in continuously engaging constituents (Smith 2008).

Partnerships with families and communities can reinforce the idea that education is important for the health and vibrancy of American Indian communities. Every student should be programmed to finish school in order to reach his or her potential, whether in technical training or academics. Only then can independent, thriving communities and school systems become a reality in Indian country (Smith 2008).

Culturally relevant pedagogy. Many teachers who are non-Native have not been exposed to culturally relevant pedagogy for American Indian students. Therefore, Native and/or non-Native educational leaders need to be sure to provide instruction to teachers to supply this information. Teachers often fail to understand problems related to the teacher's cognitive style and that of Native American students. Some teachers have not had training in multicultural education, especially in best practices for Native American students (Aragon 2002; Butterfield 1983; Cummins 1992; Ladson-Billings 2001; Nel 1994; Reyhner 1992; Stairs 1994; Swisher and Pavel 1987; Tharp and Yamauchi 1994).

Moreover, Native American students may not be motivated to participate in instructional conversations at school because they are just not interested in the materials they are supposed to be studying. Often, these materials are based on the experiences of the majority culture, and Native American students may not see the relevance of the information to their lives (Longstreet 1978; Nuby, Ehle, and Thrower 2001). Anglo teachers may interpret these differences as due to lack of initiative in learning material and consequent failure in schools as something wrong with the students.

Unfortunately, to many teachers, this has nothing to do with their teaching styles (Bowers and Flinders 1990; Nuby 1995; Nuby, Ehle and Thrower 2001; Nuby and Oxford 1996, 1997; Villegas 1991; Worthley 1987). In essence, what these teachers are doing is ignoring the cultural as well as the cognitive styles of their Native American students. Consequently, action must be taken to curtail a long series of cultural misunderstandings from emerging and interfering with the quality of education occurring in the schools where Native students are attending.

In addition, teachers then may view students as potential dropouts, disadvantaged, or "at-risk." Native students may be pushed aside because they do not meet Anglo standards. This then may create a "we" versus "them" dichotomy in the school between non-Native teachers and Native students and/or non-Native teachers/non-Native students and Native students.

The bottom line is that Native American educational leaders must provide cultural training for non-Native teachers. There is a need for ongoing seminars and professional development for teachers who are not familiar with Native American communities and their much different "ways of knowing" (Nel 1994; Smith 2008) so that they are able to provide opportunities for learning to potential future Native American leaders. In becoming more sensitized to Native cultures, teachers will be able to forge long lasting relationships with students and their communities.

Need for Emphasis on Vocational, Professional-Technical, and Academic Education

Native American leaders must convince parents, community members, the tribal council, board members, and the students themselves that a one-track academic curriculum is not for all Native American students. As in the dominant culture, too many schools stress academics. Native American schools are presently geared toward academic education only, without regard for the other abilities/preferences of their students (Smith 2008).

There is a need for academic as well as vocational or professional-technical education; both are necessary for the survival of any economy. There is no "one-size-fits-all" type of education, and the need for education in areas other than academics is becoming more apparent as the members of the "Baby Boom" generation are retiring and leaving gaps to fill in all professions. Programs are also needed that focus on agribusiness, upon which many Native communities depend.

Guidance in Preparation for College-Bound Students

Native American educators must be keenly aware of the obstacles faced by their Native American students in transitioning to the college setting (Hilliard 1989: Huff 1997; Tierney 1993, 1995; Wickett 1997). Because some of these students may lack enough preparation for college life—psychologically, socially, or academically—they may be set up for failure in completion of university studies. Many times, Native American students return home from college or university after a semester or even sooner because they may have felt out of place in predominantly white institutions.

This is especially true if American Indian students have not been exposed to the world of academia. Native American educational leaders must form partnerships with colleges and universities in order to prevent those feelings from occurring. Students should visit colleges, participate in pre-college programs, have interactions with members of other cultures, have special one-on-one advising with school counselors, meet professors in the different fields in which they are interested, visit college dorms, and much more to ensure their success in higher education (LaCounte 1987).

In many colleges and universities, Native American students are placed into an environment that does not meet their needs (Mason 1998; Sanders 1987). Native American students may also find it difficult to transition into college because of indifferent recruiting practices. Once they arrive on campus, the students may become numbers, not individuals with potential leadership qualities (Griffin 2000; Phelps and Taber 1996; Sanders 1987).

Native American educational leaders and institutional representatives must rise to the challenge of creating situations that make Native students feel welcome in unfamiliar educational environments (Butterfield and Pepper 1991; Butterfield 1994; Leveque 1994). There are many ways in which educational attainment of Native Americans can be promoted.

Among ways to do so are fostering intercultural harmony on the college or university level, improving the preparation of educators in working with diverse populations, developing instructional curricula and strategies that support diverse cultural needs and cognitive styles, and adopting a new paradigm for the evaluation of American Indians' progress and success. Native educational leaders must work with institutions of higher learning in providing comprehensive support services for mentoring and career counseling to Native students, especially effective when provided by Native counselors (Peavy 1995).

Institutions can also assist Native students with programs that bridge educational gaps. Programs can be developed that provide increased coordination and articulation between elementary and secondary schools serving American Indian students, Native community colleges, and four-year colleges and universities (Ladson-Billings 2001). Programs can include extended classes, tutorials, learning laboratories, and collaborative study groups (Gay 2000).

Institutions can also actively recruit and employ Native Americans in senior leadership positions. This sends a clear message about the value of cultural diversity among professional staff and for the institution. Effective institutions can cultivate American Indian professors by mentoring graduate students or junior faculty members and supporting them in additional graduate training. Native role models in front of the classroom can serve to validate and motivate students to attain higher levels of achievement. Native American teachers also bring with them an inherent understanding of the Native students' backgrounds, attitudes, and experiences (Lewis 1981).

Conclusion

Educational leadership and reform in American Indian communities must be developed. It is an ongoing, daunting task with no simple solutions. Although strides have been made in transforming the traditional dominant culture educational structure in the last decade, Native American educators must realize the need for a different model for Native students and accept the responsibility of preparing those students who will successfully fill leadership roles in tribal communities (Smith 2008).

Along with this, Native Americans must incorporate cultural wisdom in renewed efforts toward creating educational institutions that facilitate the complex problem of producing able and successful leaders who must function in two very different worlds (Littlebear and Martinez 1996).

In order for American Indian communities to move forward, as well as to retain traditional values and customs, leadership is critical. The challenges may be many; however, the benefits will be enormous for all members of Native American communities and the greater American community in general. The key to leadership is culturally appropriate education (Smith 2008).

REFERENCES

Adams, D. W. (1995). *Education for Extinction: American Indians and the Boarding School Experience, 1875–1928*. Lawrence: University Press of Kansas.

Aragon, S. R. (2002). "An investigation of factors influencing classroom motivation for postsecondary American Indian/Alaska Native students." *Journal of American Indian Education* 41(1): 1–18.

Austin, A. W. (1982). *Minorities in Higher Education*. San Francisco: Josey-Bass.

Barnhardt, R. (1977). "Administrator influences in Alaska Native education." In *Cross-cultural Issues in Alaskan Native Education*, ed. R. Barnhardt. Fairbanks, AK: Center for Cross-Cultural Studies, pp. 144–164.

Boloz, S., and C. Foster. (1998). "The reservation administrator." *Journal of American Indian Education*, 19: 24–28.

Bowers, C. S., and D. J. Flinders. (1990). *Responsive Teaching: An Ecological Approach to Classroom Patterns of Language, Culture, and Thought*. New York: Teachers College Press.

Butterfield, R. A. (1983). "The development and use of culturally appropriate curriculum for American Indian students." *Peabody Journal of Education* 61 (1): 49–66.

———. (1994). *Blueprints for Indian Education: Improving Mainstream Schooling*. Washington, DC: U.S. Department of Educational Research and Improvement. Education Resources Information Center. Retrieved from http://www.eric.ed.gov (accession number ED372898).

Butterfield, R. A., and F. C. Pepper. (1991). "Improving parental participation in elementary and secondary education for American Indian and Alaska Native students." In *Indian Nations at Risk*, ed. P. Cahape and C. B. Howley. Washington, DC: U.S. Dept. of Education. Education Resources Information Center. Retrieved from http://www.eric.ed.gov (accession number ED343763).

Choney, S. K., E. Berryhill-Paapke, and R. R. Robbins. (1995). "The acculturation of American Indians: Developing frameworks for research and practice." In *Handbook of Multicultural Counseling*, ed. J. G. Ponterotto, J. M. Casas, L. A. Suzuki, and C. M. Alexander, 73–92. Thousand Oaks, CA: Sage.

Churchill, W. (1994). *Indians are Us? Culture and Genocide in Native North America*. Monroe, ME: Common Courage.

Coggins, K., E. Williams, and N. Radin. (1996). *The Traditional Tribal Values of Ojibwa Parents and the School Performance of their Children: An Exploratory Study*. Ann Arbor: University of Michigan. Education Resources Information Center. Retrieved from http://www.eric.ed.gov (accession number ED400116).

Cotton, K. (1995). *Effective Schooling Practices: A Research Synthesis, 1995 Update*. Portland, OR: Northwest Regional Laboratory.

Cummins, J. (1992). "The empowerment of Indian students." In *Teaching American Indian Students*, ed. J. Reyhner, 3–12. Norman: University of Oklahoma Press.

Deyhle, D., and K. Swisher. (1997). "Research in American Indian and Alaska Native education: From assimilation to self-determination." In *Review of Research in Education*, ed. M. W. Apple, 113–94. Washington, DC: American Educational Research Association.

Duran, E., and B. Duran. (1995). *Native American Postcolonial Psychology*. Albany: State University of New York Press.

Gay, G. (2000). *Culturally Responsive Teaching: Theory, Research, and Practice*. New York: Teachers College Press.

Gilliland, H. (1999). *Teaching the Native American*. Dubuque, IA: Kendall-Hunt.

Griffin, P. R. (2000). *Seeds of Racism in the Soul of America*. Naperville, IL: Sourcebooks.

Guthrie, R. V. (1998). *Even the Rat was White: A Historical View of Psychology*. Boston: Allyn & Bacon.

Hilliard, A. (1989). "Teachers and cultural styles in a pluralistic society." *NEA Today* 7 (6): 65–69.

Huff, D. J. (1997). *To Live Heroically: Institutional Racism and American Indian Education*. Albany: State University of New York Press.

LaCounte, D. W. (1987). "American Indian students in college." In *Responding to the Needs of Today's Minority Students*. Directions for Student Services 38, ed. D. J. Wright, 65–79. San Francisco: Jossey Boss.

Ladson-Billings, G. (2001). "The power of pedagogy: Does teaching matter?" In *Race and Education: The Role of History and Society in Educating African American Students*, ed. W. H. Watkins, J. H. Lewis, and V. Chou, 73–88. Boston: Allyn & Bacon.

Leveque, D. M. (1994). *Cultural and Parental Influences on Achievement among Native American Students in Barstow Unified School District*. Paper presented at the National Meeting of the Comparative and International Educational Society, San Diego, CA. Education Resources Information Center. Retrieved from http://www.eric.ed.gov (accession number ED382416).

Lewis, R. (1981). "Patterns and strengths of American Indian families." In *American Family Strengths and Stresses*, ed. F. Hoffman. Isleta, NM: American Indian Social Research and Development Associates, pp. 101–106.

Littlebear, R., and A. Martinez. (1996). "A model for promoting Native American language preservation and teaching." In *Stabilizing Indigenous Languages*, ed. G. Cantoni, 234–39. Flagstaff: Northern Arizona University.

Longstreet, W. S. (1978). *Aspects of Ethnicity: Understanding Differences in Pluralistic Classrooms*. New York: Teachers College Press.

Lynch, G., and C. M. Charleston. (1990). "The emergence of American Indian leadership in education." *Journal of American Indian Education* 29 (2): 1–10.

Mason, N. (1998). *Project Research on the Achievement of Aboriginal Students in Reserve Schools: A Success or Disappointment*. Manitoba, Canada: Brandon University. Education Resources Information Center. Retrieved from http://www.eric.ed.gov (accession number ED427901).

McInerney, D. M. V., A. Ardington, and C. De Rachewiltz. (1997). *School Success in Intercultural Contexts: Conservations at Window Rock*. Preliminary report. Paper presented at the Annual Meeting of the American Educational Research Association, Chicago. Education Resources Information Center. Retrieved from http://www.eric.ed.gov (accession number ED407202).

Mills E., and L. Amiotte. (1995). "American Indian administrator preparation: A program analysis." *Tribal College Journal* 7 (3): 27–41.

Nel, J. (1994). "Preventing school failure: The Native American child." *Clearinghouse* 67 (3): 169–74.

Nuby, J. F. (1995). *Learning Style: A Comparative Analysis of the Learning Styles of Native American and African American Students*. PhD diss., University of Alabama, Tuscaloosa.

Nuby, J., M. A. Ehle, and E. Thrower. (2001). "Culturally responsive teaching as related to the learning styles of Native American students." In *Multicultural Education: Diverse Perspectives*, ed. J. Nyowe and S. Abdullah, 231–71. Victoria, BC, Canada: Trafford.

Nuby, J., and R. L. Oxford. (1996). *Learning Style Preferences of Native Americans and African American Secondary Students as Measured by the MBTI*. Paper presented at the annual meeting of the Mid-South Educational Research Association, Tuscaloosa, Alabama. Education Resources Information Center. Retrieved from http://www.eric.ed.gov (accession number ED406422).

———. (1997). "Learning style preferences of Native American and African American students as measured by the MBTI." *Journal of Psychological Type* 26:1–15.

Nygard, A. (2009). *A Native Leadership Perspective—Creating a Leadership System in Native Communities*. Bismarck, ND: Al Nygard Consulting.

Peavy, R. V. (1995). *Career Counseling for Native Youth: What Kind and by Whom?* Greensboro, NC: ERIC Clearinghouse on Counseling and Student Services. Education Resources Information Center. Retrieved from http://www.eric.ed.gov (accession number ED399486).

Pewewardy, C. D. (1999). "Culturally responsive teaching for American Indian students." In *Pathways to Success in School: Culturally Responsive Teaching*, ed. E. R. Hollins and E. I. Oliver, 85–100. Mahwah, NJ: Lawrence Erlbaum.

———. (2002). "Learning style preference of American Indian and Alaska Native students." *Journal of American Indian Education* 41 (3): 22–56.

Phelps, D. G., and L. Taber. (1996). "Affirmative action as equal opportunity." *Achieving Administrative Diversity: New Directions for Community Colleges* 24 (2): 67–79.

Red Horse, J. (1980). "Family structure and value orientation in American Indians." *Social Casework* 68 (10): 462–67.

Reyhner, J., ed. (1992). *Teaching American Indian Students*. Norman: University of Oklahoma Press.

Sanders, D. (1987). "Cultural conflicts: An important factor in the academic failures of American Indians." *Journal of Multicultural Counseling and Development* 15 (2): 81–90.

Smith, J. (2008). *A Qualitative Investigation into the Lack of Native Americans in Leadership Roles: Implications for Native American Education*. PhD diss., Oakland City University, Oakland City, IN.

Spring, J. (2001). *Deculturalization and the Struggle for Equality: A Brief History of the Education of Dominated Cultures in the United States*. 3rd ed. New York: McGraw-Hill.

Stairs, A. (1994). "Indigenous ways to go to school: Exploring many visions." *Journal of Multilingual and Multicultural Development* 15 (1): 63–76.

Swisher, K., and D. M. Pavel. (1987). "Styles of learning and learning of styles: educational conflicts for American Indian Alaska Native youth." *Journal of Educational Issues of Language Minority Students* 13: 59–77.

Tharp, R. G., and L. A. Yamauchi. (1994). *Effective Instructional Conversation in Native American Classrooms. Educational Practice Report: 10*. Santa Cruz, CA: National Center for Research on Cultural Diversity and Second Language Learning. Education Resources Information Center. Retrieved from http://www.eric.ed.gov (accession number ED372896).

Tierney, W. G. (1993). "The college experiences of Native Americans: A critical analysis." In *Beyond Silenced Voices*, ed. L. Weis and M. Fine, 309–24. Albany: State University of New York Press.

———. (1995). "Addressing failure: Factors affecting Native American college student retention." *Journal of Navajo Education* 13 (1): 3–7.

Tippeconnic, J. W., III. (1983). "Training teachers of American Indian students." *Peabody Journal of Education* 61 (1): 6–15.

Villegas, A. M. (1991). *Culturally Responsive Pedagogy for the 1990s and Beyond. Trends and Issues Paper No. 6*. Washington, DC: ERIC Clearinghouse on Teacher Education.

Wellstone Action. Native American Leadership Program (NALP). (2012). http://www.wellstone.org/programs/native-american-leadership-program.

Wickett, M. (1997). "Uncovering bias in the classroom: A personal journey." In *Multicultural and Gender Equity in the Mathematics Classroom: The Gift of Diversity. 1997 Yearbook*, ed. J. Trentacosta and M. J. Kenney, Reston, VA: National Council of Teachers of Mathematics.

Williams, R. A., Jr. (2000). "Documents of barbarism: The contemporary legacy of European racism and colonialism in the narrative traditions of federal Indian law." In *Critical Race Theory: The Cutting Edge*, ed. R. Delgado and J. Stefanic, 94–105. Philadelphia: Temple University Press.

Worthley, K. M. E. (1987). *Learning Style Factors of Field Dependence/Field Independence and Problem-solving Strategies of Hmong Refugee Students*. Master's thesis, University of Wisconsin, Stout.

Chapter 13

Leadership in Indian Education

Dean Chavers: Catching the Dream

ABSTRACT

The history of American Indian education is fraught with efforts to deculturalize American Indians as well as eliminate their tribal languages forever. In addition, authorities who had decision-making powers regarding how to educate Native students determined that they would only benefit from education that would prepare them for vocational roles as opposed to the professions and academics.

However, in the mid-20th century a new movement arose that began to challenge the way these authorities perceived education for American Indians. In its wake, many American Indian movements were launched, and American Indian leadership emerged to take the reins of Indian education from the exclusive jurisdiction of the United States government officials. The history of these leadership alterations and the people who effected transformations of American Indian education then and today are chronicled in this chapter.

Keywords: American Indian education, American Indian leaders, leadership in American Indian education

LEADERSHIP IN INDIAN EDUCATION

Indian education has been hamstrung on a blue-collar paradigm since before Colonel Richard Henry Pratt started Carlisle Indian School in 1878. There were a few schools on reservations before Carlisle, but within a few years after, the Bureau of Indian Affairs (BIA) had started almost two hundred federal schools for Indians. Their announced job was to assimilate Indians into the dominant society.

The Pratt model called for all instruction to be in English. Students were forbidden to speak their Indian languages. Schools were vocational, teaching students welding, carpentry, masonry, secretarial skills, and typing. In the old days, before 1960, male students had to work on the farms at the Indian schools for half of every day. They milked cows, baled hay, hoed beans and carrots, and plowed the fields. Girls worked half the day outside the classroom learning sewing, cooking, bed making, washing dishes, doing laundry, and ironing.

The students were taken away from their families for four to eight years. Often, when students came home to the reservation, they could not speak their Native languages. Some of them never relearned them and spoke only in English for the rest of their lives. They could no longer speak with their parents and grandparents.

College preparation was not part of the paradigm. The racist attitude of school people was that Indians were not capable of learning philosophy, science, medicine, sociology, and the fine arts.

Creating New Thinking for American Indian Education

One of the first traits of Indian leaders in education has been their willingness and ability to think outside the BIA-school box. Even though most educators of Indian students are still thinking inside the box, there are at least some who have been able to break out of it and challenge Indian people to do better than they have ever done in education.

Indian education stayed muddled and unchanged until the 1960s. Then several things started happening to bring about change. The movement of Indians to cities under the Relocation Program in the 1940s and 1950s, the resistance of the "fish-in" people in Washington state, and the growth of organizations of young, militant Indian people started to affect how people thought about themselves and the future of their children.

The National Indian Youth Council (NIYC) and other militants brought a new way of thinking to Indian schools. Indian students were now supposed to learn their Indian history and culture and speak their Native languages.

The occupation of Alcatraz Island in 1969 led to other occupations as well as positive movements for change. Other occupations after Alcatraz included Fort Lawton in Seattle; D-Q University near Davis, California; Pit River country in Northern California; Plymouth Rock; Wounded Knee on the Pine Ridge Reservation; Pyramid Lake, Nevada; the Gallup Intertribal Ceremonial; the BIA Central Office in Washington DC; and many other locations.

The traditional education movement. The leader of the Alcatraz occupation was *Richard Oakes* (Mohawk), who was a member of the White Roots of Peace from his teenage years. He brought the occupiers out to the Bay Area after he moved there and brought them onto all the college campuses, where they had a strong influence on the college students.

The White Roots of Peace had led a Nativist movement for three decades. Starting in the 1950s, their message was to return to Native ways, teach and learn Native languages, practice Native religions, cultivate and eat Native foods, and practice traditional Native cultures. This philosophy is the heart and soul of the new paradigm of Indian education that emerged in the 1960s, 1970s, and 1980s. Practicing Native religion, culture, and ways of life fit hand and glove with the restoration of self-government and self-determination, which came later.

Preservation of Native languages and cultures is the main touchstone of the traditional educational movement. It quickly became dogma. The new paradigm insists on language and cultural preservation to the detriment of traditional study of math, English, and science. Anyone who deviates from its tenets is certainly to be attacked as a sell-out or an Uncle Tom.

To "sell out" means that you insist on students doing well in the European subjects of literature, arts, sciences, and math to the exclusion of Native subjects. But it has been demonstrated repeatedly that the absolutely well-adjusted student can straddle both roads—attend and participate in a traditional powwow while at the same time maintaining a great record studying European subjects.

Elementary and secondary education. When *Dave Risling* (Hoopa) started college in southern California, several hundred miles from his home on the Hoopa Reservation, he had no idea of being anything except a schoolteacher. It was 1939, and war clouds were gathering over Europe and Asia. Hitler had invaded and occupied Poland and was invading Russia. The Japanese had invaded and occupied parts of China and Korea.

Dave's father, Dave Risling Sr., was one of the traditional leaders at Hoopa for decades, and he wanted Dave to be one of the first people on the reservation to have a college degree. Almost no California Indians had even finished high school.

The Indians of California had suffered terribly during and after the Gold Rush (1848–1864). The president sent three treaty commissioners to California to negotiate treaties with the 120 California tribes, which they did. They sent eighteen treaties back to Washington, where they were promptly buried. The Senate refused to ratify them under pressure from the senators and governor of California. The treaties had reserved eight million acres for Indian reservations, and the leaders of the new state thought this was way too much land for Indians to have.

The Senate locked the treaties away in a drawer, where they remained until a clerk accidentally found them in 1905. The failure to ratify the treaties meant Indians in California were thrown mostly onto their own. Many tribes, including the famous Yana and Yahi, were completely annihilated. Cowboys killed the last Yana in 1876 (Kroeber 1961).

The California legislature passed a law making it legal for whites to use Indians as farm hands, ranch hands, and indentured servants. Anglos kidnapped young Indian children and sold them as servants. Some Indians became the first braceros, predating braceros from Mexico by eighty years.

California also led the nation in massacres, with over five dozen of them. It was legal for white people to kill Indians until well after 1900; no white person was ever tried or even charged with murder during the last half century of the 1800s through the early 20th century when it became illegal to do so. The Indian population shrank from 100,000 in 1850 to only 15,000 in 1900, a death rate of over 95 percent (it had already shrunk from 300,000 to 100,000 under the Spanish).

California Indian students could attend BIA schools until 1952, when the Sacramento Area Office stopped them from enrolling in the schools. Ironically, Indians from other states were coming to Sherman Indian School in Riverside, California, but California Indians could not attend it. They were forced to attend public schools. The Indian dropout rate in the state skyrocketed, running as high as 90 percent for the Pomos around Ukiah (Chavers 2007). A whole generation of Indian students was lost, entering adulthood with little education, little ability to read, and with little chance ever to survive.

Dave Risling had been born downriver at Hoopa in 1921, where his dad was both a fisherman and a logger. But when Dave Jr. was five years old, Dave Sr. moved the whole family of eight kids to Hoopa proper so they could go to school there. By the time Dave got to high school, the BIA school had become a public school with an Indian school board— probably the first such all-Indian school board in the nation.

Risling finished high school there in 1939. He started college at Cal Poly that fall, the only Indian on the campus. He sold his two Future Farmers of America (FFA) pigs, picked out his college wardrobe at the Goodwill store in Eureka, and took the bus south to San Luis Obispo.

World War II intervened, which saw Risling become commander of his own navy ship. He went on active duty in 1942, and when he finished training, he was assigned to patrol craft (PC) 1139, the same type of ship that John F. Kennedy later made famous. They sank submarines, shot down airplanes, and rescued downed U.S. pilots. His only touch of home for almost two years came when he found his brother, Jack, on Iwo Jima. The navy released him in the fall of 1945. He and his wife, Barbara, had gotten married in 1942.

When he got home, he went back to Cal Poly and finished in 1947—the first California Indian ever to have graduated from college. He then went to teach in Fresno. In a few years, by 1952, he had earned his master's degree and moved into college teaching at Modesto.

Risling reacted to the sad situation of Indian education by teaching and then by becoming an activist. A quarter of a century after he left the navy, he decided to do something about the sorry state of Indian education. He began by talking to people he knew. These people included *Charles* and *Kay Black*, *Morgan Otis* (Kiowa), *Jack Forbes* (Powhatan), and Maidu leader *Tommy Merino*.

By the early 1960s, disturbed by the horrible conditions on Indian reservations, Risling and some other leaders prevailed on the California legislature to sponsor a study of Indian reservations. What they found was shocking. Most Indians had below a seventh grade education. Most reservations had no access to health care at all. Racial discrimination was rampant. Unemployment was massive.

American Indians Changing the Face of Indian Education

Within a few years, the study had led Risling and the other leaders to call an Indian education meeting at the little reservation at North Fork. The famous North Fork Report written by Jack Forbes (1967) set the tone for the next four decades of reform in Indian education. The ad hoc committee that held the conference quickly became the California Indian Education Association (CIEA), which is still very active in the state.

The report recommended that Indian parents become involved in the schools, that Indian communities organize around the schools and support them, and that schools "must show respect for the Indian language and heritage but at the same time must allow the Indian people to determine for themselves what 'Indian-ness' means today" (J. Forbes, pers. comm., ca. 1967).

Establishing the Native American Studies movement. Risling's sisters Vivien, Viola, and Rosalind had heard Jack Forbes speak at University of California, Berkeley, in the middle of the 1960s and were motivated by what he said. Forbes was an Indian nationalist and unusual in that he was both a historian and an anthropologist. He was able to capture people's thinking about Indian education and put it into words. His dozens of books were the initial thinking behind the Native American Studies (NAS) movement.

Formation of Indian education associations. Within five years, in 1967, Risling had led the formation of the first grassroots Indian-education group, the California Indian Education Association (CIEA). Vivien, Risling's sister, organized a chapter called the Local Indians for Education, or LIFE, in Redding, California, which lasted for years. Viv's chapter had no money for over a decade; then I wrote a proposal for them in 1976 and got them an adult-education grant from the Office of Indian Education.

Forbes drove all over the state for two years, talking to people on different reservations about the need for education and the need to get involved in education. He told me that once in a while someone would give him two or five dollars for gas, but he paid most of the expenses out of his pocket. Within a decade, there were fifteen or so states with an Indian education association, all modeled on CIEA.

CIEA held its first meeting ever in North Fork in 1967 and issued a report that has shaped Indian education to this day. The North Fork Report (Forbes 1967) called for the study of Indian history, government, culture, and language. It called for local Indian input in education and Indian control of schools. It called for preserving and promoting Indian languages. It called for racially sensitive textbooks, a subject that *Rupert Costo* (Cahuilla) and his wife *Jeanette Henry* (Cherokee) devoted years to studying and pushing (Costo 1970).

Two years later, the same thing happened on a national level when Risling, *Sam Billison* (Navajo), *Helen Scheirbeck* (Lumbee), *Will Antell* (Chippewa), and *Rosemary Christensen* (Chippewa) formed the National Indian Education Association (NIEA). Billison took up the cause. He and Antell called a group of people together in 1968 to plan the first NIEA conference. Billison told me they used the North Fork Report as their planning document.

First Native American Studies (NAS) higher education program. The CIEA North Fork conference led directly to the initiation of the first Native American Studies (NAS) program in the United States, at the University of California (UC), Berkeley, in 1969. Both *LaNada Boyer* and *Lee Brightman* (Lakota) were instrumental in founding the program at Berkeley. Within another year, both Forbes and Risling had relocated to UC Davis, where both remained for the rest of their lives.

Legislation for American Indian education. Risling was a visionary who led the way to the p_____ f the Indian Education Act (IEA) in 1972, the formation of over three hundred NAS program_ a_ _he nation's colleges, and the IEA grants to over 1,100 school districts every year. Christensen did most of the work pulling the first meeting together. She later earned her doctorate and has taught at the University of Wisconsin, Green Bay, for almost forty years. She has been a fighter for Native language preservation for half a century.

Helen Scheirbeck, at the time a staffer for Senator Sam Ervin and the mentor to the next generation of Indians on Capitol Hill, also served as the only person at the Office of Education Indian Desk for several years. She also led the fight for the Indian Civil Rights Act of 1968 (ICRA), which took seven years and many hearings to get passed.

The people in Congress had to be educated about how Indian people could not get a fair trial, how the BIA dominated and abused Indian people, and how local officials in counties and law enforcement mistreated and abused Indians (Chavers 2007). Scheirbeck also wrote the education section of the final report of the American Indian Policy Review Commission in 1976.

Will Antell helped to get the IEA passed when it looked as if it would go down in defeat. It had failed to pass the Senate in both 1970 and 1971, despite heavy support from Senator Edward Kennedy. Senator Walter Mondale of Minnesota brought Antell to Washington, DC, to work as a staff person, and they got the bill passed in 1972.

Antell served as the NIEA president for the first three years of its life. He then moved back home to work for the state department of education for the next twenty-five years. During that time, he got almost all the schools in the state with racist Indian names for their teams, such as Warriors, Squaws, and Bucks, to change their names to something that was not offensive to Indians.

Increasing the number of American Indian attorneys. Robert Bennett (Oneida), when he was commissioner of Indian affairs, started both the BIA scholarship program—contracted through American Indian Scholarships—and the American Indian Law Center at the University of New Mexico. Bennett had been one of the first Indian attorneys, finishing law school at night after he was discharged from the Marine Corps at the end of World War II. He had a national assessment done and found that there were only thirty-five Indian attorneys in the whole United States. President Lyndon B. Johnson approved both of his proposals.

Founding the Rough Rock Demonstration School. The late *Bob Roessel* (Anglo) was married to a Navajo woman, Ruth, who is still a strong leader in Indian education. A native of Webster Groves, Missouri, Roessel became fascinated by Indians from stories his grandmother told him. When he earned his master's degree, he headed west, never to return east except for a few trips home. After teaching Navajo kids for a decade, he left the reservation to run one of the first American Indian teacher education programs in the United States, at Arizona State University (ASU).

He left ASU to head the first Indian-controlled school in the United States, at Rough Rock, Arizona. *Allen D. Yazzie*, Chairman of the Navajo Education Committee, had initiated the idea for the school (Roessel 1968). The tribal education leaders were dissatisfied with the weakness of the Navajo schools and determined to improve them. They asked for and got a federal grant from the federal Office of Economic Opportunity (OEO) to start a demonstration school at Rough Rock. It would have a Navajo school board, Navajo curriculum, many Navajo teachers, and eventually Navajo superintendents (Chavers 2007).

The Rough Rock Demonstration School, established in 1964, was the leader and model for the next generation of Indian controlled schools. There are now some seventy of these schools across the nation.

Contract schools. Birgil Kills Straight (Lakota), went to college with Tom Brokaw but never met him until forty years later, when Brokaw interviewed him for the NBC newscast. Kills Straight got motivated by the school at Rough Rock and was dissatisfied with the poor quality of the schools on the Pine Ridge reservation. He started the first Lakota contract school in his home community of Kyle. The Little Wound School has become one of the best Indian schools in the nation, sending its graduates on to universities, including Stanford and the University of San Diego.

By 1972, Kills Straight, some Menominee leaders, and some Navajo leaders had formulated an organization to advocate for their needs, the Coalition of Indian Controlled School Boards (CICSB; Fitzgerald and Davis 1974). The CICSB operated for five years and closed when it ran out of money. It had operated on private and federal grants.

The Association of Contract Tribal Schools (ACTS), headed by *Roger Bordeaux* (Lakota), took up where CICSB left off. They were chartered in 1982 and are still operating.

Restoration of Menominee Treaty rights. Not totally related to education, but motivated by the loss of their land, poor education, and lack of health care, *Ada Deer* (Menominee) led the fight to reverse tribal termination on a national level. The children in the Menominee Tribe lost their right to attend BIA schools when they were terminated in 1961. They were forced to attend the local public schools. The dropout rate shot up in short order to 75 percent. Almost none of the children of the next generation finished high school. They had to be bused off the reservation to attend school in the nearby villages of Neopit and Keshena.

Racial prejudice in both villages ran rampant. School principals, teachers, white students, and white parents made fun of Indian children, belittling them. The Indian students had to ride in the back of the school buses and were beaten up if they tried to sit in the front. Students called them names all day long. They were discouraged from playing on the sports teams and participating in school activities such as plays, recitals, and dramas (Peroff 1982).

The test scores for Menominee Indian children dropped precipitously. The Indian students at Neopit tested at the eighth percentile for sixth graders and at the fifteenth percentile for third graders. The students at Keshena tested at the seventeenth percentile for sixth graders and the thirteenth percentile for third graders. The children were not used to the racist treatment they were suddenly exposed to in the public schools (Peroff 1982).

Deer quit her college teaching job in 1970 and devoted herself to the fight for restoration of treaty rights for the tribe. She traveled the nation for several years and devoted herself to lobbying on the Hill. Ada's fight, the first successful restoration of a terminated tribe, set the pattern for some sixty other tribes to reverse their termination. She served as assistant secretary for Indian Affairs (ASIA) in the first Clinton administration and then returned to the University of Wisconsin, where she still heads the Indian program.

Changes at the post secondary education level. Jack Forbes (Powhatan) invented the term *Native American* in 1963 when he was teaching in Los Angeles. When someone asked if he was Indian, Jack replied, "No, I'm a Native of the Americas. And I'm an American. I'm a Native American." By the time I got to California in 1968, the term was just starting to catch on. It wasn't going to be the Indian Studies program at UC Berkeley but instead the Native American Studies (NAS) program.

Forbes was working at the Far West Lab when I first met him in 1968. He stayed there for another year, conducting a survey on Indian education, and moved to UC Davis the next year. He had become a mentor to the staff and faculty at Berkeley while he was at Far West, which was only a few miles from the campus. He had enough time teaching that he went to Davis as a full professor of education and anthropology. Within six months, he had managed to get Dave Risling transferred from Modesto to Davis to head the new NAS program.

The occupation of Alcatraz by seventy-eight Indian college students in November 1969 electrified the college programs in California. Students from UC Berkeley, San Francisco State, UC Davis, UC Santa Cruz, and Sacramento State were in the first wave that went to the island. The idea of NAS spread like wildfire. When I got the NAS program approved by the faculty senate at CSU Hayward in 1974, we had over eighty campuses around the nation contact us for help designing their programs.

Within two years, there were a few dozen Indian programs on college campuses in the state—Chico, Humboldt, Riverside, Fresno, UCLA, UC San Diego, San Francisco State, Sacramento State, Hayward, Long Beach, Northridge, Pomona, Palomar, Redlands, San Marcos, Sonoma, Fresno, and so on. Indian college enrollment rose rapidly; at Berkeley, it went from five Indians in 1968 to over one hundred by 1973. Nationwide, it went from about 1,500 in 1963 to 30,000 by 1975. Stanford went from three Indian students in 1970 to fifty by 1975.

One of the early leaders of the NAS movements was the late *John Rouillard* (Lakota). While he was head of the NAS program at San Diego State, Rouillard was also a founder of the American Indian Language Development Institute (AILDI). NIEA memorialized Rouillard two decades ago by naming a scholarship for him.

Richard Oakes (Mohawk), the leader of the Alcatraz occupation, also got the NAS program off the ground at San Francisco State when the famous Japanese American semanticist, S. I. Hayakawa, was president. Surprisingly, the conservative Hayakawa, later a Republican U.S. senator, had a soft spot in his heart for Oakes, the young Indian radical.

Michael Dorris (Modoc) contacted me from Dartmouth in early 1973 for help in setting up his NAS program. He recruited all over the nation and immediately had a highly successful program with a 90 percent or higher completion rate. He later wrote a best seller (Dorris 1990) about adopting two Lakota children who turned out to suffer from fetal alcohol syndrome (FAS).

Leigh Jeanotte (Chippewa) started work at the University of North Dakota at the same time and is still there, having trained two generations of scholars. *Chuck Swick* (Lakota) started at the same time at South Dakota and retired three years ago after thirty-five years of service.

American Indian scholarship. Vine Deloria (Lakota) set a standard for scholarship at the college level. His best seller, *Custer Died for Your Sins* (1969), is one of only a handful of best sellers in the NAS category. Deloria taught at UCLA, Arizona, and Colorado over the years. While the Custer book was mostly tongue-in-cheek, most of his other books were very serious, laying out the framework of federal Indian law and sovereignty rights.

In addition to Forbes and Risling, there have been numerous other leaders in higher education, including *Duane Champagne* (Chippewa), *Jack Norton* (Hupa), *Donald Fixico* (Shawnee), *James Larimore* (Comanche), and *Wayne Stein* (Chippewa). Champagne at UCLA has been one of the leading Native scholars for the past quarter of a century. He has researched and written on a wide variety of subjects, including the Alcatraz occupation, the effects of P. L. 280 on Indian justice, and social change. He runs the Native Nations Law and Policy Center.

Jack Norton at Humboldt State put one of the early NAS programs together. Don Fixico at ASU has been an accomplished author on the termination of treaties and urban Indians. After Stanford's Indian program went through six directors in a decade and had a high dropout rate, Jim Larimore turned the program around and raised completion rates to above 90 percent. He left Stanford to be Dean of Academics at Dartmouth. Wayne Stein has been a tribal college president and dean and has written extensively on tribal colleges. He is a professor at Montana State.

Tribal-level leadership in education. Pat Locke (Dakota) had an amazing career. From an early start as an avid scholar and a heavy reader, Locke launched an amazing eight movements during her fifty-year career. First, she read all the books in her library at a small school in Idaho. Then she read them all again. She had one of the highest IQ scores on record. She was a visionary, a leader, a scholar, and a fighter. Indian women in education adored her.

I used to hate to try to go somewhere with her at the NIEA meetings. To go from a meeting room to the cafeteria might take half an hour or even an hour, so many people wanted to talk to her. She launched

- The movement to preserve Native languages, leading to the passing of the Native American Languages Act of 1990 (NALA). It reversed the national policy from 1869 that called for the abolition of Indian languages and said they had to be preserved, protected, and promoted. Most school people still know nothing of this law and are still carrying on in the old vein.
- The movement to establish tribal colleges (Locke 1974); she personally helped to start seventeen of them.
- The movement to unite tribal leaders, which lead to the National Tribal Chairmen's Association.
- The start of tribal departments of education (TDOEs; Executive Order no. 13175 2000).
- The movement to return sacred objects to tribes, leading to the 1990 Native American Graves Protection and Repatriation Act (NAGPRA).
- The movement to start NAS programs, which she surveyed in 1974.
- The movement to start what she called "Indian postsecondary preparation academies," or college-prep academies, which is not yet really off the ground.
- The movement to establish religious freedom for Indians, leading to the 1978 American Indian Religious Freedom Act (AIRFA).

Thus, Locke was instrumental in getting four of the most important Indian laws of the past half-century passed—NALA, TDOE, NAGPRA, and AIRFA. She knew people on the Hill better than almost any Indian leader of the past half-century. She was my mentor for thirty-five years. She was also a winner of the very prestigious MacArthur "genius" award. She also helped to found the Native American Languages Institute (NALI).

The tribal college movement. Lionel Bordeaux (Lakota) has been the leader of the tribal college movement almost from its inception. He led the fight to get legislation from Congress for tribal colleges, which took up almost all the 1970s. He is still president of Sinte Gleska University at Rosebud. The main goals of these thirty-eight colleges include preserving Native languages and cultures.

Akwesasne Freedom School. Tom Porter (Mohawk), one of the original members of the White Roots of Peace, has been head of the Akwesasne Freedom School since its inception more than a quarter of a century ago. It was one of the first Indian schools to teach all subjects in a Native language.

The Piegan Institute. Darrell Kipp (Blackfeet) has headed the Piegan Institute at Browning, Montana, for two decades. Kipp set about trying to preserve the Blackfeet language at an early age and is still at it, with great success.

Bilingual education. Lucille Watahomigie (Hualapai) launched one of the few bilingual education projects that has gained Exemplary status. The federal grant for the program ran over twenty years, and Watahomigie, one of the cofounders of AILDI, taught hundreds of other people how to develop teaching materials in Native languages and how to use them in the classroom. She and some others launched a summer language institute at the University of Arizona that is still running.

Exemplary Programs

Within the past two decades, a new initiative has started to improve schools in Indian country. The Exemplary Programs in Indian Education (EPIE) movement started by Catching the Dream (CTD) in 1988 had identified thirty-nine EPIEs in Indian country as of 2011. In 1988, there were none. The EPIE criteria demand proven student outcomes; beautiful computer programs, laboratories, and plans have no meaning if students do not improve. CTD has also made 134 grants to improve reading in Indian schools, with outstanding results.

This movement has the potential to completely transform Indian schools from islands of failure to lands of opportunity within the next two decades. Catching the Dream has published four books on the development of these programs (Chavers 1972, 1995, 1999, and 2004). These ten projects are a sample of what has happened in Exemplary Programs:

Peterson Zah (Navajo) finished at Arizona State University in 1962. After two terms as both president and chairman of the Navajo Nation, he returned to his alma mater to work directly with the president, Lattie Coor. Within five years, he had doubled the enrollment of Indians on the campus and had raised the freshman-to-sophomore retention rate from 45 percent to 77 percent, the highest of any ethnic group on the campus. Zah retired in 2010, but the programs he put in place are still going.

Roger (Ried) Riedlinger (Anglo) was superintendent of Wellpinit Public Schools on the Spokane Reservation from 1989 to 1994. He asked me to put together a school improvement plan for him in 1990 and followed it with great success for fifteen years. He raised daily attendance from 65 percent to 95 percent, raised test scores from the fifteenth percentile to the seventy-fifth, and the year before he retired, sent 100 percent of students who had started the ninth grade on to college. He had 100 percent college entry and a zero dropout rate.

Richard DeLorenzo (Anglo) and his team of people at Chugach School District in Alaska grew tired of their lack of success in 1994. They had had only one student attend college in the previous twenty years, and he had dropped out. They threw out their whole curriculum and designed a new one. Within seven years, they had achieved amazing results—very low dropout rates, high test scores, and a high college-attendance rate. In 2002, the White House presented them with the prestigious Malcolm Baldrige National Quality Award, the U.S. equivalent to the Nobel Prize.

They were in competition with IBM, General Motors, and other powerhouses for the award. Their school district is larger than New Jersey. Most of their students are Native youngsters living in isolated villages (DeLorenzo et al. 2009).

Ben Chavis (Lumbee) took over the American Indian Public Charter School in Oakland in 1999 and promptly took drastic measures to turn around a failing school. He went and got absent students and brought them to school, initiated a full period of language arts in the first class period for all students every day, and started preparing them all for college study. It is the highest achieving school in Oakland now. He has been on the national TV show *20/20* and on Fox News. Govenor Arnold Schwarzenegger called the school an "education miracle." Chavis has written a book about it (Chavis 2009).

Sigmund Boloz (Anglo) is one of the top principals of all time. In the 1970s and 1980s, he turned Ganado Primary School into a high-performance school recognized by the state of Arizona, Catching the Dream, and the White House. The mostly Navajo students were reading dozens of books every year and even had their own newspaper. Test scores had all gone from below the twenty-fifth percentile to above the seventy-fifth. Boloz is now a professor at Northern Arizona University (NAU).

Betty Ojaye (Navajo) is the founding executive director of Navajo Preparatory School in Farmington, New Mexico. The school teaches high school students in a Navajo-English curriculum and sent as many as 100 percent of them on to college one year. The tribe bought the old Navajo Methodist mission in 1992, and Ojaye was charged with improving it, which she has done in remarkable fashion. They draw from sixty-seven middle schools all over the reservation, making admission harder than for many colleges. Most students live on the campus all week and return home on the weekends.

Eileen Quintana (Navajo) is at Nebo School District, Utah. When it became apparent to the Indian parents at the schools, who are mostly Navajo, that their students were not doing well, with a 37 percent high school completion rate, they demanded change. Within five years, Quintana and her Indian Education Act staff had raised the graduation rate to 93 percent, where they have maintained it for almost a decade.

David White (Mohawk) left Brown University in 1973 with his bachelor's degree. Salmon River Central Schools hired him immediately, and he has remained there ever since. The school is just off the St. Regis Mohawk Reservation. It took a decade of trial and error, along with frustration, but the program he developed has led it to be one of the top high schools in the state of New York. They regularly send 60 percent to 80 percent of their graduating seniors to college and maintain a very low dropout rate. They make sure all students have a chance to study and learn Mohawk. This is an IEA project.

Michelle Hoffman (Anglo) went to the Fremont County School District almost thirty years ago to teach for one year. It was her first year out of college. She has stayed. When she became superintendent eight years ago, she was determined to turn around the failing math programs. She retrained all math teachers and aides and sent the math scores through the roof. Reading and language scores soon followed.

Frank Kattnig (Hispanic) got hired in 1984 as the Johnson O'Malley (JOM) counselor at Tohatchi High School thirty miles north of Gallup, New Mexico. He raised college entrance rates for the class of 1985 to 55 percent and, within another several years, raised it to 90 percent. The Gallup newspaper acknowledged that the program that year had also helped students earn $1.2 million in scholarship funds for college.

Elected Officials

There is one Native American elected official in the United States at the state level. Her name is *Denise Juneau* (Blackfeet), and she is the superintendent of education for the state of Montana. Leadership runs in the family. Her mother, Carol, was the founding president of Blackfeet Community College and is a state senator. Her father, Stan, was superintendent of the school district at Browning. He retired, and came out of retirement in the middle of the 1990s to be superintendent again for several years. Juneau was one of our scholarship students at Catching the Dream for her master of arts degree in education and her juris doctorate in law.

There has never been a Native American governor. There has been one Indian who was a state-level attorney general: *Larry Echohawk* (Pawnee) served in that capacity in Idaho for one term. He was also the assistant secretary for Indian Affairs, Department of the Interior.

Education has opened many doors in the past forty years. There are at least eighty-five Indian elected officials now at the state and local levels. Most of them are state senators (18) or state representatives (57). Two are state commissioners. *Lynda Lovejoy* (Navajo) serves as a commissioner on the Public Regulation Commission in New Mexico. *Yvonne Yazzie* (Navajo) is a member of the Board of Psychologist Examiners of New Mexico. Two are county sheriffs in Oklahoma: *Scott Walton* in Rogers County and *Bruce Curnutt* (Choctaw) in LeFlore County.

One, *Todd Gloria*, is a city council member in San Diego. One, *Sharon Drapeaux* (Lakota), is a county commissioner in South Dakota. One, *Tom Cole* (Chickasaw), is a member of the U.S. House of Representatives from Oklahoma and the only Indian in Congress, now that *Ben Nighthorse Campbell* (Cheyenne) retired from the Senate.

There has been, and continues to be, subtle and strong resistance to the new paradigm (Chavers 2009). School people, who hold almost all the power, ignore the Indian language specialists and traditional people and refuse to hire them. The mindset of non-Indian school people is clearly set in the Carlisle blue-collar mode. It is very difficult to change them.

The people who have made the changes, including the Exemplary programs, have been determined, tough-minded, and dedicated. They have found that with the right ingredients and an emphasis on the right things, a school or a district can be converted in five to eight years from a loser to a winner. The emphasis is always on the basics—daily attendance, parent commitment, reading, and challenging courses. Highfalutin theories almost never work.

Unfortunately, there are still huge challenges for Indian education. The dropout rate for Indian high school students is still 50 percent (Faircloth and Tippeconnic 2010), despite some people's refusal to acknowledge it. The college entrance rate for Indians is only 17 percent, compared to 67 percent for the nation. Test scores are below the twentieth percentile in all subjects for almost all Indian schools.

Standardized testing rules out huge numbers of Indian students from opportunities and college and for jobs (Chavers and Locke 1989). Tribal languages are dying on a regular basis; some projections say all Native languages will be dead within thirty years (Chavers 1994). Fewer than 10 percent of Indian students are exposed to their Native languages in the classroom (Chavers 2000).

Fewer than 2 percent of Indian schools have made real improvements in the past quarter-century. Only a tiny handful (5) of the 1,100 IEA projects has achieved high outcomes with students. Indian students still read fewer than one book per year outside the classroom. ACT and SAT scores average at the twentieth percentile. There is a dropout rate of 80 percent for Indian college students. There is still a long way to go.

REFERENCES

American Indian Religious Freedom Act of 1978 (AIRFA). (1978). *U.S. code.* Title 42, sec. 1996.

Chavers, D. (1972). *Exemplary Programs in Indian Education.* Albuquerque, NM: Catching the Dream.

———. (1994). *The Status of the Apache Language: An Assessment Report.* Dulce, NM: Jicarilla Apache Nation.

———. (1995). *Exemplary Programs in Indian Education.* Updated ed. Albuquerque, NM: Catching the Dream.

———. (1999). *Exemplary Programs in Indian Education.* Updated ed. Albuquerque, NM: Catching the Dream.

———. (2000). *Indian Students and College Preparation.* Albuquerque, NM: Catching the Dream.

———. (2004). *Exemplary Programs in Indian Education.* Updated ed. Albuquerque, NM: Catching the Dream.

———. (2007). *Modern American Indian Leaders.* Lewiston, NY: Mellen.

———. (2009). *Racism in Indian Country.* New York: Peter Lang.

Chavers, D., and P. Locke. (1989). *The Effects of Testing on Native Americans.* Washington, DC: Status report for the National Commission on Testing and Public Policy.

Chavis, B. (2009). *Crazy Like a Fox.* With C. Blakely. New York: Penguin.

Costo, R. (1970). *Textbooks and the American Indian.* San Francisco: American Indian Historical Society.

DeLorenzo, R. A., W. J. Battino, R. M. Schreiber, and B. G. Carrio. (2009). *Delivering on the Promise.* Bloomington, IN: Solution Tree.

Deloria, V. (1969). *Custer Died for Your Sins.* New York: MacMillan.

Dorris, M. (1990). *The Broken Cord.* New York: Harper.

Executive Order no. 13175. (2000). "Consultation and coordination with Indian tribal governments." *Federal Register* 65 (218): 67,249–252.

Faircloth, S. C., and J. W. Tippeconnic III. (2010). *The Dropout/Graduation Crisis among American Indian and Alaska Native Students.* Los Angeles: Civil Rights Project at UCLA and Pennsylvania State University Center for the Study of Leadership in American Indian Education.

Fitzgerald, P., and T. Davis. (1974). "An alternative to failure." *Journal of American Indian Education* 13 (2): 194.

Forbes, J. D. (1967). *California Indian Education.* Modesto, CA: Ad Hoc Committee on California Indian Education.

Indian Civil Rights Act of 1968 (ICRA). (1968). *U.S. code.* Title 25, sec. 1301 et seq.

Kroeber, D. (1961). *Ishi.* Berkeley: University of California Press.

Locke, P. (1974). *A Survey of College and University Programs for American Indians.* Boulder, CO: Western Interstate Commission for Higher Education.

Native American Graves Protection and Repatriation Act of 1990 (NAGPRA). (1990). *U.S. code.* Title 25, sec. 3001 et seq.

Native American Languages Act of 1990 (NALA). (2000). *U.S. code.* Title 25, sec. 2901 et seq.

Peroff, N. C. (1982). *Menominee Drums: Tribal Termination and Restoration, 1954–1974.* Norman: University of Oklahoma Press.

Roessel, R. A., Jr. (1968). "An overview of the Rough Rock Demonstration School." *Journal of American Indian Education* 7 (3). Retrieved from http://jaie.asu.edu/v7/V7S3over.html.

Final Thoughts

We have taken readers through the history of American Indian education from the earliest attempts to force Native students into learning through hegemonic Western education to current educational reforms and on towards looking at the future and the continued need to sustain education that is culturally responsive to Native students. As you have joined with us on our journey to restore the emphasis on culturally responsive pedagogy to schools serving American Indian students in the United States, we invite you to reflect on what you have read and on the reasons we have enumerated for making these changes in schools.

We also believe that the lessons that have been learned, both about what works best for Indigenous students in the course of acquiring their educations and what does not, cannot continue to be ignored in the hopes that somehow, someway, all of our students will acquire the necessary knowledge and skills needed to ensure that they will be able to reach their full potentials. The political whims of a few cannot dictate a course of action to be followed by all that benefits only a handful of citizens and damages the rest of the nation.

In light of the vagaries of politics and the push for more privatization of public schools, how do we preserve the promises of providing education that is culturally responsive to the needs of American Indian students? We believe strongly that this type of teaching represents best practice for schools attended by our Native students. Additionally, we believe that this type of teaching is good for all students and should be available in schools serving all ethnicities in this country.

As educators, we need to align ourselves with advocates for American Indian education and not be afraid to make our voices heard in order for this goal to be accomplished. We have a clear vision of the pathways that need to exist for our students, of how following these pathways will lead to the enfranchisement of Native Americans throughout the country as a whole, as citizens capable of making decisions regarding the wants and needs of their children. We cannot continue to act as a nation in a paternalistic fashion of "father knows best"— clearly this is not only unctuous for Native peoples but strips them of their rights as citizens of sovereign nations to declare what they know is best for their peoples.

It is our sincere hope that education for all of the citizens of this great nation will be the most efficacious for each and that together we may create a future that will include social justice for all of our populace. Thank you for engaging with us in our dreams as readers of our work.

Biographies

ABOUT THE AUTHOR

Beverly J. Klug is associate professor at Idaho State University. She has specialized and published in the areas of literacy, American Indian education, teacher education, and the arts; as well as co-authored a book on culturally relevant pedagogy.

CONTRIBUTORS

Freddie A. Bowles is associate professor of education at the University of Arkansas, Fayetteville. Her interests focus on foreign language education, language preservation, and language acquisition.

Dean Chavers, Lumbee, is founder and director of the Catching the Dream foundation. He is a former president of Bacone College and author of 27 books on grant writing, exemplary programs in Indian education, racism, and Indian leaders.

Angela Jaime, Pit River and Maidu, is associate professor of education at the University of Wyoming. She specializes in American Indian education, native women in higher education, multicultural education, and social justice.

Helene Johnson, Navajo, born to the Ashii clan, is an experienced educator in the Piñon Unified School District in Nevada. She has been a teacher-leader and coach in the Accelerated Schools Project for more than ten years.

Stephen T. Marble is associate professor of education at Southwestern University in Georgetown, Texas. He has specialized in improvement of math and science education and in teacher preparation and the philosophical concepts of Gilles Deleuze.

Jane McCarthy is professor of education at University of Nevada, Las Vegas, where she is director of the Accelerated Schools Project. She has published widely in the areas of school reform, classroom management, and teaching at-risk students.

Teresa L. McCarty is the Alice Wiley Snell Professor of Education Policy Studies, and professor of applied linguistics, Arizona State University. Her many journal articles and books focus on issues in indigenous/multilingual education.

Jacqueline F. Nuby is professor emeritus at University of Montevallo in Montevallo, Alabama. She has published in the areas of diversity, culturally inappropriate pedagogy, and learning styles.

Leann Putney is professor of education at the University of Nevada, Las Vegas. She co-founded a K–12 public charter school for linguistically and culturally diverse learners in Las Vegas and has published works focusing on diversity and Vygotsky.

Jon Reyhner is professor of education at Northern Arizona State University. He has published extensively in the area of American Indian education including books about teaching Native students and the history of American Indian education.

R. Timothy Rush is professor of education at the University of Wyoming. He directs the Teachers of American Indian Children (TAIC) certification and endorsement program and has published in the areas of literacy and diversity.

James Smith, Cherokee, has worked as a director and instructor of cultural arts for Cherokee high school students and taught at Oakland City University. A well-known sculptor, he was instrumental in establishing an art institute in Cherokee, North Carolina.

Jeanette Haynes Writer, Cherokee, is associate professor of education at New Mexico State University in Las Cruces. She has focused on Tribal Critical Race Theory, multicultural teacher education, social justice, and indigenous education.

William Young is assistant professor at Oglala Lakota College. His research interests include best practices in teaching Native American youth, teacher self-efficacy, and culturally responsive pedagogy.

Index